Public Needs and Private Behavior in Metropolitan Areas

Public Needs and Private Behavior in Metropolitan Areas

Edited by
John E. Jackson

Papers presented to a Meeting of the Metropolitan Governance Research Committee, sponsored by Resources for the Future and the Academy for Contemporary Problems, October, 1973.

Ballinger Publishing Company • Cambridge, Mass.
A Subsidiary of J.B. Lippincott Company

JS
422
.P83

International Standard Book Number: 0-88410-035-9

Library of Congress Catalog Card Number: 75-6732

Printed in the United States of America

Library of Congress Cataloging in Publication Data

Main entry under title:

Public needs and private behavior in metropolitan areas.

    1. Metropolitan government—United States—Addresses, essays, lectures. 2. Metropolitan areas—United States—Addresses, essays, lectures. 3. Municipal services—United States—Addresses, essays, lectures. I. Jackson, John Edgar. II. Metropolitan Governance Research Committee. III. Resources for the Future. IV. Academy for Contemporary Problems.
JS422.P83   301.5'92'0973   75-6732
ISBN 0-88410-035-9

Contents

List of Figures

List of Tables

Metropolitan Governance Research Committee

Membership

Preface

The Metropolitan Governance Research Committee was started in February 1973 as an RFF-sponsored activity with financial support from the Academy for Contemporary Problems. The Committee's aim was to identify problems of metropolitan governance, to find new research, results of which would bear on these problems, and to provide a means whereby this research and its implications could be discussed, evaluated, and applied to practical problems. The Committee also hoped to be able to point out where additional knowledge is needed and offer suggestions as to analytic methods that might provide insights for new policies.

This first conference sponsored by the Committee deals particularly with the interrelated processes of residential mobility and the capacity of communities to meet public service needs. Variations in public services and tax rates do influence the spatial distribution of the population; at the same time the number of people locating in any town, along with their characteristics, determines the need for and provision of public services in that community. The interesting questions are: what is the relative importance of public services in the locational decisions of different families; what limits the ability of various political institutions to respond to citizens' needs; in what ways do locational decisions, political activity and other behavior interact to reinforce or frustrate public policies. Every local public official, as well as most citizens, understands how frequently the meeting of a general need for better schools, housing, or police protection can be thwarted by private decisions to move out beyond the reach of city taxes and thereby to compound yet other public service costs like sewer, water and transportation.

The research discussed in these papers aims to expose many of the choice processes people in metropolitan areas employ to satisfy their demands for public services and attractive living environments. It also shows that each of these processes works better for one type of family or in particular part of the metropolitan area than for others. Because of the restrictions on housing in many suburban communities, minorities and lower income groups are denied some of the options available to upper income groups. Growing suburbs face different demands and needs than do central cities. The papers also illustrate how attempts to legislate certain public policies, such as equalizing expenditures in different areas, can be frustrated by important segments of the population able to exercise other choice mechanisms. Some families may find a new location or may resort to the private market for services, and thus avoid the public responsibility they are being asked to carry. The lesson to be learned from these observations is that policy makers must be aware of all the choice processes people have at their disposal and how they exercise them before making changes which deal with only one process.

As was known from the outset, the research reported here cannot be considered definitive, although it represents some of the most advanced work being done on these related topics. Limitations of data and of the conceptual models of the different choice processes restrict the confidence the policy maker should place in the results reported here. One only hopes that the research findings, which are an advance over previous work, and the policy implications will spur further analytic modeling and data collection activities. If so, the Committee will have met one of its principal objectives, that of focusing the attention of researchers on questions of importance to policy makers. At the same time, even the preliminary results discussed here should alert policy makers to the need for additional and better research.

Joseph L. Fisher
Member of Congress
Tenth District—Virginia

Public Needs and Private
Behavior in
Metropolitan Areas

Chapter One

Public Needs, Private Behavior, and Metropolitan Governance: A Summary Essay

John E. Jackson

The purpose of the conference sponsored by the Metropolitan Governance Research Committee was to consider what demands people have with regard to local public services and environments; what ways they have of satisfying these demands; how alternative means interact, reinforce, and conflict with each other; and what people concerned with governing metropolitan areas should learn from these considerations.

It is not hard to see what constitutes people's demands for public services, living conditions, and amenities in an urban area. The obvious items are housing; accessibility to work, shopping, and leisure time activities; pleasant physical and social surroundings; good public services such as schools, libraries, and personal and property protection; and the ability to alter some or all of these things as incomes and needs change.

The distinguishing characteristic of all these items is their collective nature and the conflicts inherent in the decisions about their provision. People may agree on what constitutes a desirable neighborhood, and then argue that its creation requires the exclusion of certain other people who want to live there. Providing some people with accessibility to workplaces or other activities may mean reducing the physical attractiveness of others' neighborhoods. Similar conflicts exist for all the services and amenities listed above. The essence of the problem is to decide what people want, to understand the constraints imposed by limited resources, to ascertain the conflicts in these desires and constraints, and to find means for people to resolve these conflicts and to balance satisfaction of their own demands with the costs imposed on others.

The alternative means to satisfy demands for physical, social, and public service amenities and to resolve their inherent conflicts and the way the alternatives interact to reinforce and frustrate each other is the central theme of this book. Political activity and the behavior of public institutions is the usual process suggested by this discussion. The obvious forum for political behavior is the voting booth: citizens vote on everything from new capital expenditures, to school boards, to mayors; voting gives people both the opportunity and the institutional structure to make their opinions and demands known and presumably felt. Voting also makes other forms of political activity such as meetings, picketing, and lobbying more effective because most elected officials know they can be held accountable to these demands in the future. One can question how well the voting process works in reality, but its intent surely is to provide for this type of demand expression.

There are additional ways to express demands through public agencies. Litigation against municipalities and public officials is a current method to obtain satisfaction for certain types of demands and for certain groups of people. Lawyers claim local governments have denied equal protection to its citizens. In cases where discrimination in the provision of public services is based on a suspect classification, such as race, the courts have ordered this discrimination to cease and have used the yardstick of equalized expenditures to measure compliance with the order. This approach has proved effective in changing the behavior of public agencies in certain instances so that the needs and demands of individual citizens are better served. This strategy is only viable for specific groups, however, and its long run success depends upon community reaction to the redistribution of public services.

A much practiced alternative to political action is the move to an area with more desirable amenities, public services, and neighbors. Individual communities in a metropolitan area offer different types of housing, neighbors, social environments, and public services. Families "purchase" the desired activities with their housing purchase and their residential site selection. Housing prices in towns possessing desirable characteristics that are not easily duplicated by other towns, such as accessibility or desirable neighbors, will be relatively higher. This approach requires a variety of communities within the metropolitan area so that each family can find the desired environment, given their willingness and ability to pay for housing and associated services. The consequences will be many smaller, homogeneous communities with people sorted out geographically by their income and taste differences.

A third alternative is simply the private market. This option, though quite powerful, is often overlooked for many services. Short of neighbors and neighborhood characteristics, most of the services people want can be obtained without political action and without changing their residences. People certainly change their housing consumption by adding rooms, redecorating, and similar actions. They also engage in the purchase of conventional public services such as private schools, country clubs, and now even burglar alarms and private protection services. The availability and private purchase of these services will decrease the use of other options by reducing the propensity to move and the willingness to vote for additional public expenditures. Reliance on private purchase, however, ignores the community interest inherent in the availability of these services.

Political processes, residential location, and private markets as options by which we satisfy people's demands for public goods are all highly related and have comparative advantages in different situations and for different groups of people. Their simultaneously complementing and conflicting effects must be comprehended by those who propose, evaluate, and implement public policies if we are to realize any improvement in metropolitan living conditions. Understanding these processes, their interactions, and the relative importance of each in different circumstances will lead to better use of all approaches and to a greater ability to meet the demands of metropolitan residents. This knowledge should also minimize inconsistent policies and forestall efforts to implement one set of policies without considering the effects of people exercising alternative options. Conflicting policies and more extensive use of other options will prevent realization of the desired objectives and possibly result in an actual worsening of conditions.

The chapters in this volume develop empirical evidence about these processes and how they relate to each other. This introductory chapter, in addition to outlining the topics and summarizing the empirical findings and associated discussions, points out their implications for deciding how metropolitan areas should be organized and governed. It also presents the weaknesses of the chapters' analyses so their results and implications can be appropriately qualified, and points out areas where we do not have sufficient information to make authoritative statements.

INDIVIDUAL DEMANDS

It is relatively easy to suggest services and amenities that people value and that are relevant to our study of metropolitan government. The most important one is housing. There are a variety of factors that combine to create a "unit" of housing; they include the number and type of rooms, amount of land, age of structure, and overall quality and type of construction. The availability and cost of these characteristics in a metropolitan area result from many private decisions on the part of builders, landlords, and individual homeowners. Housing demands are satisfied through the private market, either by residential location decisions or by alterations to existing housing units. The only public policies bearing directly on housing services are local zoning rules and the small publicly subsidized housing programs. However, the consequences of the behavior in this private market have substantial impacts on most other decisions, both public and private.

An important amenity considered in location decisions is accessibility to workplaces and possibly to other activities such as shopping and recreation.- Changes in accessibility, with their expected consequences for metropolitan development, result from both public and private actions. Employment location decisions are dominated by private institutions, which depend primarily upon access to markets and the availability of the necessary production inputs, and are only marginally influenced by public policies. These decisions determine the workplace accessibility of each geographic area.

The second determinant of accessibility—the transportation network—is largely publicly determined. Mass transit is administered by state or local agencies, and state and federal governments control the building and location of major expressways; thus transportation service decisions and the resulting accessibilities are made by governmental agencies. Within the constraints imposed by public policy, individuals can vary their accessibility. The most obvious way to increase accessibility is to switch from bus or public transportation to private automobile, or from car pools to individual ridership. Second and third cars also increase a family's overall accessibility to activities, including shopping and recreation as well as workplaces. Finally, accessibilities can be altered by changing residence: one can always move closer to work or these other activities.

In addition to the physical characteristics of their housing, people are clearly concerned about the social and environmental characteristics of their neighborhoods. For reasons of prejudice, prestige, and simple commonality of interests, people care who their neighbors are and want to live in certain neighborhoods and avoid others for this reason. People also avoid certain physical surroundings, such as noisy, smoky, and smelly factories. Most people find dense, congested areas undesirable so the proximity of a shopping area or major highway, although accessible, is objectionable on esthetic grounds.

Neighborhood characteristics are extremely difficult for individuals to control. People can, and surely do, consider their neighborhood characteristics when they select their housing unit. Once located though, it is impossible for people acting individually to change their neighbors, eliminate a shopping center, or stop population increases. At this point, people's only control over these factors is the collective decision to exclude certain types of land use and, indirectly, certain types of neighbors, through zoning. Zoning and land use controls are usually established and enforced by local governmental units, subject to the constraints imposed by higher level authorities. One important issue for metropolitan governance (not specifically addressed here) is the whole question of land use controls: their effects, people's reaction to them, and the proper role for each governmental level. However, present and potential variations in land use patterns and neighborhood characteristics do affect people's decisions.

The final set of activities over which people are expressing concern is the level and type of local public services such as education, public recreation, public safety, sanitation, and so on. These activities are economic in nature, in that government agencies are responsible for taking inputs such as raw materials, labor, and capital and providing a service to the residents of that community, just as business firms process similar raw materials into goods and services for private consumption. Governments must decide how much of these services to provide, how to finance them, the best way to provide these services, and how to distribute them among the relevant population. Many proposals for improving local government focus on questions of increasing the efficiency of these institutions in providing services and the proper distribution of their cost.

Proposals reforming local governments and establishing metropolitan governments must consider many more issues than just their ability to provide a few public services. The decisions of governmental agencies affect land use, accessibility, neighborhood composition, and to some extent housing services, in addition to the more conventional public services. These help determine the satisfactions of people living in metropolitan areas. It is crucial to understand the determinants of these demands, what people advocate them, and how metropolitan governments function to facilitate their satisfaction.

DETERMINANTS OF PEOPLE'S SERVICE DEMANDS

The determinants of people's demands for housing, public services, and other amenities is the first link in the metropolitan political economy. Demands vary with individuals' income, social characteristics, and the price of the service. These variations are important because of the interaction between public policies and behavior designed to satisfy demands. The distribution of services and amenities influences residential location decisions and thereby the demographic composition of the metropolis. Coincidentally, the geographic distribution of the population affects the demands and problems faced by local governments and their abilities to respond to them.

For example, families with school age children want good schools and will pressure local governments to provide them. But the quality of public education depends upon the social and economic characteristics of the families sending their children to the public schools as well as on local education policy. At the same time, school quality influences location decisions and affects the local school committee's ability to provide good schools. Thus people's demands, their location decisions, the characteristics of the metropolitan area, and local government policies are tightly bound together. The place to begin unraveling these interactions is with the structure and determinants of people's demands.

The important demand determinants include income, number of school age children, age, education level, and race and ethnic background. Income is the most important because demands for most services increase with income, although demands for certain items are more income sensitive than others. The number of school age children, education level, and age will be specifically related to demands for specific housing attributes and for educational versus other public expenditures. Education levels may indirectly influence housing demand because of its relationship with people's expected future income. People with higher education levels expect their future incomes to rise and thus buy housing characteristic of people in their future income class rather than their current income group. This is particularly true of younger households. Ethnicity is included because investigators have concluded that some ethnic groups have different views on the role of the public sector and demands for various services, as well as an affinity for neighbors with the same heritage.

Race is included explicitly because blacks have been forced into certain decisions and different behavior patterns because of discrimination in the housing market, the political process, and by private organizations. This discrimination badly biases the choices open to blacks and severely limits their ability to obtain the services and amenities that others consume. It is important to know the consequences of this discrimination, both for blacks and the metropolitan community generally.

The emphasis in looking at these social and economic characteristics is their effect on the relative demand for various services. We expect higher incomes to result in increased demands for all services, but are education expenditures more sensitive than housing expenditures and so on? Similarly, do people with more education have a higher demand for education services than people with less education but the same income? These questions are important in determining the demands placed on public institutions, the different social environments existing among areas with different groups of residents, and the amount of social and economic stratification of the population, given variations in services within a metropolitan area.

The second important determinant of people's demands for urban services is cost. The standard economic model predicts that people's demands for goods and services depends upon the price of that item relative to the price of other items. This same principle should apply to public services and the other attributes that make up the metropolitan environment. For our concerns, these prices are much harder to see than prices in the private market because of the nature of the commodity. In some cases, prices are determined by the conventional market mechanism, are quite visible, and can be measured directly. Land prices may fit the traditional model. The cost of housing may also approximate this model, although one must be careful about interpreting any term called "housing price" because we do not know what constitutes a unit of housing. Housing expenditures are purchasing a wide variety of things, such as a physical structure, accessibility, neighbors, and public services, and these characteristics are obtained in very different combinations. Consequently, it is extremely difficult to determine the price of housing, as compared to a person's housing expenditure. Eventually we need to know the "price" of the individual components.

Public service prices are the most difficult to accurately estimate. They are determined by the cost and manner of combining the inputs necessary to produce these services. Thus increased wages in the public sector increase the cost of these services, and presumably lead to decreased demand for them, and possibly decreased expenditures depending upon the price elasticity.

A more difficult question is the price individuals face. These prices depend upon the tax structure and the other revenue sources used to finance the services and the sources' impact on the individual. It is quite possible for the same family with all the same demands and consumption of other items to face quite different "prices" for public services in different parts of the metropolitan area. The best example of this is the property tax. People's taxes and the costs of additional public services depend upon the valuation of other property in the community as well as on their own housing.

Tax price differences in metropolitan areas, their systematic variation among social and economic groups, and the extent to which public decisions such as zoning cause and reinforce them is a matter of serious public concern. Local variations in public service prices due to tax base differences is a problem confronting metropolitan governments. It should be pointed out that this problem is not unique to the property tax. Sales and income taxes will also produce variations in the price of local services among jurisdictions. However, these variations will not be so closely related to the other characteristics that constitute urban policy, such as land use and the consumption of housing. Metropolitan policy must take into account these price variations' influence on the demand for public services, on the responses of people trying to satisfy their demands at the lowest possible cost, and ultimately on the development of the metropolitan area.

WAYS OF SATISFYING INDIVIDUAL DEMANDS

The real metropolitan governance question is the effectiveness of alternative means to satisfy public demands and how the presence or absence of these alternatives influence metropolitan development. The principle alternatives are private purchase, the choice of a residence location, and political action, including voting, political pressure, and legal action.

Private Markets

The option of direct, private purchase of services, other than the decision to purchase housing, has not received enough empirical study, although there are private options available for most of the items we have discussed, such as private schools, garbage and refuse collection, security forces, country clubs, automobiles, and so forth. Most discussions of these services and amenities start with the private purchase option and conclude it is not viable. Its major deficiency is the neglect of the collective nature of the items and the need for group rather than individual decision making.

The clearest example is the desire of people for certain types of neighbors and neighborhoods. Neighborhood availability depends upon the location decisions of other people and nonresidential land users, which is beyond any one person's control. Similarly, individual attempts to insure the safety of their property, to provide fire protection, or to obtain recreational services may also make those services more available to other people living in proximity. The process is also symmetrical. If other people purchase these services, they are automatically available to this individual, who consequently has an incentive to wait and try to get others to provide them.

The number of people who decide to obtain a service and the way the service is delivered also changes the price to individuals. For example, police and fire protection can be provided more cheaply, on a per unit basis, to all the residents of an area than if each person purchases the protection separately. Consequently decisions about the purchase of services are dependent upon the decisions of other people.

Private purchase is also viewed as an unattractive solution because many of the services, such as housing and education, are considered "merit" goods. As a society, for a variety of reasons, we have decided that it is important for all people to have at least minimum levels of housing and a certain amount and type of education. Purely private decisions lead to certain people, for reasons of income or tastes, not purchasing "enough" or the proper type of these services. Consequently we make these services available to all—even requiring they be consumed, controlling their content, and financing them publicly, implying some income redistribution. The best illustration is public education with its compulsory attendance, curriculum review, accreditation, and partial administration by higher level governments.

Private purchase must be remembered both as an available option and as a possible way to provide services. Its continual availability means private alternatives cannot be ignored when evaluating the effects of changes in other processes. For example, manipulating the political process to guarantee a certain distribution of public expenditures may encourage some people to increase their private purchase of these services. This increased private purchase may then lead to reduced demands for the public service. For example, people who opt for private education may become reluctant to increase their support for public schools.

Increased access to and use of private alternatives may decrease pressures on other options. A wide variety of such services available throughout the metropolitan area may reduce both the services public agencies must offer and administer, and the incentives for residential relocation. This is one of the arguments put forth for the voucher type of public support for education. The vouchers take care of the merit good or distributional aspects while the presence in all areas of a variety of private schools with different curriculums, philosophies, and resources make it possible for people to get the type of education they want for their children without resorting to political pressure or a move to certain suburbs. Thus even with its difficulties, private purchase is a real and possibly useful alternative that will affect our evaluation of the other means of satisfying demands.

Residential Location

People can get the desired services and environment through their residential location decision, if there are enough communities offering different types of housing, neighborhoods, and public services at different accessibilities from major workplace concentrations. Families simply pay the price required to get housing at the desired location. Housing prices will reflect the relative demands for different neighborhood environments and the ability of communities to provide those environments. Increased housing values provide the incentives for communities to offer the types of neighborhoods and services being demanded. For example, if families are demanding better schools, then a community can increase rents and real estate values by increasing the amount spent on public schools, which presumably provides better schools to residents of that town. In the long run, these service increases must be provided if a town is to maintain its housing values.

The locational approach is in effect making the demand and supply of public services and neighborhood characteristics a private market. The producers in the conventional sense are the owners of land and housing who maximize their profits (housing revenue minus operating costs, which include tax payments) by creating and selling desirable locations. The consumers are the people buying commodities—e.g., neighborhoods—based on the "market" price and their own demand for better locations. The purchase price of housing and gross rents will reflect the value of different services and neighborhood characteristics if services and amenities strictly determine locations and if community characteristics are fixed. These prices will homogeneously stratify the population both by income and by service and neighborhood preference.

Community characteristics are not fixed, and only attributes that other towns cannot duplicate are permanently capitalized into property values. The best example of such an attribute is accessibility to workplaces. Land values are higher in areas with greater accessibility and it is impossible for landowners in less accessible areas to raise the value of their land by increasing its accessibility. The same process holds for other relatively unique characteristics, such as scenic views, beachfronts, and so on.

A town's ability to provide public services at a lower cost than other communities can be permanently capitalized into local land and housing prices. For example, a community with a few large property taxpayers, such as a private utility company or a few very wealthy families, can provide public services at a relatively lower cost to residents because the few taxpayers are paying a large portion of the costs of those services. These lower tax rates become capitalized in the value of housing in that community because people are willing to pay more for housing in an area with lower tax rates for a given level of public services.

Attributes other towns can replicate are not permanently capitalized in housing values, although there is short run capitalization of temporarily scarce attributes. People will pay a premium for housing in a particular town if it is the only one with good schools. However, other towns can increase the quality of their schools. Families then have several "good school" areas to choose from and are unlikely to pay a premium to live in any particular one. Any model of housing prices estimating the price effects of neighborhood amenities and public services must take into account the availability of these characteristics in the metropolitan area as well as people's demands for them. This is an extremely difficult problem, which remains unsolved.

Regardless of the capitalization question, families' residential location decisions are influenced by variations in public services, neighbors, and other amenities as well as differences in housing stocks, accessibilities, and prices. The important considerations are the relative magnitude of these influences on location decisions, whether the importance varies among income and demographic groups, and the subsequent implications for metropolitan governance. The chapters by Mayo and Bloom, Brown and Jackson provide some evidence about these questions.

In Chapter Two, Stephen K. Mayo examines the probability of people in different income and family size groups with the same workplace residing in each census tract in the Milwaukee metropolitan area in 1960. These probabilities are related to the characteristics of the individual tracts; distance to workplace, type of housing stock, public expenditures and taxes, average achievement level in the local elementary school on a standardized test, accessibilities to shopping centers, and neighboring land uses. Housing characteristics and travel time to the workplace are the most consistently important variables in influencing where people locate. This result was particularly true for the lower income groups. Only among the families with incomes in excess of $12,000 (this is in 1960) did school expenditures become important in where a family resided.

There are several explanations for this behavioral difference. Perhaps lower income groups do not care enough or have sufficient information about public expenditures to include them in their locational decisions. Alternatively the Milwaukee housing market may be such that within the constraints on their residential choice imposed by other considerations, such as total housing expenditure, the need for public transportation, etc., it is impossible to find an area that both satisfies the constraints and has "good" schools. Consequently, differences in schooling cannot influence their location.

Upper income individuals are not so constrained. They can afford a wider range of housing choices and second cars, for example. Families with a larger set of possible geographic locations have more variation in school expenditures, or other amenities, among areas that are roughly comparable in other aspects such as travel time and housing stocks. With this greater choice among service levels, and possibly greater interest in school expenditures, it is not surprising that upper income families show a greater sensitivity to such differences in their residential location decisions.

There are several important qualifications to Mayo's results which indicate the implications should be viewed cautiously. First, a majority of Mayo's census tracts, which are the units of analysis, are located within the city of Milwaukee. His expenditure data is computed for whole political jurisdictions so there is no variation in these public expenditure variables for the Milwaukee tracts. Thus even though service variations exist within the city, and people may respond to these differences, Mayo's data will not reflect these variations and their subsequent behavior. There is one important exception to this problem, however: the school achievement data is by individual neighborhood, which has some variation within Milwaukee. If people constrained to live within the city for reasons of income, travel time, etc., are sensitive to educational differences, this variable should measure those sensitivities, even though the expenditure data do not.

A second difficulty with Mayo's model is the interpretation given to the expenditure variables. People in the lower income groups may be willing to give up some housing consumption or increased travel time in order to get better schools, as measured by larger school expenditures. However, given their income constraint there is a limit as to how much they can spend on public education and still have enough income to buy a house, food, clothing, and other private services. Consequently, these families cannot continually give up housing, accessibility, and other consumption for higher school expenditures. Thus we should not find people in the lower income groups locating in areas with large school expenditures simply because they cannot afford them.

Mayo's model, which shows that a low income family's probability of locating in a given tract does not increase with school expenditures in that tract, includes tracts with very high as well as low expenditures. The result may simply indicate that poorer families do not locate in tracts with expensive schools because of their inability to afford them, and not that education is unimportant in their location decisions.

An alternative interpretation of the model says that inclusion of the local school tax rate in the analysis accounts for this income constraint. People restricted in their choice of residence because they cannot afford expensive schools, may still want the best school within their budget constraint. If true, the school expenditure term should be positive while the tax term is negative, indicating that for a given tax rate, these people will give up some housing or accessibility to get better (more) school expenditures or a school with better average achievement scores. If the included tax variable does not measure the true cost of public services, then the interpretation problem remains.

Mayo's data has one other difficulty. The sample consists of households already residing in an area; it is not a sample of families who recently made a locational decision and picked that particular area. The problem is twofold: it is possible that some longtime residents originally selected the site for reasons and under a set of conditions that no longer apply, but have just not bothered to move. A classic example would be a family who ten or fifteen years ago, when their children were young, selected an area with good schools. The children have now grown and are no longer in school, but the couple has remained in the neighborhood, even though if making the locational decision today they would not have chosen that site.

There may also be families who chose an area given their income at that time. In the intervening years their income has increased but for a variety of reasons they have not relocated but have done without some services or found other ways to obtain them. A model that predicts location on the basis of neighborhood characteristics for different income groups and family sizes would not accurately reflect the locational decisions of these families.

The data will more accurately estimate the influence of neighborhood characteristics in the locational decisions of groups with the greatest residential mobility. The upper income groups are the most mobile because of their higher incomes and because they are more likely to move from metropolitan area to metropolitan area. Consequently the models that Mayo estimates may more accurately reflect the locational decisions of the affluent.

By not measuring people's location decisions, but simply their current location, Mayo may confuse the effects of current services on these decisions with decisions made about public services after people have moved into an area. For example, higher income people may locate in a particular area because of the area's housing stock, accessibility, and land prices, following the traditional urban economics residential location model. Once there, these families, who very likely have high demands for certain public services such as public education, may vote larger school expenditures and tax rates in order to get those schools. This produces a systematic relationship between income, location, and school expenditures even though school expenditures were not an important part of the *location decision.* One needs to study the location decisions of recent movers and the neighborhood characteristics and public service levels in the community when the family made its location decision. This would give a more accurate picture of the role played by the different factors in these location decisions and the viability of the locational models as a way of satisfying people's demands for various services.

Bloom, Brown, and Jackson do not analyze the location decision per se. In Chapter Three they relate changes in the population composition, housing stocks, and fiscal behavior of Boston suburbs between 1960 and 1970 to each other and to changes in accessibility, industrial employment, and state revenue transfers. Their analysis tries to disentangle statistically the simultaneous interactions of these effects because individual location decision and political activity data were not available.

Their results also suggest that accessibility and housing characteristics are the most influential determinants of location; however, their analysis shows more responsiveness to public school expenditure differences than does Mayo's. Towns with higher educational expenditures, at a given tax rate, had larger increases in median incomes, college educated people, and families with school age children, than did towns with lower expenditures but similar valued housing stock and populations in 1960. This strongly suggests that these families, whom we expect to have higher demands for education services, are being attracted to and settling in communities with better schools. Thus this chapter finds that public expenditures and changes in housing values, which incorporate the effects of accessibility and housing characteristics, are influential in changing the composition of the population in these suburban towns. Variations in public school expenditures result in a residential sorting process leading to more homogeneous communities.

The difficulty with the Bloom, Brown, and Jackson work is the use of highly aggregated data that only measures changes over a ten-year period. The data is highly collinear, with changes in income levels, housing prices, and public services all rising in certain areas and more so in a few towns, generally located in specific geographic areas. Consequently it is very hard to indicate precisely those changes that cause other changes. Their results could in substantial part be due to the particular patterns of variation in their variables and inaccurate measures of the effects of the hypothesized influences. To become more reliable estimates, their work needs to be supplemented and supported by additional studies at a less aggregated level, such as the type that Mayo undertook.

The Mayo and Bloom, Brown, and Jackson chapters provide some empirical support for the argument that residential location decisions are sensitive to differences in public services and other amenities. Mayo, however, suggests that this influence may be limited to the upper income groups. The evidence in Chapter Three does not conflict with this observation, although it is impossible to examine this effect with their aggregate data. If only the higher income groups (who also have more college experience) are influenced by school expenditure differences, it would give the aggregate result that communities' median income and proportion with some college would increase if their school expenditures increased, relative to other towns.

The characteristics of the local housing stock and accessibility also play a very important role in people's location decisions. Thus people may sacrifice a better school system to live in a town that is closer to their place of work, or which has the type of housing structure they want (the reverse trade-off is also present). This means that people may still move into an area with the hope of changing the level of public expenditures to conform to their needs because that town had better housing and accessibility characteristics than other towns with better schools.

Both chapters estimate the effects of differences in housing and community characteristics on housing prices. The physical characteristics of the dwelling, such as number of rooms and age, work accessibility, and neighborhood characteristics are the important determinants of these prices. The exception is that rooms had little effect on the gross rent in the Bloom, Brown, and Jackson study. Neighborhood effects were noticeable in that communities with high densities and large amounts of nonresidential land use—which is associated with greater congestion and other environmental problems—exhibited lower rents and housing prices than did lower density, completely residential areas with similar housing and accessibility characteristics. The Bloom, Brown, and Jackson study shows large increases in owner occupied housing values in towns with large houses in 1960, as measured by the average number of rooms. This result could indicate that demand for large houses increased faster than for housing generally during that decade. However, if communities considered "desirable" for social and environmental reasons have larger houses, then the result could be another estimate of the value placed on neighborhood quality.

Neither study finds very strong evidence that differences in public services and tax rates have an influence on housing prices. The value of owner occupied units is not related in any important way to differences in tax rates, school expenditures or standardized achievement scores. The one exception to this conclusion is the Bloom, Brown, and Jackson estimate that gross rents in the Boston area increased more in towns with large school expenditures. They explain the contrary results for owners and renters by arguing that in the Boston area there are many suburban towns with "good" school systems and that these towns offer a substantial variety of owner housing. Consequently, people can obtain both a house and good schools without paying a premium. Renters, on the other hand, had considerable difficulty finding units in towns with good schools, since most were predominantly owner occupied towns. Thus the limited rental property in towns with good schools commanded a premium.

The three authors contend this is not a long run or permanent price differential unless towns with good schools can prevent the development of multiunit housing. If rental units in "good" school towns are commanding a premium rent, developers profit by building in one of those towns until that premium no longer exists. At that point, there should no longer be an association between school expenditures and rents.

The strongest implication of these two chapters is that the distribution of public services, as measured by per person expenditures, though not the most important factors, do influence people's location decisions. This is particularly evident in the role of school expenditures on the population composition of each community. These results strongly suggest that for at least one population group, the residential location decision offers a viable option for obtaining the type of neighborhood and public services desired.

Political Activity

The political process is the final option open to people to satisfy their demands for public services and neighborhood quality. Dissatisfaction with reliance on private purchase of these goods and services results because individuals do not take into account the collective nature of their decisions and because certain services and amenities cannot be obtained individually. Governmental institutions and the political process, in its broadest terms, are the conventional means for making decisions about collective matters and resolving the conflicts inherent in such decisions.

The most important element of the political process in metropolitan areas is the voting process. Voting is clearly not the only means of influencing public decisions and by itself, it may not even be the singly most effective way. However, elections and their threat to public officials, gives much greater weight to other means, such as lobbying, public forums, new media efforts, and so forth. In addition, voting can constitute the final decision, as in the case of public referenda on new capital expenditures and even operating budgets in some cities.

The suppositions behind the political approach to satisfying individual demands is that people will vote for those policies or for administrations whose policies coincide with their needs and demands. The same individual characteristics that are used to predict the response of location decisions to patterns of public expenditures and neighborhood compositions should also relate to people's voting behavior on these issues. Citizens who want additional education expenditures, for example, will vote favorably in school referenda, or for public officials who support those services. Thus we should find people with higher incomes and education levels and families with school age children voting for additional education expenditures.

Cost to the individual will be important in demands for public services, and thus in voting behavior. In the case of the property tax, which is used to finance most local governments, this individual price or tax price is the proportion of the total assessed evaluation of the town on which the individual must pay taxes. For owners this is simply the assessed value of their house divided by the total assessed valuation in the community. For a renter this tax price is determined by the taxes the landlord pays on the unit and how much of these taxes are passed onto the tenant in higher rents. By this argument, people with more expensive homes in a given community have larger tax prices. Similarly, residents of communities with large nonresidential tax bases face lower tax prices than families with the same housing consumption in totally residential towns because the nonresidential land user pays some proportion of the cost of public services, reducing the amount that individual families must pay.

As with all price theory, we expect people with lower tax prices to favor larger public expenditures than people with higher tax prices, other characteristics such as income being the same. By a similar argument, people with larger homes should favor policies that increase the tax base and thereby reduce their tax prices, so long as those additions do not add more in expenditure demands or create undesirable land uses. People presumably express their demands by voting new expenditures, defeating proposed projects, and by electing public officials committed to the desired policies. We should find voting behavior related to demand characteristics and tax prices if these arguments hold.

Chapters Four, Five, and Six demonstrate that voting, both for specific expenditure items put on referenda and for incumbent public officials, reflects the expected demands for public services. The votes studied include school bond issues, zoo and welfare levies, and the attempts of an incumbent mayor identified with certain policies to seek further public office. In all cases, variables included to represent individual demands for the specific service or for the policies being followed by the incumbent administration, as well as variables measuring the cost of these services and policies to individual voters, are quite important in explaining electoral outcomes.

The chapters can be broken into two groups. The chapters by Peterson (Four) and Hanushek (Five) deal solely with referenda on specific issues, so that the only thing being voted on is additional public expenditures. In these cases it is quite logical to expect variables related to the demands for services and the price of these services to be important determinants of individual voting decisions. Jackson's work (Chapter Six) complements these two by looking at attitudes towards an incumbent mayor and the subsequent votes cast for him in the city during a statewide primary. His chapter, although with weak data, looks at a voting situation where considerations of public expenditures and taxes are not so obvious determinants of political behavior, given the presence of personality differences, ethnic cleavages, and the usual conflicts inherent in local elections.

Peterson's work shows quite clearly the importance of both demand and price effect variables on the level of school expenditures in different towns and in people's voting on these issues. People with higher incomes, school age children, and those in professional and managerial occupations all want additional school expenditures and vote for higher expenditures. At the same time, people in areas with small nonresidential tax bases have lower per person school expenditures and are less likely to vote for increases in those expenditures.

Hanushek provides similar conclusions in his study of referenda voting on welfare expenditures and a zoo proposal in Cleveland, Ohio. His results are not as clear or as concise as Peterson's, but demonstrate some of the same underlying effects. In the welfare case, lower income and black areas were more likely to favor such expenditures while higher income areas expressed greater opposition. These variables reflect the groups most and least likely to benefit from such expenditures respectively. At the same time, most people of central European origin, with the exception of German ancestry, were likely to oppose these additional expenditures.

This opposition could be reflecting a combination of antiblack feeling or a traditional adherence to a work ethic antiwelfare position. In a city such as Cleveland, these people are very likely blue collar lower middle income people who do not benefit from additional welfare expenditures and may object to others being given subsistence without working. The only difference on the voting for the zoo levy was that both upper and lower income groups were more likely to favor its passage. It is quite possible that this difference is reflecting the demand of upper income people for this recreational activity.

Hanushek did not find the expected tax effects that Peterson found, however. Homeowners were more likely to vote against both proposals, as expected, since the property tax was to be used to finance both services. However, support did not decline as the value of homes increased as would be expected by the price model. The effect of the value of homes is quite small relative to the effect of the simple ownership variable. It takes median housing values of over $35,000 before a tract's support for either referenda increases with increasing home ownership. This value is three times the city average and over ten standard deviations above this average. Thus homeowners are less likely to support these expenditures than renters.

These coefficients and their implications need to be interpreted cautiously, as Hanushek points out. The extreme levels of collinearity among the income, value, rent, and home ownership variables make it hard to have great confidence in these estimated coefficients. If there is any misspecification in the model itself, such as in the description of the income or housing effects, this collinearity will almost insure that the estimated coefficients will be biased.

For example, if support for the proposals increased among much wealthier individuals, this support might not be captured by the variable measuring the proportion of the population with income over $10,000, but might be better expressed by the housing value variable, leading to a positive coefficient. Second, since the likelihood of voting is strongly related to individual characteristics such as income, education, and home ownership, and because the census tract variables used to estimate the voting equations refer to all residents of the tract and not just to voters, it is possible that the home value variables are reflecting some of the errors due to systematic turnout differences and not just the expected voting effects.

Hanushek's analysis of voter turnout raises an interesting and important point in our discussion of using the voting process to satisfy individuals' demands for public services. His results show that upper income and better educated people have the greatest propensity to vote, or at least did in 1960. These are also the people who Mayo found most sensitive to differences in public school expenditures in selecting a residential location. If we accept the point that voting is one of the ways people express their demands for public services, as is changing residential locations, then the fact that lower income people seem less sensitive to these differences in selecting a location and are less likely to vote implies either that they simply care less about public services and the accompanying taxes or simply are not aware of how to make their demands felt.

For reasons of public policy, it is important to know if these parallel findings represent lower income people's indifference to public services because they feel unaffected by these services and the taxes used to finance them or whether they lack an understanding of how to use the different approaches to get better services.

The exception to the above observation is Hanushek's results that blacks and people with less than five years education were more likely to vote on the welfare issue. These are the people at the very bottom of the occupational ladder and the ones most likely to benefit from the welfare proposal. Their increased participation is even more significant because the vote took place during a primary election and not during a presidential election, as did the zoo levy. Conventional wisdom has it that these people are much less likely to vote in nonpresidential elections, and certainly not in primaries. The increased participation of blacks and those with low education levels suggests that they *are* aware of public service decisions that affect them and do vote in such cases. The fact that their location decisions do not depend upon school expenditures (Mayo's result), and that people further up the occupation and income scale do not vote or locate in response to school expenditure differences, simply indicates that these public services are not important to them and consequently they do not vote.

Jackson's chapter uses a completely different situation to show the same results as Peterson and Hanushek. He examines homeowners' attitudes towards an incumbent Boston mayor, John Collins, and aggregate voting behavior in a subsequent primary election in which Collins tried for higher office. The expenditure and tax implications of policies associated with a mayor are more ambiguous than school or welfare referenda. However, Jackson finds that surveyed attitudes among homeowners are consistent with those one would expect, given the service and tax policies followed by Collins. The voting patterns follow these expectations and those in the attitude data.

The most important effect, for our purposes, is that home ownership and home value affected attitudes and voting behavior in the manner predicted by both the tax price model and that found by Peterson in his study of school voting. Collins followed a policy of decreases, or slight increases, in the local property tax. Jackson's analysis finds that the mayor's support among homeowners increased as the assessed valuation of their homes increased, other things such as evaluations of the adequacy of public services being equal. Collins's support was lowest where people felt they were not getting adequate public services.

Jackson's analysis has several weaknesses however. The election data are the same type used by Hanushek, and of course have the same liabilities. The problems created by differences in turnout rates among the census tracts are compounded by the fact that Jackson is studying a partisan primary that excludes Republicans. The use of the survey data to corroborate the election analysis is helpful in this regard, but the survey itself has difficulties. Only homeowners were surveyed and they constitute a small and unrepresentative segment of the Boston population. This weakens the link between the survey findings and the voting analysis. In addition, the survey has a limited number of relevant items, and the reliability of these is debatable. Jackson has little success in explaining the responses to these questions with variables representing both the model we are discussing and the more traditional urban politics explanations, such as ethnic and neighborhood ties.

The statistical significance of our voting model based on people's public service demands in this situations increases its credibility, but cannot validate it. However, the model's extension to the case of an incumbent mayor and to voting in a more general election suggests its applicability to a broader and more important class of political decisions. The results support the contention that elections are important as a way for people to express their demands for public services and that electoral results reflect these demands.

The three voting papers provide corroborating evidence for the public service discussions of the Bloom, Brown, and Jackson chapter. Their work argues that changes in a community's population composition, tax base, and intergovernmental transfers result in changes in per household school expenditures and in equalized tax rates. The contention is that people locate in or maintain residence in an area because of its housing stock, accessibility, or neighborhood characteristics, even though that town may not have the most desired public services. These people express their demands by advocating and voting for the desired changes in public services and taxes. The exercise of their political franchise leads to changes in the level and type of public expenditures available in that community. The voting papers provide evidence that people do use their votes and political access to alter a town's public services and to make them conform to individual demands.

An important result of the three voting studies, worth reemphasizing, is the consistent observation that the distribution of the costs of public services is an important determinant of individual demands. All three studied situations where the property tax was the sole or predominant source of revenues for the proposed project or where an attempt to hold down the property tax was a major policy. Homeowners, more than renters, opposed additional expenditures and favored the mayor who kept property taxes low. Both Peterson and Jackson also find this support for nonspending increases as the individual homeowner's share of additional expenditures increases. Thus the price individuals must pay for public services is an important determinant of their desired service level, as measured by expenditures, and consequently of their votes.

People weighing changes in local tax structures should clearly consider these effects. Such changes alter individual tax prices, and shift demands for public expenditures. This affects local voting behavior, which ultimately changes the pattern of public services. For example, Peterson presents a case where local voting on school referenda changed markedly following the introduction of a circuit breaker provision, which substantially reduced the cost of additional school expenditures to poor people and the elderly. According to Peterson's analysis, these people switched their votes in large numbers from an election prior to introduction of the circuit breaker clause to one following. The switching was sufficient to reverse the earlier defeat of the referenda. The subject of alternative revenue sources is the topic for a subsequent conference,[1] but suffice it to say, shifts in local taxes have major impacts on local expenditures. One might want to consider a policy that provides local governments much greater discretion in how they raise revenues so as to provide a means for building support for various service proposals.

Legal Approaches

In the final chapter, Fessler and May present an alternative to voting and its associated political activity to redress discrimination in the access to conventional political methods (such as denials of voting rights) and in the delivery of public services. This method is the suit against local governments and their officials. Suits are predicated on the basis of demonstrable and glaring differences in the provision of services to specific minority groups. They have been filed largely under the equal protection clause of the federal constitution, although the emphasis is shifting towards the state courts and state constitutions after recent decisions by the United States Supreme Court. Suits filed on behalf of blacks citing clear racial discrimination have been upheld. Litigation has not been as successful where the basis of discrimination is argued to be economic.

Equal protection suits have so far only been successful at fighting discrimination in the delivery of services within individual jurisdictions. Other than the *Serrano vs. Priest* decision on school financing in California and some roughly similar cases, the equal protection suits have not touched the question of differences in services among jurisdictions, even though the jurisdictions are within—and thus controlled by—a single state government. So far, successful cases have rested on demonstrated local government discrimination in the distribution of expenditures on certain services to particular residential areas within the jurisdiction. For example, successful suits have developed from situations where street paving, sewer services, and sidewalks have been provided in one area and not another, and this second area is identifiable by the race of its residents.

The courts have only gone so far as to judge services on the basis of equal expenditures, not some measure of equal services. In one case, a suit against the mayor of the City of New York claimed that although residents of a certain area of the city were receiving expenditures on a local park equal to those in other areas, they were not receiving equal services because the park was always in poorer physical condition due to breakage and vandalism. The court held that the city was not responsible for providing equal services, somehow measured, but simply equal inputs of expenditures. Likewise, in requiring action on the part of local governments subsequent to successful equal protection suits, the courts have only demanded that the local jurisdiction provide equal expenditures, not equal services to each area. The courts have finessed the same question that most researchers have—namely, how to get measures other than simply expenditures of public services.

Litigation filed on their behalf provides poor and minority groups a way to express their demands for public services. The attractiveness of this approach for these groups should be evident from the discussions of the previous approaches. Because of economic constraints and overt racial discrimination, these people find it very difficult to get the desired public services by changing their residential location. Blacks of all income levels are systematically excluded from most suburban communities and forced to live in central city areas. They are then unable to take advantage of the better neighborhoods and public services offered in outlying areas and to lengthen their journey to work to gain access to a wider variety of communities, and unable to use the locational approach to satisfy their demands. The conventional political approach also has not proved to be completely satisfactory. In some cases minorities have been explicitly discriminated against in gaining access to the political system. The various barriers to voter registration, including poll taxes or the need to own property, are blatant examples of such discrimination.

There are other causes for their nonparticipation, however. Articulating demands and converting them into a credible number of votes is required before public officials will begin to respond to individual demands. The organizational skills, resources, and experience needed to accomplish this articulation are generally absent from minority and lower income groups. This deficiency—the feeling that voices are not heard, and possibly a lack of understanding of how the political system should and does work—provides further reasons why these groups are unable politically to satisfy their demands for public services and neighborhood quality. Consequently, they have resorted to legal action, particularly since it is now possible to find lawyers and legal scholars willing and able to find the proper justification for these suits. The filing of successful suits, and even the threat of legal action, quickly overcome these other barriers. The remedies sought are not just a redresss in the operation of the political process, or an end to discrimination in metropolitan housing markets, but an immediate equalization of expenditures by the local government to compensate for historical discrimination.

METROPOLITAN GOVERNANCE AND THE
SATISFACTION OF PUBLIC NEEDS

Given the various ways people can obtain the types of neighborhoods and public services they want, the important question is, what are the uses, advantages, and limitations of these approaches from the standpoint of metropolitan governance. The difficulties with relying on private provision and purchase were outlined earlier and it is these difficulties that create the need for other alternatives. However, it is important to keep in mind that this method is neither impossible nor unavailable: it merely has certain difficulties, as do the other solutions.

The notion that residential mobility in a metropolitan area can satisfy people's demands for neighborhoods and public services has a certain appeal, as well as validity; but there are disadvantages. First, it necessitates a large variety of communities in the metropolitan area. The combination of attributes influencing location decisions are extremely numerous and varied. People want accessibility, a certain type and size of house and adjacent land, particular amounts of different public services, and neighbors of a certain social and economic class. Even if all employment were concentrated at the center of a radially designed metropolitan area, there must be the different housing, neighborhood, and public service combinations available at each accessibility level (distance from the city center), so that people can make the conventional trade-off between accessibility and housing costs and still have a large choice among the other considerations. In more realistic metropolitan areas, where workplaces are scattered throughout the region, it is even more difficult to envision providing everyone the choice of services and neighbors at each accessibility level and at an affordable housing price.

Given the complex attributes affecting location decisions, the variations in people's tastes, and the difficulty in providing enough options, people exercising the mobility solution must still sacrifice some attributes in their location choice. These trade-offs go beyond the simple housing cost-accessibility exchange which is the core of traditional locational and land allocation models. Communities with the desired type and price of housing and accessibility may not offer the right public service package. Conversely, communities with the desired public services may only have housing that is too large or too expensive, and so on. People are thus forced to make compromises among their desired attributes. Even after making the "best" locational choice to satisfy their various demands, given the alternatives, families may still want to alter their life style—either with an additional room on the house, increased taxes for more public school expenditures, the extra cost of private transportation, and so on. Certainly, a larger variety of communities leads to greater satisfaction of individual needs but people will still be left with demands to satisfy through other means once a location is chosen.

The greater the number of individual communities in a metropolitan area, and the greater the similarity of tastes, income, etc., within each community, the easier it will be for most people to select a community that most nearly fits their demands. However, once this happens, there are many unresolved problems and decisions of a collective nature, which are outside the jurisdiction of the individual communities. The best example of such problems and ones that greatly affect the satisfaction of the individual residents are environmental quality, transportation, and land use. These activities provide appropriate illustrations because any decisions on these matters affect most parts of the metropolitan area: one community cannot improve its accessibility to other parts of the metropolitan area without also improving the accessibility of many other communities. Or if one town either strengthens or weakens its environmental controls, many other towns will share in the benefits or the costs. Land use decisions have generally been left to individual communities but decisions by one town to attract or exclude certain types of housing and nonresidential activities influence the pressures on other towns' land use decisions. The need for some form of metropolitan body to consider the spillover effects of these decisions should be obvious.

The locational approach to meeting people's demands for public goods has an additional deficiency. This method essentially converts the problem of providing public goods into conventional private goods market where the commodity is a complex composite good consisting of housing, services, neighbors, and accessibility. Prices are set by the interaction of aggregate demand and the ability of landowners and communities to provide the parts of the composite good. In this scheme, the individual family is merely a passive consumer, deciding how much to spend on housing and other services, assessing the marginal value of these attributes, and then buying accordingly.

As with all private market solutions, this one assumes that income is properly distributed, that people have no interest in others' decisions, and that everyone has equal access to the market. The maldistribution of income and the interdependence of decisions are manifest in beliefs that a metropolitan area's welfare is increased if everyone receives at least certain minimum levels of shelter, health care, education, and so on. Our extensive public housing, health, and education programs attest to these concerns. With a series of small, "balkanized" governments it becomes virtually impossible to deal with these problems. There are very clear and strong incentives for each community to ignore the question of merit goods, to hope others will take care of providing them, and thus to avoid the associated costs. The net result is that only the government where the needy are located provides the services—which generally is the older, poorer, central city.

Discrimination in the housing market, whether by social or by income groups, exacerbates the above problems as well as presenting difficulties of its own. If one is going to rely on the residential location decision to provide people with the public services they want, we cannot deny people access to communities that offer the desired services—just as we now prevent producers of other goods, such as food, public accommodations, and so on, from practicing discrimination. The forms and type, if not the extent, of discrimination against blacks and other minorities in the housing market is obvious and it prevents them from obtaining desired public services.

A less obvious, but more serious, form of housing market discrimination is on the basis of wealth. Suburban towns systematically exclude housing in low income families' price ranges. A most important contributor to this income discrimination is the property tax, which is used to finance virtually all local public services. The property tax distributes the cost of public services among families on the basis of their housing consumption. Within any given community, the smaller one's housing consumption, the less one pays for these public services, with the cost shifted onto the consumers of larger houses and nonresidential users. Thus people with large housing consumption demands have incentives to maintain towns with little or no low cost housing.

Because of the systematic correlation between housing consumption, income, and levels of public services, those communities with larger housing units are generally the ones with larger public expenditures. For example, Boston suburbs with large school expenditures have virtually no rental units. Limiting the housing stock in these towns to the larger and more expensive units prohibits people with low demands for housing (because of either taste or income reasons) and high demands for public services from obtaining the desired service levels. They must either buy more housing than they want or pay a premium for the few available units of the type they desire.

Every tax structure has distributional implications requiring some people to pay more than others for the same services. Unfortunately the property tax and the restrictions on the housing market tie these distributional considerations to the level of housing consumption. This consumption, along with the spatial distributions of housing type, determines access to public services. In terms of the "voting with one's feet" model, housing prices become a form of poll tax—and a fairly high and inequitable one. Effective application of the location model requires that we find ways of insuring the access of all people to every community.

The incentives to exclude lower cost housing from individual communities lead to a grand "beggar thy neighbor" policy by individual communities in the absence of any metropolitanwide authority to restrict zoning controls and other exclusionary practices. The consequences of these practices are the concentration of low income people and blacks in specific areas of the metropolitan region without the ability or the resources to get necessary services.

High concentrations of these groups result in very high costs and inefficiencies in the provision of public services, not necessarily as measured by per capita expenditures, but in a more realistic output sense. We know very little about the process of converting expenditures in the public sector into actual services and the impact of the number, types, and mixes of people in a community on this conversion process. However, research strongly suggests that the type of people in a neighborhood and the other children in a classroom have important effects on the quality of the services available and produced for any given expenditure of money.

The best example of this is current work in the field of education. Most of these studies show that one important factor in children's performance is the nature of the peer group. Given the decreasing (though still positive) productivity of large expenditures of money in schools with high concentrations of children from poor and minority backgrounds, and with the high concentrations of these children in central cities, it becomes increasingly costly to try to provide them an adequate education.

A better policy is to have the currently homogeneous schools absorb small numbers of disadvantaged students. The same arguments can undoubtedly be made for attempts to provide safe neighborhoods, housing, and other facilities. Metropolitan areas currently lack any means to prevent the creation of these high concentrations of poor and minority families and to disperse the existing ones. Without such means, the only choice is to spend considerable amounts of money to provide the necessary services and environments—or to neglect the problems entirely and provide grossly inadequate services. To achieve both efficiency and equality, it is better to prevent towns from excluding lower income and minority families.

The political process and reliance on voting procedures is not without its problems and difficulties. Consideration must be given to these difficulties when proposing political processes as a means of satisfying individual demands. The most serious liability is that without substantial participation in the political process by all people affected by decisions, and by those who have demands for public services, the final results will not reflect their demands. This need for widespread participation is not confined to excursions to the ballot box once or twice a year, even though these chapters examined only explicit voting behavior.

No one argues that voting is the only means people have for controlling public decisions. Effective operation of the political system requires that people's demands be articulated and be well understood by policy makers as they make budgets and administer services. Articulation of these demands requires organizations, political parties, and other citizen interest groups able to bring pressure to bear on officials. For the most part, this pressure insures that officials understand people's demands *and* know that the groups' members will appear at the polls with the appropriate political information. Voting legitimizes and enforces these lobbying efforts.

The political approach puts a premium on what political scientists have begun to call issue voting. If people are always voting on the basis of symbolic differences in candidates or other nonissue related matters, then officials have no need to take those individuals' positions into account when making decisions. The chapters on voting behavior discussed in this volume strongly indicate that in referenda voting, and even in a Democratic primary in the model of a symbolically oriented city, voting is issue oriented. However, it is still up to educators and other commentators on our political life to get across the point that the purpose of political behavior is to express individual demands with respect to public activities, and that citizens are largely responsible for the activities of officials and the performance of the system.

The structure of the political system and the types of elections influence how governments respond to variations in demands. Although not the topic of these chapters, this subject warrants a few brief comments. We have already pointed out that jurisdictions that are too small geographically are not able to cope with problems such as land use, transportation, and environmental quality. Jurisdictions that are too large also create difficulties. Large jurisdictions will have more heterogeneous demands, and thus more conflicts among individuals than small ones. This diversity creates a serious problem: if the government tries to promote uniform services, taxes, and environments throughout the area, there will be little satisfaction of individual demands. However, governments have difficulty varying the types, amounts, and financing of public services among neighborhoods in response to these variations in demands. The current trend is to enforce equal expenditure levels within jurisdictions because it is impossible to separate a government's efforts to respond to demand differences from efforts at outright discrimination.

In addition to frustrating individual demands, large jurisdictions that include activities that could and should be decided in smaller, separate jurisdictions are politically inefficient. People spend their political energy and influence resolving conflicts that would not exist if decisions could be made in smaller units. For example, it is quite likely that most decisions on education policy, safety, and recreation can be made by relatively small units, while decisions on transportation, land use, and environmental quality should be made at the metropolitan level.

However, in a metropolitanwide government responsible for administering education, safety, and recreation programs, public officials and voters will spend a considerable portion of their time, energy, and political capital determining local services rather than developing the appropriate metropolitan policies. The representatives from areas concerned about getting better schools must sacrifice some of their influence over transportation and land use decisions in order to get the type of schools desired. Consequently, transportation policy will not adequately reflect all interests. If school decisions are made at the appropriate level, all the members of the metropolitan government could insure that their constituents' interests in the metropolitan issues are being represented. The metropolitan government officials have the responsibility of dealing with the problems of spillovers among towns, but this is a substantially different concern from having metropolitanwide services.

The difficulties with large jurisdictions illustrate the problems involved in a political solution. Unless a jurisdiction's population is homogeneous with respect to the type and amount of services desired, conflicts over the services will remain. Such conflicts are inherent in public goods and are the motivation for the small homogeneous communities of the location model.

The structure and organization of local governments affects how well it can cope with these diversities. One of the key elements in the heterogeneity of local demands is the different priorities people assign to each service and even aspects of each service. For example, families with children may be primarily concerned with education policies; the elderly with public safety; and the very poor with public housing. Some of the diversity and conflicts within a jurisdiction can be accommodated if policies on all services and programs are adjusted in response to the more intense feelings. Thus if public decisions can provide good schools, additional personal safety protection, and public housing, each of the above groups may be better off because they are receiving the service about which they are most concerned, even though it "costs" them in the form of paying for additional services they may not want.

Intense concerns are better accommodated in multifunction governments than by independent, single purpose agencies who have no way to package changes in several services. In a general government the representatives and executives campaign for office on the basis of decisions and platforms encompassing all services; the elements of past decisions and platforms can be selected to appeal to the different intensities of feelings.

The clearest illustration of single issue decision making is Hanushek's analysis of the welfare and zoo referenda in Cleveland. Decisions about welfare spending, the development of a zoo, and presumably other services not voted on that year, were decided by separate referenda. This procedure allows virtually no interaction of demands and makes coordinated decisions on several services impossible. People who strongly wanted a better zoo had no way to exchange their willingness to support other proposals to gain support for the zoo. At the same time, those who felt strongly about services voted on in other referenda could not obtain the necessary votes by agreeing to vote for the zoo. By combining positions on many services and issues into one platform, as in a general election, it is possible to create the coalitions and accommodations demanded by the variations in intensities. Thus general elections, rather than individual referenda, seem to offer more hope of being responsive to the priorities and variations in demands that exist in a nonhomogeneous community.

The examples used in the above discussion reiterate the difficulties mentioned previously with the property tax. These examples all illustrated situations where the people most concerned about a particular service generally wanted to increase the level of that service. The result of the coalition building was to increase the level of all services. This imposes a burden on those who did not want any of the services, and who were only concerned about their tax payments. With the current structure of the property tax the only way to express this concern (short of moving to another community with low taxes and low services) is to reduce housing consumption by getting a smaller house or an apartment. However, more flexible local tax instruments, whose incidences could be varied to take into account the distribution of demand for the services being provided, would alleviate some of this problem. As it is now, tax payments are tied to people's housing consumption rather than to the nature of the services being provided. However, we would need reform of both the local tax structure and the voting process to insure that decisions about services *and* taxes are related and sensitive to the distribution of demands within each community.

The legal remedies for redressing the problems created by people being denied access to both the locational market and the political process are not without their difficulties. In the short run, the mandate to equalize expenditures on various services within a single jurisdiction will have either of two effects. One is to raise the tax rate so that expenditures can be raised in the area discriminated against. Alternatively, expenditures can be reduced in the better served areas. Both actions involve a redistribution of wealth within the community. This redistribution, whether or not it is desirable and necessary, is likely to evoke responses from citizens in that community. The obvious responses are for various people to move to other jurisdictions where the demands for redistribution will not be so strong, or simply to substantially reduce public provision of services and resort to private purchases where possible. The new result in either case will be far less redress than initially desired.

In the long run this type of legal action is not likely to be a productive alternative to the problem of satisfying individual demands. As long as suits are restricted to the behavior of officials within individual jurisdictions, the possibility of being sued to equalize expenditures on various services throughout the metropolitan area will certainly provide incentives not to create the type of metropolitanwide government desirable on other grounds. As metropolitan government becomes more highly integrated with respect to geographic coverage, services, and financing arrangements, it becomes more susceptible to equal protection suits.

CONCLUSION

The workings of the different approaches to satisfying individual demands, their presence in all metropolitan areas, and their strengths and limitations, have important implications for people involved with developing and administering metropolitan institutions. One important lesson is for policy makers to be aware that all approaches exist and that people will use whatever means seem best or most available to try to satisfy their demands. Attempts to implement one set of plans or policies without understanding people's desires and motivations (as well as how they might use available alternatives to meet those desires) can lead to frustrations of the desired policy.

The best example of this is the attempts to rectify the exclusion of blacks and the poor from access to public services by suing local governments and requiring an equalization of expenditures. On the surface this seems to solve the problem. However, if it results in the wealthier people leaving the particular community or substituting private for public provision of services wherever possible, it is not likely to lead to much improvement for the minority groups. There are any number of other ways in which these different alternatives can interact to circumvent policy.

There are other cases where policies fail because policy makers do not recognize the different ways people have of pursuing their own interests. Here it is not so much that the policy will not succeed in doing what was intended as it is that the accompanying and unintended consequences more than offset the gains. The best example of such a result would be if the locational approach were followed by creating a large number of small, relatively homogeneous communities, which then developed their own package of public services, tax rates, and land use policies without regard to metropolitanwide impacts. The end result would likely be a few very attractive and exclusive communities, with the poor and minority groups concentrated in a few areas and not receiving adequate services and everyone wondering why the cities are in such a state.

Hopefully policy makers and people concerned with metropolitan environments in general will recognize the variety of ways available for satisfying people's desires for decent homes, neighborhoods, and environments, and will try to use all the alternatives to reach this end. Certainly the more alternatives available, the better they are understood, and the more imaginatively they are used, the more likely we are to develop viable metropolitan governments.

Chapter Two

Local Public Goods and Residential Location: An Empirical Test of the Tiebout Hypothesis

Stephen K. Mayo

Choosing a place to live is a complicated matter. It involves choosing both a location and a multidimensional bundle of residential attributes the components of which are embodied in the residence itself, its surrounding neighborhood, the governmental and private services that are provided to the residence, and its proximity to places of employment, shopping, and other activities. The choice depends not only on the attributes of a particular location but on the costs of living there as well: housing and land costs, commuting costs, and local taxes. According to economic theories of location, the choice depends ultimately on a balancing of costs and benefits at various locations subject to a household's income and its tastes, the latter being determined by household characteristics other than income such as family size and race.

One would hope for such a theory to be well articulated and tested by now. A review of the literature, however, leads to an impression of not so much competing theories of location as compartmentalized theories. It appears that frequently the factors held constant by one theory under ceteris paribus assumptions are at the core of another. For example, residential location theory, identified with Alonso, Kain, Muth, and others, places great stock in the notion that locations are determined in large measure as consumers trade-off increased commuting costs for greater amounts of residential space. Britton Harris has asserted of such theories that they are "almost wholly unsupported by careful empirical studies."[1] In their place he suggests a greater emphasis on residential attributes other than space, especially physical characteristics of housing, as determinants of location. Charles Tiebout,[2] in a pioneering study, suggested the importance of local public goods and taxes in determining residential choices, asserting that households shop among potential locations for a preferred combination of local public goods and taxes and choose where to live accordingly.

Empirical research has paralleled such theoretical compartmentalization to a considerable degree. With few exceptions empirical tests of residential location choice have relied on rather narrow sets of explanatory variables, leading to the possibility of biased evaluations of the effects of particular variables or types of variables. For example, in a recent review, Ball[3] presents results of eleven studies of the determinants of housing prices (and by implication, residential choice), no two of which include the same sets of independent variables and most of which omit local public goods and tax variables altogether. Not surprisingly, the results of such studies differ greatly.

Further, most empirical studies fail to consider one of the most important and unresolved issues of location theory: the degree to which different groups of people are influenced by particular residential attributes. One reason is a result of the most common type of econometric model used to test residential location hypotheses—the hedonic price index. At the heart of such models is the notion that the bundle of residential attributes offered at a particular location will influence its attractiveness to potential residents and will therefore be reflected in its market value.[4] Thus property values are regressed on housing characteristics, sometimes but not often including local public goods and taxes, and the results are presented as a test of the influence of various housing characteristics on residential choice. It is likely, however, that the poor and the rich, large and small families, blacks and whites, and other groups are affected in considerably different ways by changes in the characteristics of areas and the costs of living there. Consequently, if local authorities or private interests succeed in changing the character of an area, they are likely to change its relative attractiveness to different groups and eventually the composition of the population living there.

Because of such a possibility, the limitations of most empirical studies to general market effects, excluding effects on population subgroups, appears to be quite serious. What is needed to evaluate the appropriateness of alternative explanations of residential choice is a model that controls for a wide range of locational influences—those suggested by the many compartmentalized theories—and that permits consideration of different locational behavior by different groups.

The following analysis presents results of one such model. Effects on various population subgroups of changes in an area's characteristics are estimated, and the results are compared to those of other empirical studies of residential location.

A MODEL OF RESIDENTIAL CHOICE

The neoclassical theory of residential choice presents the process of site allocation within urban areas as one of competitive bidding, whereby various housholds participate in a hypothetical auction with sites allocated to the highest bidder.[5] In theory, household bids depend upon households' income, tastes, the distance that a potential residence is located from the workplace of the household head, and on the prices of goods other than housing. The hypothetical auction of the neoclassical model takes place on a featureless plain where there are neither structures nor public goods and services.

In the interest of greater realism, given the long lives of housing structures and the presence of a public sector, the naïve neoclassical model may be generalized to take account of the characteristics of housing and services offered at a particular site.[6] Depending on the relative preferences of various household types and upon their incomes, the market clearing process represented by the hypothetical auction of sites results in the observed spatial distribution of households.

One way of describing the observed distribution of households is as a family of discrete probability distributions. For example, suppose that there exist a finite number of residential sites in a given city denoted by $i = 1,2, \ldots, I$, and a finite number of workplaces, denoted by $j = 1,2, \ldots, J$. Further suppose that the population may be divided into behaviorally distinct submarkets on the basis of household incomes and other characteristics such that there are K groups denoted by $k = 1,2, \ldots, K$. We may then denote the probability that a household whose head works at j and whose income and other characteristics place him in submarket k lives at site i as p_{ijk} where:

$$\sum_{i=1}^{I} p_{ijk} = 1$$

To completely describe the residential distribution of a city's population, J times K distributions suffice.

Such distributions represent the outcome of competitive processes and may therefore be expressed in terms of those factors that influence the level of competing bids. For a particular submarket/workplace group the probability of locating at a particular site will depend on the level of its own bid at that site and on the levels of competing bids; if its bid increases, the level of competition remaining the same, the probability that it locates at a given site would increase. Its own bid depends on factors mentioned above—distance from workplace, the prices of goods other than housing, and the characteristics of housing and public goods and services offered at that location. Competing bids depend on accessibility not to a particular workplace but rather to all possible workplaces, and also on nonhousing prices and characteristics of housing and public goods and services at the site in question. If a particular household type is attracted by a particular site attribute to a greater degree than are other groups, so that its bid changes more rapidly with respect to that attribute than do the bids of others, then the observed probability of locating at those sites where the attribute in question is in relatively greater supply will be high.

The model just described lends itself to empirical estimation according to the following:

$$p_{ijk} = f_{jk}(Z_{li}, t_{ij})$$ (1)

where,

p_{ijk} = the proportion of all workers of type $k = 1,2,\ldots,K$ who are employed at workplace $j = 1,2,\ldots,J$ who live in residential subarea $i = 1,2,\ldots,I$

Z_{li} = a vector of residential attributes defined for each subarea i and where $l = 1,2,\ldots,L$

t_{ij} = distance from workplace j to residential subarea i.[7]

For convenience it is assumed that nonhousing prices are equal for all subgroups and thus do not need to be considered in equation (1). Estimates of p_{ijk} may be gotten by dividing the number of workplace j, subgroup k workers who live in residential subarea i by the total number of workplace j, subgroup k workers. The vector of residential attributes should include housing and neighborhood characteristics, a measure of a site's accessibility to employment opportunities (to account for competing bids), local public goods and services, and, without loss of generality, local tax levels.[8]

It may be shown that the coefficient of commuting time (t_{ij}) will vary monotonically with the slope of the bid rent function in the neoclassical analysis of Alonso.[9] The greater, in absolute value, the slope of the bid rent function, the greater will be the change in the probability of living at a particular location with respect to distance. Thus empirical tests of the model provide a direct test of the neoclassical theory, which suggests that the derivative of the slope of the bid rent function with respect to income is positive.

The model just described permits one to test directly the impact on location of variables suggested both by neoclassical location theory and by proponents of other theories concerned with residential location such as Tiebout. Further, it permits consideration of differential impacts of such variables on different groups defined in terms of household characteristics and workplace location. It represents an alternative to hedonic price studies, which focus only on measuring broad market price effects to test the relevance of alternative locational influences.

EMPIRICAL ESTIMATION OF THE MODEL

The Data

The area studied in this analysis is the Milwaukee Standard Metropolitan Statistical Area (SMSA). Milwaukee was chosen because it offered an exceptionally rich source of data assembled by the Southeastern Wisconsin Regional Planning Commission (SEWRPC) as part of a transportation and land use study. In spring of 1963, a household interview survey was conducted by SEWPRC within the Milwaukee "urbanizing area," which included most of the Milwaukee SMSA, and parts of Ozaukee, Racine, and Kenosha Counties. The sample consisted of roughly 17,000 households of which some 10,000 were within the Milwaukee SMSA. Because much of the collateral data employed in this analysis was not available for outlying counties, only the Milwaukee SMSA was considered here.

The sample was chosen randomly from a listing of electrical meters within each geographical area; the sampling ratio was about 3 percent within the Milwaukee SMSA. Data were collected on socioeconomic characteristics of households such as income, family size, race, age, and occupation, and on trip patterns of household members. Included in the trip data was information on residence location classified by census tract, quarter section, and "traffic analysis zone" and workplace location of the primary wage earner and any secondary wage earners. Information on the socioeconomic characteristics of the 10,000 households living in the Milwaukee SMSA was used to stratify the sample according to distinct behavioral groups. Information on the primary wage earner's workplace was used to further stratify the sample.

Some households included in the sample failed to respond to one or more questions regarding socioeconomic status. There were hardly any instances of failure to respond to questions of race, sex, family size, or the number of household members contributing to income—stratification variables used in this analysis. There was a nonresponse rate of about 8 percent on the question of household income, however. Households who failed to reveal income were arbitrarily assigned to the income category which contained the median of the income distribution, $4,000 to $8,000 per year, and which, according to the 1960 Census of Population and Housing, contained nearly 50 percent of all households in the Milwaukee SMSA. This arbitrary procedure would bias the results for the $4,000 to $8,000 income group if there were a systematic relationship between nonresponse and income. Examination of the data revealed no convincing evidence that any significant relationship in fact exists.

Socioeconomic Variables

Many attributes of households can be hypothesized to affect residential location choices. The attributes of the decision making unit that are important in determining residential location act either through their effects on preferences for residential characteristics or on costs of locating in particular places. Attributes which affect preferences are practically innumerable and range from relatively important variables such as income and family size to whether or not a family has pets or strong feelings about the frequency with which their trash is removed. Costs of location are also affected to a greater or lesser degree by each of many household attributes.

The stratifying variables that have been used and their categories are given in Table 2-1. There are 96 different possible mutually exclusive categories. Many of the categories had so few members that they could not be analyzed. The analysis therefore concentrated on only twelve categories, which account for somewhat more than three-quarters of the sample population. The initial criterion for including a group was that it include at least 50 observations from the sample when further stratified according to workplace location. In actuality a group was included if it merely had a sample size greater than 50 at only the most central workplace location of four workplace locations considered. Consequently some groups actually had fewer than 50 observations for outlying workplaces.

The groups that were actually considered are shown in Table 2-2. The groups included represent all four income classes, both sexes, all three household sizes, and both classes of "contributors to income." In the case of the highest income group households both "contributors" categories were combined to reach the minimum sample size.

There were too few observations for nonwhites to meet the minimum sample size of 50 for any group. For nonwhites to have been included would have required combining roughly a dozen of the original 96 categories in order to meet the required sample size. Combining households across socioeconomic categories was felt to be undesirable insofar as it lumps together groups whose behavior is not likely to be homogeneous. It is not possible, therefore, to directly compare the behavior of whites and nonwhites on a finely stratified basis.

Table 2-1. Stratification Variables

1. Household income
   a. less than $4000
   b. $4000 - $8000
   c. $8000 - $12,000
   d. more than $12,000
2. Race
   a. white
   b. nonwhite
3. Household size
   a. one or two
   b. three to five
   c. six or more
4. Sex of household head
   a. male
   b. female
5. Persons contributing to family income
   a. one
   b. two or more

Table 2-2. Socioeconomic Analysis Groups

Group	Income	Race	Household Size	Sex	Contributors to Income
1	$0-4000	white	1 or 2	male	1
2	$0-4000	white	1 or 2	female	1
3	$4-8,000	white	1 or 2	male	1
4	$4-8,000	white	1 or 2	female	1
5	$4-8,000	white	2	male	2
6	$4-8,000	white	3-5	male	1
7	$4-8,000	white	3-5	male	2
8	$4-8,000	white	6+	male	1
9	$8-12,000	white	2	male	2
10	$8-12,000	white	3-5	male	1
11	$8-12,000	white	3-5	male	2
12	$12,000+	white	3-5	male	1 or 2

The variables used to stratify the population are to a large degree conventional in studies of residential location and housing demand, and would seem in most cases to have easily understood and powerful effects on housing preferences and costs. Other variables that have been considered in the literature are age, occupation and industry, religion, social class, kinship ties, and stage in a family's "life cycle." Failing to stratify according to these other variables introduces a misspecification into the estimated models that may be more or less serious. If the omitted stratification variables are not in fact important, there is little cause to worry; if they are important behavioral characteristics, they may both bias estimated parameters and result in a greater proportion of unexplained variance than had they been controlled for.

Workplaces

The model developed earlier required that behavioral relationships be stratified not only by socioeconomic characteristics of the population, but by workplaces as well. The reason for stratifying by workplace is simply that households are assumed to optimize their locational choices with respect to a predetermined workplace location. The desirability of one residential area vis-à-vis another depends on its distance from the fixed workplace, and households will bid on residential sites accordingly. For a given level of competing demand, a household will be more or less likely to acquire a site depending upon its own evaluation and bid.

The workplace zones that were chosen are based upon groupings of "traffic analysis zones" utilized in the transportation land use study done by the Southeastern Wisconsin Regional Planning Commission. Four workplace zones, containing nearly 80 percent of the employment of the Milwaukee SMSA, were chosen. For each zone a representative workplace was chosen from which travel times to residence zones were measured. In each case the representative workplace was chosen with an eye toward choosing the "employment centroid" of the zone: that point about which employment was relatively evenly distributed.

Figure 2-1 portrays the four workplace zones that were chosen and

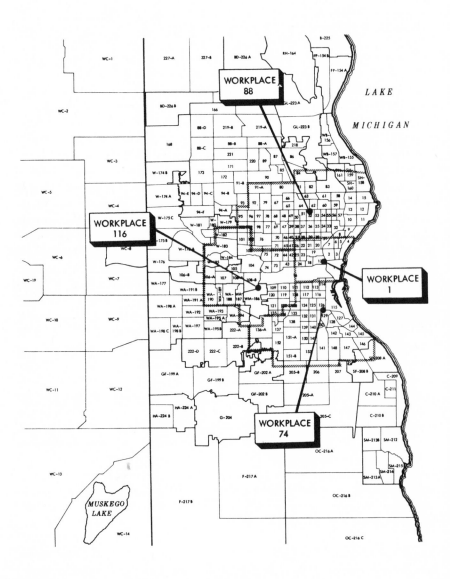

Figure 2-1. Workplace Locations

the representative workplace for each zone. Workplace 1 has boundaries of roughly 1-3/4 miles by 2-1/4 miles and is the smallest zone in strictly areal terms. Workplace 88 is the largest in area and is roughly 3-1/2 by 5 miles between its widest boundaries. In terms of peak hour travel time, however, both workplace zones have roughly the same "time dimensions"—that is, the time that it takes to get from boundary to boundary is roughly the same for both zones. The census tracts that are most widely separated within workplace 1 are roughly 32 minutes from each other at peak travel hours. Within workplace 88, the greatest time separation is about 33.6 minutes. The time dimensions of the other two workplaces, 74 and 116, are comparable to those of workplaces 1 and 88. All in all, none of the four workplaces should have markedly different travel time measurement errors from the others.

One possible source of error in the estimated equations for multiple worker households exists, since households were stratified only according to the workplace of primary wage earners. Stratifying by the workplaces of other employed household members would have made multiple wage earner sample sizes statistically negligible. If one believes that workplace locations of secondary wage earners are an important determinant of residential location, then multiple wage earner households should be stratified by secondary workplaces as well, and travel time to the secondary workplaces should be included as a variable that affects location. If secondary workplace locations are unimportant, then there is no cause for concern. The estimated equations should provide some indication as to the severity of this problem. If secondary workplaces are important, predictive equations for multiple worker households will consistently have less predictive power than will those for single worker households.

Residential Attributes

The observational unit for residential locations in this study is the census tract. All residential attributes on which data were collected were transformed to "census tract variables," since the census tract was the smallest observational unit for which most data were available. Methods of prorating data that were not initially collected on a census tract basis varied, based on assumptions concerning the nature of their external effects. For example, elementary school achievement levels were assigned to census tracts on the basis of assigning a census tract to the elementary school district whose boundaries included the largest single share of the census tract's population. Variables that measure the percentage of a census tract's land in various uses were created by prorating the area of "traffic analysis zones" in each use to the census tract based on the area of the census tract within the boundaries of each component traffic analysis zone.

Groups of variables included in the analysis are suggested by a wide variety of disciplines that have dealt with questions of residential choice, demand for housing, and urban social structure. Broadly categorized, the following groups of variables have been considered:

1. Housing and socioeconomic characteristics
2. Public services
3. Education
4. Taxes
5. Land use and topography
6. Accessibility to shops
7. Location rent
8. Travel time

The full set of residential attributes, how each was measured, and what the effect of each is likely to be on residential choice is discussed below.

1. Housing and Socioeconomic Characteristics. Two important sets of attributes that may affect location are physical characteristics of the housing stock, and the economic or social characteristics of its occupants. There is such a wide variety of possible variables that fall into these categories that it is likely that persons consider no more than a few broad indicators of the physical or social quality of neighborhoods when choosing where to live. Further, it appears that because of a high degree of intercorrelation among housing and socioeconomic variables, in a statistical sense there may be far fewer dimensions by which neighborhoods may be characterized than there are possible housing and socioeconomic variables to be found among the original data. For these reasons a principal component analysis was performed on a number of housing and socioeconomic variables (Table 2-3), and the first five (significant) components were used as regressors in place of the original data. (All data for original variables came from the *1960 U.S. Census of Population and Housing.*)

Principal component loadings are shown in Table 2-4. Variables which are significant according to a test proposed by Meyer are indicated by an asterisk.[10] Because this report must be short, a full discussion of the interpretation of the principal components is not possible. The names given the components and brief statements of significant hypotheses are given below in the table.

2. Public Services. The services provided by local governments to residents represent another important set of possible influences on location. Various groups of consumers may have different preferences for public versus private goods which they express by their residential choices. Ideally one would like to have data on output measures of local services rather than on inputs; unfortunately output data for most services were unavailable for this study. Consequently municipalities were characterized according to five expenditure variables:

1. Total annual expenditures per capita (XPC).
2. Percent of expenditures on police and fire protection (MPF).

Table 2-3. Housing and Socioeconomic Variables

Housing Variables

1. Percent owner occupied
2. Percent available vacant
3. Percent nonwhite occupied
4. Percent "sound"
5. Percent with more than one bathroom
6. Median rooms
7. Percent with more than six rooms
8. Percent with less than four rooms
9. Percent single family
10. Percent of units in apartment buildings with more than ten units
11. Percent built before 1939
12. Percent with central heat
13. Percent with more than one person per room

Socioeconomic Variables

14. Percent foreign stock
15. Percent married couples and children
16. Percent of children in public school (except college)
17. Median school years completed by the adult population
18. Percent of population living in the same house as in 1955
19. Median income of families and unrelated individuals
20. Percent of employed persons "professional" or "managerial"
21. Percent of employed persons "clerical" or "sales"
22. Percent of employed persons "operatives" or "craftsmen"

3. Percent of expenditures on recreation (MRec).
4. Percent of expenditures on schools (MSch).
5. Percent of expenditures on highways and roads (MHwy).

Data were gathered from unpublished reports of the state of Wisconsin, Department of Administration, Bureau of Municipal Audit. Expenditure variables were calculated as the average of 1962 and 1963 expenditures divided by the 1960 population given by the U.S. Census of Population. "Investments" and "payments on indebtedness" were excluded from consideration and were deducted from total municipal expenditures for the basis of computing expenditures per capita and for computing the four "percent of expenditures" variables. "Investments" were excluded because of their heterogeneity and their lumpiness from year to year. "Payments on indebtedness" were eliminated for similar reasons and because the services they are in effect securing occur over a long and highly variable time period. Any attempt to characterize the service output of a municipality by its capital investment or debt management programs over only a two-year period would be foolish.

Hypotheses concerning these public service variables may be briefly stated thus:

Table 2-4. Principal Component Loadings

Variable[a]	PC1	PC2	PC3	PC4	PC5
1	.30*	−.16	−.07	.15	.10
2	−.23*	−.03	−.22*	.18	−.29*
3	−.18	−.25*	.18	−.15	.53*
4	.24*	.13	−.13	.24*	.16
5	.26*	−.09	.28*	−.15	−.23*
6	.24*	−.16	.01	−.38*	.11
7	.18	.04	.28*	−.44*	−.17
8	−.23*	.27*	.18	.15	−.20
9	.26*	−.21*	.05	.16	−.26*
10	−.17	.33*	.23*	.17	−.13
11	−.21	.16	−.09	−.41*	.09
12	.17	.25*	.05	.22	.35*
13	−.16	−.37*	.02	.17	−.03
14	.02	.34*	−.33*	−.11	−.22*
15	.24*	−.24*	−.21	.08	.02
16	−.08	−.22*	.30*	.04	.11
17	.27*	.07	.23*	.20	.09
18	.14	.11	−.34*	−.26*	−.10
19	.29*	−.08	.01	.05	−.13
20	.26*	.14	.30*	−.08	−.09
21	.18	.30*	−.11	.16	−.33*
22	−.14	−.25*	−.36*	.14	−.18

[a]For identification of variables, see Table 2-3.
*Significant according to a test proposed by Meyer (see Reference note 10).

Key to Table 2-4

PC1–*General residential quality* should tend to attract high income residents and possibly families with children.

PC2–*High density-good quality* characterizes primarily a middle class renters market and should be important for households in the smallest household size category.

PC3–*High mobility* lumps together two kinds of areas, both of which have high rates of mobility of persons within the housing stock–high prestige professional areas and ghetto areas. It is not clear which effect will predominate a priori. It seems reasonable to expect that PC3 will exert a negative influence on low to middle income white workers who desire neither the "status" attributes of the component nor the neighborhood instability of the ghetto and high income areas. If the status attributes of the component prevail, the component will likely exert a positive influence on the locational tendencies of the highest income classes.

PC4–*Expanding middle class* is similar to PC2 in that it identifies sound middle class areas, but predominantly those that are growing and those where the dominant tenure relationship is owning rather than renting. PC4 should be important for most middle income groups but more so for those with larger household sizes.

PC5–was not given a name, accounts for only 3 percent of the variance of the data, and is difficult to make hypotheses about. It loads very heavily on the "percent nonwhite" variable and may on that basis exert a slightly negative effect on all white groups, although such a hypothesis appears to be quite tenuous.

Expenditures per capita, insofar as it is able to measure service variations, is likely to influence higher income families and households with children to a greater extent than other groups.

Expenditures on police and fire protection as a percent of the municipal budget will tend to influence positively those more likely to own property than to rent. Higher income groups and those with children should be positively influenced.

Expenditures on recreation as a percent of the municipal budget should also tend to influence positively high income groups and those with children.

Expenditures on schools as a percent of the municipal budget should tend to influence households with children to a greater extent than other groups.[11]

Expenditures on highways and roads as a percent of the municipal budget should influence positively those who value commuting time savings relatively more highly—lower income groups.

3. Education. The quality of schools would seem to be an important variable in influencing the location of families either with or anticipating children. The measure of school quality used in this study was a measure of achievement test scores of elementary school pupils. The specific measure used here was an average of standardized test scores for reading and arithmetic for sixth grade pupils, based on the Iowa Test for Basic Skills. The test is administered to pupils in all public elementary schools in the Milwaukee area about one month after the beginning of the school semester. Test results were for the most part based on the 1961-62 school year and were provided by the individual school districts in Milwaukee and Waukesha Counties. The measure of "average achievement" used was in terms of "grade equivalents" of education which students had acquired.[12] The major hypothesis being tested is that households with children will locate in areas where the quality of education is highest. A secondary hypothesis is that the effect of high quality education will be greater for high income households.

4. Taxes. Property taxes may affect residential location in several ways. The influence of public services on residential location depends not just on what level of services are offered in various communities, but on the price of those services as well. Property taxes are a major source of revenue for most municipalities; proceeds are used to provide services. Variations in property tax rates among municipalities may be looked at as variations in the price of local public goods. Presumably, households will be less inclined to live in areas with high local tax rates than in areas where they are low, for a given bundle of public services.

On the supply side, the property tax tends to lower the return to investment in housing with the result that optimal densities of development are likely to be affected; net densities at which land is developed will vary inversely with the tax rate. If net density affects the desirability of areas, then the tax rate will have an indirect effect on residential choice through its supply side effect.

Both demand and supply side effects of the property tax may be mitigated by the degree to which property tax differentials are capitalized into property values, however.[13] If taxes are fully capitalized, the net value of housing after tax will fall by the full (capitalized) amount of the tax, leaving total payments—rental plus taxes—the same as before the imposition of the tax. Consequently, tax differentials will leave relative costs of locating at any given site unaffected, and the net locational impact of the taxes will be negligible. To the degree that taxes are not capitalized, differential taxes will influence location decisions.

The tax variable included in the model was the "full value tax rate" on real property. The rate is calculated by adjusting nominal tax rates by sales-assessment ratios in each community and was provided by the State of Wisconsin Department of Taxation. Rather than use only the one rate for each community, the rate was separated into its two major components—(1) school tax, and (2) "pure" property tax. This was done in order to control further for differences in public benefit structures among communities: the amount of school tax may be an important indicator of the commitment the community has made to public education. Households may react differently to the imposition of different taxes; households with school age children will presumably be less put off by higher school taxes than are single persons or childless couples.

5. Land Use and Topography. An important element in defining the character of residential areas is their physical attractiveness. Scenery, proximity to bodies of water, and the relative degree to which an area is "residential," "commercial," "industrial," or "pastoral" in part determine residential quality and may influence location decisions.

For this analysis a number of variables were selected that permit comparison of areas based on the "land use externalities" that prevail within them. Data were obtained from the Southeastern Wisconsin Regional Planning Commission on acres of land in each of the following uses, by census tract.

1. Residential
2. Commercial
3. Industrial
4. Transportation and utilities
5. Governmental and institutional
6. Recreational
7. Open land
8. Agriculture

Variables were created for each category expressing the percentage of total census tract land area in the particular use.

The hypotheses with regard to land use variables are straightforward. Some uses are assumed to be obnoxious, and proximity to them is undesirable because of noise, pollution, heavy traffic, and so on. Some uses are assumed to be desirable because they do not give rise to obnoxious side effects and may yield useful services. Land uses in the obnoxious category are commercial, industrial, transportation, and utilities. The other land uses are probably neutral at worst in their external effects and may be strongly positive. Recreational land use would certainly seem to exert positive "neighborhood effects," and to be highly desirable for upper income groups especially.

Such neighborhood effects of land uses are not wholly unambiguous in their hypothetical effects. It may be the case that while effects in the immediate vicinity of an "obnoxious" use such as a shopping center are negative, areas outside the immediate vicinity may be much sought after because of positive effects. Depending on the size of the area over which the effects are observed, the average effect on residential quality may be positive, negative, or completely neutral. There is a real danger of finding such indeterminacies in the empirical estimation of this model due to the relatively large unit of observation employed—the census tract.[14]

In addition to the land use percentages two other variables were included to measure the physical attributes of census tracts. One was net residential density (persons per residential acre) which, when high, might be expected to exert some of the same negative externalities as the obnoxious land use variables. Noise, traffic, and a general lack of openness and residential ambience are products of high net densities of occupancy and are generally considered to be undesirable neighborhood attributes. The other additional variable was a dummy variable, which designated census tracts that bordered on Lake Michigan. There may be both scenic and "status" advantages to lakefront addresses, so this variable was included to test their importance.

6. Accessibility to Shops. Proximity to shopping areas is undoubtedly important to some households. Two measures of shopping accessibility are used here. The first is an index of "shopping trip accessibility," which was calculated by SEWRPC for use in a trip generation model for the Milwaukee area. The index for residential zone i is defined as:

$$Acc_{4,i} = \sum_{j=1}^{n} \frac{S_j}{t_{ij}^{\alpha}}$$

where

$$S_j = \text{shopping trip destinations in zone } j$$

$$t_{ij} \quad = \quad \text{travel time from zone } i \text{ to zone } j \text{ by private automobile}$$

$$\alpha \quad = \quad \text{a positive constant}$$

The index is defined so that it varies directly with the number of trip ends and inversely with travel time.

The second measure of shopping accessibility is a measure of relative accessibility to shopping by way of public transportation as compared to private automobile. It is calculated by first computing an index of accessibility such as that for $Acc_{4,i}$ using travel time by public transportation in place of time by private auto, and then dividing the public transportation index by the private auto index. This should serve as a rough measure of the relative cost of shopping by way of public transportation as compared to private auto. It is unlikely that the "relative shopping accessibility" variable will be important for any but very low income groups.

7. Location Rent. The importance of location rent in determining location was noted in the previous analysis. In locations where the "competing bids" against a particular household type are high as a result of accessibility to many possible employment locations, location rents will be a good indicator of competitive pressures. Location rents are accounted for by a surrogate variable, "employment accessibility," the calculation of which was accomplished by the SEWRPC transportation-land use study. The index is defined in the same fashion as the shopping accessibility variable but with employment (E_j) substituted in place of shopping trip destinations:

$$Acc_{1,i} = \sum_{j=1}^{n} \frac{E_j}{t_{ij}^{\beta}}$$

where the parameter β is a positive constant different from the exponent of the shopping accessibility variable. The hypothesis suggested by the model presented earlier is that the greater the measure of location rent in a particular census tract (and thus the higher the average level of competing bids) the less likely is it that households from whatever stratum will live there. In the context of the model, the greater the generalized accessibility measure the lower the proportion of a given type of households who will live there

8. Travel Time. Travel time from workplace to residence will influence the evaluation that households make of various places of residence. Because of the cost and bother of traveling, bids will tend to be highest near workplaces and lowest far from them. For any given residential site one would expect that persons who are employed near the site are more likely to be successful bidders than those who are employed far away. Thus one expects the partial derivative of residential densities and the probability of choosing a particular location with respect to travel time to be negative.

For the empirical analysis travel time t_{ij} was specified both untransformed and also in an exponential form $e^{kt_{ij}}$ where k was initially specified as an arbitrary negative constant equal in absolute value to 0.01. Data on travel times were computed by the SEWRPC transportation-land use study group by means of an algorithm, which finds the minimum travel time between any two nodes in a transportation network given peak hour travel times along all possible linkages.

For those for whom private automobile transportation is not the relevant travel mode, some modification must be made. Rather than enter a separate "public transport time" variable for those groups likely to use public transportation to get to work, an index of "relative transit accessibility" $Acc_{2,i}$ was used. The index was formed by first constructing an index of employment accessibility such as that described in the previous section, but using peak hour public transportation time in weighting employment densities. The "generalized transit accessibility" index was then divided by the "generalized auto accessibility" index to form a ratio of relative accessibility to concentrations of employment by public transportation. The larger the index in an area the more likely are persons who use public transport to live there.

As was noted earlier, estimated coefficients of commuting time will be related monotonically to the slopes of bid rent functions in the neoclassical analyses of Alonso and others. Because of the importance of commuting costs in the neoclassical model it is useful to specify in detail hypotheses concerning the possible effects of each stratification variable on the slope of the bid rent function and thus on the estimated coefficient of commuting time.

> *Income*—may be expected to flatten the slope of the bid rent function. A positive income elasticity of demand for housing which is greater than the income elasticity of marginal transportation costs will cause smaller slopes (in absolute value).

> *Household size*—will also tend to flatten the bid rent function. Demand for more space (as opposed to simply demand for more "housing services") by larger household sizes will cause the slope of the bid rent function to decrease in absolute value.

> *Sex of the household head*—will result in female-headed households having bid rent functions steeper than those for male-headed households. This will be true insofar as demand for housing services is affected by "permanent" rather than "transitory" income and since at given current income levels females are likely to have lower permanent incomes. Further, female heads of household are likely to have higher marginal costs of transportation because of greater reliance on transit rather than private automobile transportation.

> *Persons contributing to family income*—will have the effect of increasing bid rent slopes. Tastes for housing are likely to be less for

households with multiple income earners. Further, having stratified as well by total household income, it is true by definition that the income of each income earner is less than that of a single income earner in the same total household income category. This will tend to increase the slope of the bid rent function as well.

The Final Set of Variables

Based on preliminary analysis of the data, it was concluded that certain of the discussed variables were not likely to be useful in further analysis because of consistently insignificant results or because of severe multicollinearity with other variables. In particular, two land use variables—open land and agricultural land—were dropped from the analysis, and three "obnoxious" land uses were combined to form one variable, *LBad.* The three were land in use in industrial, commercial, and transportation and utilities. In addition, it was found that the exponential form of travel time gave consistently better results than did the untransformed variable, so that only the exponential form was used in the final analysis. The final set of variables is given below in Table 2-5.

Table 2-5. Independent Variables

Symbol	Description
PC1	Principal component 1—general residential quality
PC2	Principal component 2—high density-good quality
PC3	Principal component 3—high mobility
PC4	Principal component 4—expanding middle class
PC5	Principal component 5
Avach	Average 6th grade school achievement (years)
XPC	Expenditures per capita by municipalities (hundreds of dollars)
Ptax	Property tax rate (except school levy) (percent)
Stax	School tax rate (percent)
MPF	Expenditures for police and fire services (percent)
MRec	Expenditures for recreation (percent)
MSch	Expenditures for schools (percent)
MHwy	Expenditures for highways (percent)
LRes	Residential land use (percent)
LBad	"Obnoxious" land use (percent)
LRec	Recreational land use (percent)
Lake	Lakefront dummy
Acc 1	Generalized employment accessibility by auto
Acc 2	Shopping accessibility by auto
Acc 4	Relative employment accessibility by public transport
Acc 5	Relative shopping accessibility by public transport
NDen	Net residential density (households per thousand acres)
Area	Area (thousands of acres)
T_{ij}	Exp $(-.01\ t_{ij})$ where t_{ij} is peak hour auto travel time from workplace to residence

RESULTS

The model (Equation 1) was estimated using ordinary least squares in a linear additive format. Other overall functional forms such as a log-linear specification and a form embodying threshold effects were tried for several behavioral equations, and resulted in no better results than did the linear additive equations. Initially 48 separate equations were estimated, one for each workplace/socioeconomic group (WSEG) combination. (Regression coefficients for the 48 equations are given in the appendix tables.) Results for each equation were analyzed separately. The data were then pooled across workplaces, and twelve equations were estimated using the pooled data. Analysis of covariance was performed on the pooled estimates to determine whether or not the pooling was valid. In addition to the pooled and unpooled estimation, actual and predicted values of the dependent variable were grouped according to broader geographical areas than census tracts to evaluate the ability of the model to explain residential distributions over larger than tract-size areas. Because of space limitations pooled equations and results of grouping are not presented.

General Results

The results of the model varied widely among groups. The proportion of variance explained, corrected for degrees of freedom, ranged from 0.04 to 0.45 with an average of about 0.22. These results are shown in Table 2-6. The corrected R^2 statistics should not be greatly emphasized, however. The proportion of variance explained generally tended to vary with the number of nonzero observations in the data group for which equations were estimated. The reason for such variability is related to the linear specification of the model. In the case of small sample sizes, a large proportion of census tracts exists for which the observed proportion of a group residing there is zero. In such a case the linear specification of the model results in an error component independent of the "true" error component of the regression. At sample sizes of about 60, there is a dramatic change in the value of corrected R^2. Up to that point R^2 statistics are uniformly small; beyond that point they are much larger and are completely unrelated to sample size. The only exception to this phenomenon is in the case of groups with large family size and with multiple wage earners, all of which had consistently lower R^2 irrespective of sample size. (Reasons for these discrepancies will be explained later.) For the other groups there are no significant tendencies for R^2 to vary by either workplace or by socioeconomic group.

Individual parameters must be cautiously interpreted since a considerable amount of multicollinearity exists in every estimated equation. Tests for the singularity of the correlation matrix indicated that potentially dangerous collinearity was present for every equation. Inspection of the inverse of the correlation matrices indicated that multicollinearity was most likely to be "harmful" to both parameter estimation and hypothesis testing for the following variables: (1) general residential quality, (2) school quality, (3) property tax,

Table 2-6. Corrected R^2 by Socioeconomic Group and Workplace

Group	Workplace			
(defined in Table 2-2)	1	74	88	116
1	.34	.44	.32	.32
2	.27	.40	.36	.31
3	.20	.28	.37	.28
4	.32	.13	.30	.17
5	.04	.08	.17	.14
6	.31	.43	.33	.32
7	.10	.27	.18	.14
8	.12	.15	.09	.10
9	.06	.06	.11	.10
10	.25	.12	.28	.32
11	.11	.12	.11	.16
12	.45	.06	.33	.15

(4) school tax, (5) general (auto) accessibility, (6) general (transit) accessibility, (7) shopping (transit) accessibility, and (8) travel time. In spite of the high degree of multicollinearity inherent in the estimates, it was felt that parameters could be estimated with reasonable confidence for outlying workplaces.

Before discussing in detail the effects of particular attributes, a general overview of the effects of housing attributes on residential choice is appropriate. Results were similar enough among workplaces that general patterns of significance of attributes may be inferred from particular workplace estimates. Table 2-7 presents parameter estimates for Workplace 88, one of the outlying workplaces. In interpreting the coefficients of particular attributes, one must bear in mind that most coefficients depend on two separate effects. Coefficients of distance from workplace (T_{ij}) and the location rent proxy (Acc_1) are exceptions in that they represent "pure" effects. For a given level of competing bids, represented by Acc_1, and a given bundle of attributes, accounted for by other included variables, distance from workplace unequivocally reduces a household's bid for a site and hence its probability of locating there. Similarly, for a given level of a household's bid, which is determined by distance from workplace and the levels of attributes offered at a site, greater competitive pressures—as evidenced by higher location rents—will unequivocally reduce the chances of a household's choosing to live at a site.

For other attributes, the net effect of changes in the level of a given attribute from place to place depends both on how a given household type's hypothetical bid changes and on how the bids of competing groups change. The first effect may be referred to as the "own bid" effect; the second as the

Table 2-7. Linear Regression Coefficients for Workplace 88

Variable	Group											
	1	2	3	4	5	6	7	8	9	10	11	12
Const	-3.540	-3.830	-3.230	-2.810	-3.480	-2.030	-3.510	-3.192	0.280	-1.330	-5.240	-5.840
PC1	.015	-.055+	-.005	.045	-.077*	.027	-.044	-.010	.048	.060+	-.063+	.056
PC2	.090**	.147**	.084**	.139**	.099**	.037**	.055**	-.009	.074**	.010	.030	-.002
PC3	-.138**	-.082**	-.044**	.022	-.141**	-.017	-.104**	.010	.052+	.071**	-.012	.134**
PC4	.015	.089**	.042*	-.003	.042	.121**	.062*	.116**	.152**	.155**	.068*	-.012
PC5	.012	-.007	-.020	.070	.054	-.087**	-.090*	-.172	.031	-.087+	-.043	-.144**
Avach	-.149	-.059	.045	-.127	.161	-.097	.080	.134	-.186	-.116	.423	.519**
XPC	-.091	-.021	-.081+	-.001	-.052	-.076+	-.032	-.076	-.170*	-.220**	-.120+	.047
Ptax	-.248+	-.175	-.137	.019	-.397*	.027	-.067	.085	-.176	-.597**	-.222	.046
Stax	.008	.013	.000	.161	.014	-.150	-.194	.132	-.024	.045	-.031	-.327
MPF	1.343	.417	1.190	2.844	1.466	1.118	-.168	1.473	3.746	6.097**	4.084+	-2.122
MRec	-2.209	-3.313	-1.532	-3.091	-.423	-5.007	-.389	6.615	-.849	-1.603	-1.632	-1.972
MSch	-.345	.070	-.560	-.352	-1.209	-.019	.009	-.329	-.861	-1.512*	.076	.705
MHwy	4.568+	3.019	2.803	.293	2.251	2.682	2.454	-.002	1.248	6.016*	8.437**	-1.086
LRes	.192	.515+	.262	-.172	.345	.166	-.122	-.078	.533	.423	.221	.131
LBad	.446	-.150	.228	.151	-.135	.111	-.160	.413	.395	.853*	-.095	1.077**
LRec	-1.192+	-1.038*	.146	1.760**	-.455	-.410	-.411	-1.084+	-.086	.889+	-.717	-.410
Lake	-.064	.100	.018	.416**	.091	-.089	-.015	.092	.208	.115	.091	.231
Acc₁	-.136**	-.079*	-.093**	-.093*	-.081+	-.103*	-.111**	-.070+	-.007	-.074*	-.055	-.076+
Acc₂	-.076	-.109**	-.015	-.034+	.037	.001	-.016	-.017	.027	.084**	.041	-.024
Acc₄	-3.834	-4.989**	-5.128**	.523	-1.568	-5.377**	-.089	-6.596*	-3.017	-.067	-5.392+	-1.876
Acc₅	-4.556*	-5.442**	-1.997	-2.006	-2.879	-3.638	-4.165*	-5.243**	-2.431	-3.632+	-2.722	-2.599
NDen	.001	-.001	-.000	-.002*	-.000	.000	.000	.000	-.002	-.001	-.000	-.000
Area	.008	.011	.006	.013	.014	.002	.009	-.013	.014	.005	-.007	.004
T_{ij}	8.479**	7.456**	5.991**	6.140	5.900**	5.327**	6.035**	4.547**	2.780**	5.014**	4.062**	4.261**

+Significant at 0.20 level.
*Significant at 0.10 level.
**Significant at 0.05 level.

"market effect." If the coefficient of an attribute is negative for a particular group, it may be inferred that "the market" is capable of outbidding the group in question for the attribute over a wide range of values of the attribute. Conversely, a positive coefficient indicates that the group is able to outbid most competitors ("the market,") over a wide range. If a coefficient is close to zero, or statistically insignificant, it may be inferred that the group's evaluation and the market's evaluation are similar over a wide range.

The validity of the Tiebout hypothesis depends on whether or not different groups respond differently to changes in local tax and public service variables. Thus an appropriate test requires one to examine the pattern of coefficients for such attributes across socioeconomic groups. If coefficients differ, then it is apparent that the sorting out of groups implied by the Tiebout hypothesis is in fact going on; if not, explanations for observed residential stratification of socioeconomic groups must be sought elsewhere.

Analysis of results for Workplace 88 indicates that most "sorting out" of groups is by variables other than those suggested by the Tiebout hypothesis. Public service and tax variables are not often significant and many have coefficients whose sign is opposite that suggested by theory. Variables suggested by the neoclassical model, in contrast, are uniformly powerful in their effects on various groups. Distance from workplace (T_{ij}) is, for example, not only highly significant for all groups but markedly different in magnitude among groups. The location rent proxy (Acc_1) behaves according to a priori hypotheses in that larger values are significantly associated with lower probabilities of choosing a location. Other variables that appear to be significant in sorting out households are neighborhood housing and demographic characteristics as embodied in the five principal components PC1-PC5. In the following sections the effects of each residential attribute are discussed in greater detail. Following that, results of this model are compared with the results of other empirical studies of residential choice.

The Effects of Independent Variables

1. Distance to Workplace. Distance to workplace (t_{ij}) was measured by peak hour automobile travel time between the census tract of residence and the workplace centroid. The original variable was modified so that the variable which entered each equation took the form:

$$T_{ij} = e^{-.01 t_{ij}}$$

The estimating equation was then linear in T_{ij} rather than in t_{ij}. Larger coefficients are associated with more rapidly declining residential distributions and, therefore, with steeper bid rent functions.

The initial results that were achieved using all of the variables given in Table 2-5 are shown in Table 2-8. The most important aspect of the table is

Table 2-8. Coefficients of T_{ij}

Group (defined in Table 2-2)	Workplace				Average of 74,88,116
	1	74	88	116	
1	3.94[a]	9.58	8.48	11.68	9.91
2	1.91[a]	9.15	7.46	10.81	9.11
3	3.27[b]	5.56	5.99	6.04	5.86
4	4.10[a]	8.95	6.14	7.28	7.46
5	−1.22[a]	5.13	5.90	6.56	5.86
6	2.95[b]	6.04	5.33	4.96	5.44
7	8.04	8.05	6.04	5.51	6.53
8	1.86[a]	5.03	4.55	5.09	4.89
9	5.11[a]	4.49	2.78	5.53	4.27
10	−0.10[a]	5.13	5.01	2.43	4.19
11	5.79	5.98	4.06	5.62	5.22
12	5.58[b]	3.97	4.26	4.86	4.36

Horizontal lines separate income groups. Except as indicated all coefficients are significant at the 0.05 level.

[a]Insignificant at 0.10 level.

[b]Significant at 0.10 level.

the almost total agreement of the estimated coefficients with a priori hypotheses. Furthermore the parameter of every T_{ij} coefficient for the outlying workplaces is significant at least at the 0.05 level. The T_{ij} coefficients for Workplace 1 are however greatly affected by collinearity between T_{ij} and the accessibility variables. The partial t-statistic between T_{ij} and Acc_1, computed from the $(x'x)^{-1}$ matrix, was 6.56 and therefore caused great problems in estimating both T_{ij} and Acc_1 coefficients for Workplace 1. In spite of the severe collinearity, ten of twelve Workplace 1 coefficients had the correct sign, and five were significant at 0.10 or better.

Some of the more important hypotheses related to the effect of distance from workplace on residential choice are related to the supposed differences in response according to household characteristics. The coefficients given in Table 2-6 above indicate that there is substantial variation in the response among the twelve analysis groups. The most apparent variation is among income groups. Figure 2-2 illustrates graphically the variation in T_{ij} coefficients for outlying workplaces.

For the lowest three income groups the average value of $\beta_{T_{ij}}$ drops considerably from an average for the six low income WSEG categories of 9.53 to an average of 4.56 for the nine \$8-12,000 income groups. There is a small drop

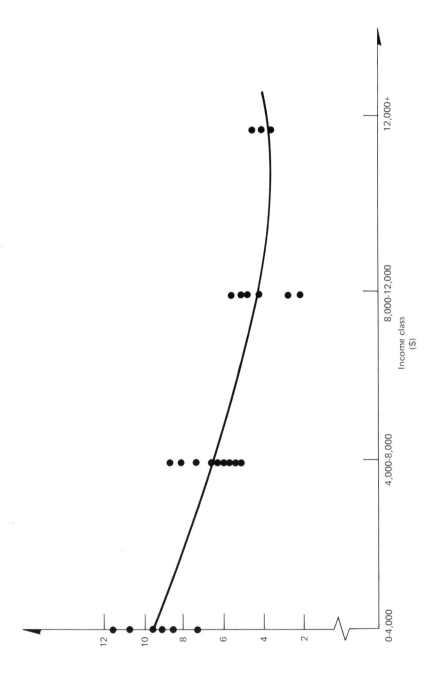

Figure 2-2. Variation in T_{ij} Coefficients.

from the average for the latter category to that for the highest income group, 4.56 to 4.36, although such a drop can hardly be considered significant. In line with the model developed previously, the decline in coefficients of T_{ij} is indicative of bid rent functions having slopes that decline in absolute value with income. What is indicated is that, as hypothesized, bid rent functions do in fact decline in slope with increasing income, although not over the full range of income. From Figure 2-2 it appears that bid rents become less steep with income only up to the $8-12,000 class; beyond that there is little change.

The effects of other household characteristics on T_{ij} coefficients are not as striking as the effect of income. Nevertheless, the results tend to agree generally with a priori hypotheses. Table 2-8 portrays the average value of $\beta_{T_{ij}}$ for each group for outlying workplaces. The effect of household size is as was hypothesized: greater household size is associated with smaller values of $\beta_{T_{ij}}$ and therefore with bid rent functions of flatter slopes. Increases in contributors to income are associated with steeper slopes.[15]

Differences in the sex of the household head are ambiguous and probably unimportant. The variation in coefficients among family size, contributors to income, and sex groups occurs within a much narrower range than that within income groups, indicating that variations in income are likely to produce more far-reaching changes in residential location than are variations in other household characteristics.

It is interesting to compare the relative importance of T_{ij} in explaining the residential distributions of various groups. This may be done by comparing the partial correlation coefficient of T_{ij} and the residential distribution variable r_{ijk} to the total proportion of variance, which the entire set of regressors is capable of explaining. The squared partial correlation coefficient of T_{ij} is a measure of the proportion of variance that T_{ij} alone is capable of explaining after removing the influence of other variables. The ratio of the squared partial to R^2 may be taken as a measure of the relative contribution of distance from workplace to the total explainable variance in r_{ijk}. Results of computing such a ratio are shown in Table 2-9. The figure given is the average ratio computed using outlying workplace equations. The interesting point to note in evaluating the table is the general decline in T_{ij}'s relative importance with income. Aside from changes attributable to income variation, there are no other household characteristic changes that are systematically related to changes in the relative importance of T_{ij}.

Between the two lowest income categories there is not a very large change; between the two lowest categories and the two highest there is a fairly considerable change. The implication is that higher income groups are relatively more concerned with locational attributes other than distance from workplace. Even though, as was previously mentioned, there is little systematic variation among groups in the overall degree to which residential distributions may be

Table 2-9. Relative Importance of T_{ij}

Group	Squared partial of T_{ij} and r_{ijk} ÷ Proportion of explained variance (R^2)
1	.541
2	.488
3	.522
4	.380
5	.383
6	.535
7	.556
8	.382
9	.164
10	.231
11	.337
12	.121

explained (except for multiple worker and large household groups), there is a large shift in the relative importance of different residential attributes. In the following discussion the effects of other attributes on each group is explored.

2. **General Accessibility.** The "general accessibility" variable Acc_1 was included as a measure of the intensity of competitive pressure at various locations. As such, it is a proxy variable for location rent which was hypothesized to affect the probability of choosing a particular location negatively. The coefficients of Acc_1 are presented in Table 2-10. Of the 48 estimated coefficients, 34 had the correct a priori sign. Of those with the correct sign, 26 were significant at least at the 0.2 level. As was mentioned before, Acc_1 was particularly subject to the influence of harmful multicollinearity. For the CBD, Acc_1, had a multiple correlation coefficient of 0.95 with other variables included in the set of regressors; for outlying workplaces the multiple correlation was only slightly lower. In light of such severe collinearity it is somewhat surprising to see Acc_1 perform as well as it does. The most consistent results are those for workplaces 74 and 88, which between them have only one incorrect sign. The magnitude of the coefficients for particular groups appears to be quite similar for those two workplaces, and even for those significant coefficients that exist for the other workplaces.

Because of the effects of collinearity it is difficult to make firm statements concerning the effect of changing household characteristics on the response to general accessibility. It does appear that there is probably less systematic variation in β_{Acc_1} with household characteristics than there was in $\beta_{T_{ij}}$. Given the size of the standard errors of the β_{Acc_1}, it is not possible to

Table 2-10. Coefficients of Acc_1

| Group | Workplace | | | |
	1	74	88	116
1	.071	−.153[b]	−.136[b]	.058
2	.048	−.138[b]	−.079[a]	.045
3	.006	−.115[b]	−.093[b]	−.107[b]
4	−.010	−.136[a]	−.093[b]	.019
5	.133[a]	−.046	−.081[a]	.018
6	−.065[a]	−.080[b]	−.103[a]	−.087[b]
7	−.167[b]	−.110[b]	−.111[b]	−.120[b]
8	.003	−.117[b]	−.070[c]	−.038
9	−.048	−.133[c]	−.007	−.070[c]
10	.008	−.072[c]	−.074[b]	.039[c]
11	−.113	−.094[c]	−.055	−.049[c]
12	.055	.110[c]	−.076[c]	.015

[a]Significant at 0.10 level.
[b]Significant at 0.05 level.
[c]Significant at 0.20 level.

reject the hypothesis that the coefficients are equal for all groups. This would tend to indicate that an increase in general accessibility (or in the general schedule of location rents) will leave the relative composition of areas relatively unchanged with respect to the socioeconomic groups who live there.

The general result of correct a priori signs on the coefficients of Acc_1 must be taken as further confirmation of the validity of the general precepts of the neoclassical model of location theory. Between the effects of T_{ij} and Acc_1, a considerable amount of the "explainable" variation in residential distributions may be accounted for, especially for lower income groups.

3. **Demographic Variables.** The demographic variables in the models are embodied in five principal components of 22 census variables on housing and socioeconomic characteristics of census tracts. The results are extensive and are not gone into in great detail here. In general, however, the results tended to indicate that for upper income groups and households with children, demographic variables were highly important. While some principal components were significant for other groups, the coefficients tended to show some instability among workplaces. For the high income groups with families, however, results were highly consistent across workplaces.

To illustrate, the coefficients are presented below in Tables 2-11 and 2-12 for Groups 10 and 12, which differ only according to income. Group 10 is

Table 2-11. Coefficients of Principal Components for Group 10

Variable	Workplace			
	1	*74*	*88*	*116*
PC_1	$.071^b$	$-.003$	$.060^c$	$.042$
PC_2	$-.004$	$.012$	$.010$	$-.023$
PC_3	$.084^b$	$.041$	$.071^b$	$.018$
PC_4	$.083^b$	$.146^b$	$.155^b$	$.093^b$
PC_5	$.006$	$.109^c$	$.093^b$	$.056$

[a]Significant at 0.10 level.
[b]Significant at 0.05 level.
[c]Significant at 0.20 level.

Table 2-12. Coefficients of Principal Components for Group 12

Variable	Workplace			
	1	*74*	*88*	*116*
PC_1	$.168^b$	$.080$	$.056$	$.139^b$
PC_2	$-.044^c$	$-.071$	$-.002$	$-.098^b$
PC_3	$.167^b$	$.064$	$.134^b$	$.049$
PC_4	$.005$	$.048$	$-.012$	$-.015$
PC_5	$-.188^b$	$-.118$	$-.144^b$	$-.092$

[b]Significant at 0.05 level.
[c]Significant at 0.20 level.

in the $8-12,000 per year category; Group 12 is open-ended at $12,000 and above. For Group 12, three of the principal components have consistent and significant effects on residential choice. Both PC_1, general residential quality, and PC_3, high mobility, are consistently positive in their effects. The other component which consistently affects Group 12 is PC_5 which is heavily weighted positively on nonwhite occupancy and negatively on having more than one bathroom and single family housing. The effects of all three significant components appear to agree fully with a priori hypotheses concerning their effects.

The interesting thing to note with regard to Table 2-11 is the way in which the response of upper middle income families differs from that of high income families as portrayed in Table 2-12. The two significantly positive variables, PC_1 and PC_3, tend still to be positively related to residential choice though their effects are only half as large numerically for Group 10 as for Group 12. Group 10 responds very positively, however to PC_4, the component associated with an expanding middle class. As with Group 12, the coefficients for Group 10 are consistent across workplaces.

Results for other groups, while somewhat inconsistent among workplaces generally tended to indicate the following:

1. PC_1, *general residential quality*, was significantly negative in its effect on low income households. This is undoubtedly the effect of competition from other groups and further indication of the relative importance of transportation cost/location rent tradeoffs relative to the influence of residential quality for low income households.

2. PC_2, *high density-good quality*, was generally significant and positive for small household groups—Groups 1, 2, 3, 4, 5, and 9, and insignificant for households with children.

3. PC_4, *expanding middle class*, was almost always significantly positive in its effects on the residential choices of every group with the exception of the highest income group. For the eleven other groups: of 44 PC_4 coefficients, 36 were significantly positive.

4. PC_5 was never a consistent influence on the choices of any group except for the highest income group.

4. School Quality. School quality, *Avach*, was never a consistent influence on the residential choices of any group, with the exception of the high income group. The pattern of signs was seemingly random across both workplaces and groups except for Group 12. The values of β_{Avach} for Group 12 were 0.22, 0.47, 0.52, and $-.03$ for the four workplaces, of which the first three coefficients were significant. It is interesting to look at the implicit trade-off between school quality and other variables for the high income group. In particular we may ask what price in additional commuting time high income households will pay for greater school quality. Assume that a representative value for β_{Avach} is 0.4, and assume that the average travel time for a household head in Group 12 is 24 minutes. If school quality, as measured by grade equivalents at the sixth grade level, increases by one full grade, $\Delta Avach = 1.0$. The change in the probability of living at the location where the change occurs is thus $1.0 \cdot \beta_{Avach} = 0.4$.

We may compute the increase in travel time that a high income household head would be willing to accept to just offset the increased probability due to higher school quality. Taking 4.36 as a representative value for $\beta_{T_{ij}}$ from Table 2-8 and solving for $\Delta r_{ijk} = 0$ gives a required increase in commuting time of 10.5 minutes. That is, one grade level equivalent has the same effect at the mean as 10.5 minutes of commuting time; a high income household will be willing to increase commuting time by as much as about 45 percent to achieve significantly greater school quality.

This result must be cautiously interpreted however, in light of the collinearity among *Avach* and other variables. School quality is highly correlated with general residential quality in particular, and may be proxying some of the effects of general quality on high income households.

5. Public Service and Tax Variables. Public service variables, including the proportions of municipal budgets allocated to various activities and expenditures per capita have extremely variable and, in general, insignificant coefficients. Significant coefficients for *MPF, MRec, MSch,* and *MHwy,* are so high that they may be serving as gross proxies for accessibility rather than as tax variables per se. Coefficients of *Ptax* and *Stax* are given in the appendix tables. The "school tax" rate, *Stax,* is almost never significant. The property tax rate exclusive of school levies is not often significant either, although for upper income groups there is a rather consistent pattern of negative signs. If we could be confident of the effect portrayed by the coefficients of *Ptax,* we could assert that property tax differentials are less completely capitalized in the upper income markets than they are in the lower income markets, possibly a result of greater housing supply elasticities for the high income submarket. Thus in the lower income markets such differentials have no effect on residential choices; for upper income groups they have a negative effect.

6. All Other Variables. It is roughly fair to say that of the variance in residential choice accounted for by the independent variables in this analysis, the variables that have already been discussed account for 90 percent or more. The effects of other variables are, in general, not significant or variable across workplaces. Many are highly collinear both among themselves and also with previously discussed variables, and so must be carefully interpreted in any case. The effects of the remaining variables are summarized in the following discussion.

1. Accessibility variables other than general accessibility—Acc_2, Acc_4, and Acc_5 are highly collinear among themselves and with Acc_1 and T_{ij}. Their effects are highly variable and appear mainly to explain nonlinearities in the response to Acc_1 and T_{ij} which are not otherwise accounted for.

2. Land use variables are in one case extremely consistent among equations though not highly significant, but in general are insignificant. The percentage of land in residential use, *LRes,* almost always has a positive effect on the probability of choosing a location, although the effect is frequently statistically insignificant. Obnoxious land uses, *LBad,* and recreational land use, *LRec,* are generally insignificant. The dummy variable representing lakefront census tracts is highly unstable across workplaces, and bears little relationship to a priori hypotheses.

COMPARISON WITH OTHER STUDIES

Two major conclusions emerge from this study with regard to the influence of local public goods and services and taxes on residential choice. The first is that public service variables—at least as measured here—do not appear to matter much in determining residential locations. The only possible exception is that the quality of education appears important to higher income groups. The second is that local taxes, general property taxes, and levies especially for schools, do not seem to matter either. Again, there is slight evidence that higher income groups respond to property tax differentials. It is appropriate to ask whether or not such conclusions are consistent with other recent empirical studies of residential choice, and also whether the evidence from this study, taken with those other results, brings us farther along the road to a definitive test of the Tiebout hypothesis.

Other studies have most often been based on empirical estimation of hedonic price indexes that express housing values or rental prices as functions of housing characteristics that include location, quality, and neighborhood characteristics including local tax and public service measures.[16] As mentioned earlier, the choice of independent variables is hardly universal in such studies, and concern only with the general market (or price) effects of particular variables severely limits testing the richer Tiebout hypothesis that groups are affected differently by particular variables. Nevertheless, the conclusions of such studies are generally consistent with the results presented here.

Hedonic price studies have generally been confined to either rental or owned housing; few studies have examined both at once. Such a distinction, however, highlights one of the major side issues of the debate over the empirical validity of the Tiebout hypothesis—namely, that of capitalization and shifting of property taxes and local benefits. It has been argued that insofar as such variables affect the relative costs and attractiveness of locating in particular communities, their relative variation will be capitalized in property values. To the degree, however, that tax and service differentials are borne by owners of rental property as opposed to tenants, rental levels will not reflect the differentials.

Traditional incidence theory suggests that the degree of capitalization and shifting will depend on elasticities of supply and demand for housing.[17] Under what seems to be a reasonable assumption in many American cities—namely, highly inelastic supply of rental housing—it would seem theoretically that full shifting of taxes and service benefits to tenants is unlikely. Similarly, rent differentials attributable to public service differentials would be small.

Empirical evidence generally supports the notion that effects on rents of tax and service differentials are small, although there is some evidence to the contrary.[18] Such evidence suggests that the relative costs of living in various communities are unlikely to be greatly different as a result of tax and service differentials. Consequently, one could argue that there is little incentive for renters to adjust their locations to local variations in such variables, at least on the basis of relative cost differentials. Such a result is supported by the results of this study: for those groups most likely to be renters (the lower income groups), tax and public service variables are hardly ever significant. On the other hand, incidence theory suggests that, other things being equal, the greater the supply elasticity of housing the greater the degree of tax and benefit capitalization. To the degree that the supply of owner occupied housing is more price elastic than rental housing, evidence of capitalization would be more forthcoming. Tax differentials would be perceived as significant cost differences among communities if supply were elastic, and households would be expected to adjust their locations accordingly.

Some empirical evidence supports the notion that property taxes are capitalized significantly for owner occupied housing, though also suggesting that the net effect of taxes and the benefits they finance may have a small net effect on property values.[19] Again the evidence of recent hedonic price studies is supported by the results presented here; only groups with the highest proportion of owners show any pattern of influence whatsoever by tax and service levels.

For comparative purposes it is useful to present a hedonic price index using data for the Milwaukee SMSA. Table 2-13 gives the results of regressions estimated with the value of single family homes as a dependent variable and using the independent variables employed earlier to explain residential choice. Results are shown both including and excluding tax and service variables. While several of the local fiscal variables are significant and have the expected sign, it is interesting to note that the level of general property taxes—as opposed to levies specifically for schools—is significantly positive. It is most likely that such a result is attributable to the high degree of geographic aggregation of the tax variable.

All census tracts within the City of Milwaukee have the same value for *Ptax*, and it is considerably higher than that of surrounding areas. *Ptax* is likely then to be serving as a broad proxy for centrality not accounted for by the accessibility index, Acc_1. It should be noted as well that as a group, the local fiscal variables do not add greatly to the explanatory power of the hedonic index, increasing the corrected R^2 by 0.007. The predominance of housing and demographic characteristics of neighborhoods and of accessibility to employment concentrations in determining housing values is apparent. Thus, on the basis of their effects on relative prices alone, one would expect such variables to be more powerful locational influences than are local fiscal variables.

There is still, of course, the possibility that the variables that matter most in determining property values also matter considerably in determining patterns of local fiscal effort and budgetary allocations. Thus choosing a community on the basis of its housing characteristics and the socioeconomic

Table 2-13.   Determinants of Housing Value

	Coefficients of Variables	
Variable	*Equation 1*	*Equation 2*
Constant	3,021.0[a]	10,370.0[a]
PC1	1,076.2[a]	1,160.0[a]
PC2	279.6[a]	251.7[a]
PC3	1,242.7[a]	1,299.0[a]
PC4	219.4[a]	253.2[a]
PC5	−803.8[a]	−963.1[a]
Avach	561.0[b]	434.8[a]
XPC	8.3[a]	
Ptax	1,233.2[a]	
Stax	295.2	
MPF	−13,663.0[a]	
MRec	42,950.0[a]	
MSch	6,754.7[a]	
MHwy	−6,578.1	
LRes	290.8	1,664.0[a]
LCom	−3,135.0	−2,667.0
LInd	−812.7	1,255.0
LTr	−1,485.4	−1,137.0
LRec	655.0	1,331.0
Lake	−121.9	45.5
NDen	−19.9[a]	−20.2[a]
Acc$_1$	206.1[a]	333.1[a]
R_c^2	0.909	0.902

[a]Coefficient significant at 0.05 level.

[b]Coefficient significant at 0.10 level.

characteristics of its inhabitants is, in effect, choosing a bundle of local goods and services that is complementary to privately provided goods. In that case, however, it is not the tax-local goods package that is the operational variable in residential choice but rather the land value-housing-socioeconomic attribute package that both facilitates the provision of local public goods and establishes what level of fiscal effort is required to provide them.

CONCLUSIONS

This has been an attempt to examine empirically the extent to which local public goods and services and tax rates influence the location of different groups. Empirical testing has required that other location influences be held constant.

To that end a wide variety of possible influences on locational choice have been accounted for: housing and socioeconomic characteristics of neighborhoods, land use and topography, accessibility to shops, location rent, and commuting time, in addition to local public goods and services and taxes.

The general results of the model that was tested give great support to the neoclassical model of residential location, which emphasizes the importance of trade-offs between housing costs and journey to work costs. Distance from workplace and a location rent proxy consistently affect residential distributions in the ways one would expect from the neoclassical theory. The only exception was for the highest income group, for which other variables were more powerful and consistent in their effects.

In spite of the support for the neoclassical theory, there is support for the notion that other variables are important as well. There is a general tendency for the combined influence of distance from workplace and location rents to decrease with increasing incomes, suggesting that housing quality rather than housing quantity (in terms of space or net density) becomes relatively more important for higher income groups. The physical quality of neighborhoods and their social attributes as well appear to be significant for every group investigated. The influence of education quality seemed to be confined to the highest income group, although problems of collinearity with other data require cautious interpretation of that result.

One more serious limitation remains, however. Residential choices of the entire population and not simply recent movers have been related to residential attributes. If "stayers" are on average more out of equilibrium with respect to housing attributes than are recent movers, then lumping movers and stayers together would bias results.

Two recent analyses, however, give evidence that such concerns are unlikely to be important empirically. In a study of housing demand Carliner[20] found that cross-sectional price and income elasticities of demand for movers and stayers were practically identical. In a national survey Butler and others[21] found that, contrary to expectations, stayers and recent movers had very similar levels of satisfaction with both dwelling unit and neighborhood attributes. Such analyses are not directly comparable to this one but do tend to support the notion that confining analysis of residential choice only to recent movers because they are nearer "equilibrium" is overly cautious. Definitive testing of the influence of public service variables and taxes should, however, await the development of output measures and measures of fiscal effort that are geographically disaggregated.

It seems likely that the measured effects of highly aggregated expenditure measures underestimate the direct influence of local public services. Because most low and middle income households in the sample live within the municipal boundaries of the City of Milwaukee, they are characterized by identical levels of public services (expenditures) and local tax rates. It is only insofar as such households are willing to choose to live in suburban municipalities that have expenditure and tax levels different from Milwaukee that they will appear to be influenced by expenditure or tax differentials.

It is undoubtedly true that budgetary allocations for particular types of services and tax assessment ratios vary geographically within the boundaries of a city as large as Milwaukee. Even if expenditures were equal and taxes uniformly assessed, however, service levels could still vary significantly, and households respond to perceived differentials. Such responses will not be detected within municipal boundaries until service and tax burden measures are disaggregated.

On the other hand, the results of this study have been shown to be in strong agreement with those of other analyses using different empirical techniques, particularly those using hedonic price indexes to measure the influence of alternative housing characteristics on property values and rents.[22] This analysis has gone farther than hedonic price index studies, though, in that an attempt was made to measure the direct influence of particular variables on many population subgroups and not simply their effects on observed market values or rentals. In spite of the data limitations of this study, the evidence is that local public goods and tax differentials are not major determinants of households' residential choices.

**Appendix Tables
Linear Regression
Coefficients for
Workplaces 1, 74, 88,
and 116**

Workplace 1

Group

Variable	1	2	3	4	5	6	7	8	9	10	11	12
Const	-.550	-.070	-1.130	-.120	-.960	-3.690	-4.690	-.330	-4.560	.390	-3.730	-4.690
PC1	-.136**	-.142**	.034	-.014	-.043	-.006	.018	.064	.068+	.071**	.017	.168**
PC2	.224**	.257**	.089**	.213**	.101**	.000	.021	.005	.023	-.004	.017	-.044+
PC3	.109**	.086+	-.002	.060+	.015	-.011	-.051*	.020	-.060+	.084**	-.031	.167**
PC4	.244**	.224**	.076**	.165**	.088**	.108**	.072**	.168**	.087*	.083**	.144**	.005
PC5	-.278**	-.220**	.034	.123*	-.034	.005	-.010	-.087+	.117*	.006	.044	-.185**
Avach	-.037	-.138	-.149+	-.207	.176	.179**	.020	-.240+	.259+	-.072	.093	.218+
XPC	.037	-.012	-.008	-.032	.110	-.008	-.035	-.088	-.030	-.150**	-.014	.021
Ptax	-.088	-.019	-.158	-.061	.043	.054	-.063	.107	.013	-.275*	.001	-.249
Stax	-.038	-.140	.081	-.225	.212	.300*	-.217	.045	-.036	-.103	.162	.375
MPF	2.239	.991	3.535*	.819	-1.350	5.264	3.302+	4.907*	.244	3.760+	1.304	2.612
MRec	-.410	-3.452	-5.288	-2.891	-5.586	-5.418	-6.574	-4.299	-1.085	-6.398	-3.534	-1.067+
MSch	-.046	.123	-.676	-.530	-.471	-.529	.018	.911	.035	.574	-.664	-1.426**
MHwy	-1.531	-1.492	1.346	-3.172	.444	1.289	2.935	3.226	.855	2.736	-.167	-8.280
LRes	1.421**	1.983**	.247	.729*	.066	.496**	.449+	.228	.743*	.378	.889**	.503
LBad	-1.450*	-2.086**	-.465+	-1.016*	-.448	.098	.005	-.445	-.410	.593+	-.202	.303
LRec	-.410	-.297	-.557	.477	-.210	.479	-.228	-.231	-.655	-.144	.741	-.706
Lake	-.078	-.130	-.012	.335+	-.062	-.163+	-.177	-.187	-.375+	-.033	-.371**	.321+
Acc1	.071	.048	.006	-.010	.133*	-.065*	-.167**	.003	-.048	.008	-.113*	.055
Acc2	-.063	-.054	.030+	-.050+	-.023	.043**	.032	.015	.016	.098**	-.007	.056+
Acc3	-4.930	-1.151	1.269	.657	.681	.135	-4.699*	.858	1.121	2.201	-4.993*	-4.477+
Acc4	12.730**	10.120**	3.299*	7.370**	-3.650	-2.373*	-.909	-4.115*	1.322	-.510	.184	1.719
Acc5	-.008**	-.004**	-.002**	-.004**	-.001	.000	.000	.000	-.000	-.001	-.001	-.000
NDen												
Area	.014	.019	.017**	.030**	.012	.004	.011	.005	.010	.002	.007	.012
Tij	3.935	1.906	3.270*	4.100	-1.220	2.946*	8.044**	1.858	5.110+	-.098	5.786**	5.578*

+Significant at 0.20 level.
*Significant at 0.10 level.
**Significant at 0.05 level.

Workplace 74

Variable	Group											
	1	2	3	4	5	6	7	8	9	10	11	12
Const	-5.910	-7.330	-1.900	-8.210	-2.320	-3.240	-6.120	-5.450	-4.750	-2.920	-6.070	-6.420
PC1	.007	-.034	-.030	-.082	.093+	.050*	-.006	-.044	-.031	-.003	.074+	.080
PC2	-.013	.020	.033	.083+	-.035	-.016	-.020	-.028	.062	.012	-.056+	-.071
PC3	-.112**	-.076**	-.067**	-.043	-.083+	.004	-.029	.067+	.209**	.041	-.018	.064
PC4	-.097**	-.085**	.050+	.077	.036	.094**	.043	.123**	.179**	.146**	.082+	.048
PC5	.007	.029	.106**	.110	.032	-.026	.068	-.066	-.148	.109+	.074	-.118
Avach	.085	.251	.019	.426	-.003	-.073	.230+	.201	-.063	.082	.195	.468+
XPC	-.080	-.060	-.080	.150	-.200+	.000	-.110	.020	.020	-.080	.000	-.300*
Ptax	-.234	-.199	-.011	.221	-.157	.156+	-.145	.301+	.120	-.152	.181	-.974**
Stax	.338	.229	-.457	-.340	-.408	-.068	.105	.261	.527	-.169	-.015	-.561
MPF	12.095**	11.646**	2.025	7.700+	6.627+	2.337	9.032**	.888	5.089	.133	7.258*	13.018**
MRec	1.281	.942	.247	-2.396	1.405	-.490	4.006	-2.990	-23.145**	-1.117	.605	38.707**
MSch	-2.769**	-1.891**	-.122	-.581	-.123	-.045	-.901	.950	.272	.405	.467	1.583
MHwy	-3.577	.759	-7.298**	-5.021	1.305	-2.062	-5.897+	.671	16.570**	3.798	.722	8.026
LRes	.130	-.379	.325	-.478	-.045	.348+	-.054	.449	-.019	.800*	.050	.385
LBac	-.366	-.616	-.431	-1.531*	.040	-.329	.357	.727+	-.348	-.558	-.315	-.659
LRec	-.458	-.937	-1.347**	-1.651	-1.713*	-.482	-.929	.406	.214	-1.614*	-.085	-.572
Lake	-.026	-.216	.041	.013	.198	-.372**	-.113	-.366*	-.798**	.025	.003	-.003
Acc1	-.153**	-.138**	-.115**	-.136*	-.046	-.080**	-.110**	-.117**	-.133+	-.072+	-.094+	.110+
Acc2	.064**	.062*	.010	-.025	-.052	-.012	.041	-.042	.024	.013	-.020	.010
Acc4	6.454**	8.006**	5.260**	9.633+	3.458	2.176	2.798	-7.383*	6.181	-8.820**	.536	6.025
Acc5	1.334	-2.564	-.948	-2.185	-.125	-1.363	-2.768	-5.667*	-11.314**	1.292	1.739	1.621
Nden	.001	.001	-.001	.002	-.000	-.000	-.000	.001	-.000	-.001	-.001	-.000
Area	.012	.011	.018*	.032+	.006	.011+	.012	-.007	-.013	.003	.010	-.011
T_{ij}	9.576**	9.150**	5.556**	8.945**	5.129**	6.036**	8.045**	5.032**	4.489**	5.127**	5.978**	3.970**

+Significant at 0.20 level.
*Significant at 0.10 level.
**Significant at 0.05 level.

Workplace 88

Variable	Group											
	1	2	3	4	5	6	7	8	9	10	11	12
Const	-3.540	-3.830	-3.230	-2.810	-3.480	-2.030	-3.510	-3.192	0.280	-1.330	-5.240	-5.840
PC1	.015	-.055+	-.005	.045	-.077*	.027	-.044	-.010	.048	.060+	-.063+	.056
PC2	.090**	.147**	.084**	.139**	.099**	.037**	.055**	-.009	.074**	.010	.030	-.002
PC3	-.138**	-.082**	-.044**	.022	-.141**	-.017	-.104**	.010	.052+	.071**	-.012	.134**
PC4	.015	.089**	.042*	-.003	.042	.121**	.062*	.116**	.152**	.155**	.068*	-.012
PC5	.012	-.007	-.020	.070	.054	-.087**	-.090*	-.172	.031	-.087+	-.043	-.144**
Avach	-.149	-.059	.045	-.127	.161	-.097	.080	.134	-.186	-.116	.423	.519**
XPC	-.091	-.021	-.081+	-.001	-.052	-.076+	-.032	-.076	-.170*	-.220**	-.120+	.047
Ptax	-.248+	-.175	-.137	.019	-.397*	.027	-.067	.085	-.176	-.597**	-.222	.046
Stax	.008	.013	.000	.161	.014	-.150	-.194	.132	-.024	.045	-.031	-.327
MPF	1.343	.417	1.190	2.844	1.466	1.118	-.168	1.473	3.746	6.097**	4.084+	-2.122
MRec	-2.209	-3.313	-1.532	-3.091	-.423	-5.007	-.389	6.615	-.849	-1.603	-1.632	-1.972
MSch	-.345	.070	-.560	-.352	-1.209	-.019	.009	-.329	-.861	-1.512*	.076	.705
MHwy	4.568+	3.019	2.803	.293	2.251	2.682	2.454	-.002	1.248	6.016*	8.437**	-1.086
LRes	.192	.515+	.262	-.172	.345	.166	-.122	-.078	.533	.423	.221	.131
LBad	.446	-.150	.228	.151	-.135	.111	-.160	.413	.395	.853*	-.095	1.077**
LRec	-1.192+	-1.038*	.146	1.760**	-.455	-.410	-.411	-1.084+	-.086	.889+	-.717	-.410
Lake	-.064	.100	.018	.416**	.091	-.089	-.015	.092	.208	.115	.091	.231
Acc1	-.136**	-.079**	-.093**	-.093*	-.081+	-.103*	-.111**	-.070+	-.007	-.074*	-.055	-.076+
Acc2	-.076	-.109**	-.015	-.034+	.037	.001	-.016	-.017	.027	.084**	.041	-.024
Acc4	-3.836	-4.989*	-3.123**	.523	-1.568	-5.377**	-.089	-6.596*	-3.017	-.067	-5.392+	-1.876
Acc5	-4.556*	-5.442**	-1.997	-2.006	-2.879	-3.638	-4.165**	-5.243**	-2.431	-3.632+	-2.722	-2.599
NDen	.001	-.001	-.000	-.002*	-.000	.000	.000	.000	-.002	-.001	-.000	-.000
Area	.000	.011	.000	.013	.014	.002	.009	-.013	.014	.005	-.007	.004
T_{ij}	8.479**	7.456**	5.991**	6.140	5.900**	5.327**	6.035**	4.547**	2.780**	5.014**	4.062**	4.261**

+Significant at 0.20 level.
*Significant at 0.10 level.
**Significant at 0.05 level.

Workplace 116

Variable	Group											
	1	2	3	4	5	6	7	8	9	10	11	12
Const	−9.60	−10.02	−3.62	−4.47	−4.51	−2.68	−3.17	−2.87	−6.10	−.94	−.94	2.09
PC1	−.071+	−.159**	.028	−.069+	.010	−.0002	.034	.036	−.037	.042	.118**	.139**
PC2	.081**	.197**	.014	.151**	.055*	.0003	−.031	−.044+	−.033	−.023	−.027	−.098**
PC3	.081*	.095*	−.078**	.137**	.010	−.039*	−.057*	−.049+	−.016	.018	−.019	.049
PC4	.195**	.242**	.059**	.108**	.123**	.084**	.081**	.109**	.156**	.093**	.121**	−.015
PC5	−.080	.010	.095**	−.031	−.018	−.004	.028	−.112*	.024	.056	.026	−.092
Avach	.158	.213	−.063	−.063	.166	.119	.020	−.055	−.164	.502**	.048	−.263+
XPC	.002+	.003**	.001**	.000	.000	.0006	.0009	.001+	.000	−.0004	−.0004	.0005
Ptax	−.204	−.199	−.017	−.019	−.191	.105	.098	−.010	−.086	−.621**	−.297+	−.556*
Stax	.020	.009	−.430*	−.498	−.161	−.299+	−.164	.126	−1.072**	.318	−.400	−.594
MPF	2.031	2.037	−2.976+	−1.450	.547	−2.807	.638	−1.391	.455	−.229	1.762	−9.365**
MRec	4.904	−1.266	−6.826	−4.882	−1.477	−4.117	−5.729	−4.330	−2.130	−20.435**	−10.489	−8.278
MSch	.089	1.108	1.172	−.644	−.723	.094	.037	.672	1.263	−2.280**	−1.085	−4.090**
MHwy	−4.059	−4.194	−.163	−2.640	5.117	−1.231	−4.197+	−4.405	5.258	9.696**	5.840+	−9.097+
LRes	−.042	.148	.557**	.021	.414	.558**	.547*	.351	1.109**	.736**	1.102**	.261
LBad	.358	−.040	.158	−.384	.025	−.042	.861*	.180	−.260	.485	.732+	.692
LRec	3.256**	.856	.763+	.531	−1.328+	−.303	.990+	.668	1.199	.902+	.550	.132
Lake	.103	.224	−.086	.070	−.010	.007	.112	.035	.134	−.323+	.065	−.039
Acc_1	.058	.045	−.107**	.019	.018	−.087**	−.120**	−.038	−.093+	−.050	−.095*	.020
Acc_2	−.216**	−.216**	−.023	−.109	−.104	−.026+	−.020	−.038	−.070+	.039+	−.049+	.015
Acc_4	−5.252	.432	−.784	.610	−4.981+	−1.711	.133	−.008	−.638	6.545**	.432	−1.816
Acc_5	−12.331**	−18.103**	3.213+	−8.508	−3.708	−.718	−1.015	−1.571	1.023	−.406	1.516	4.573
Nden	−.001	−.001	−.001	−.002+	−.001	−.0002	.0002	.0003	−.0009	.0000	−.0005	.0004
Area	.032	.041**	.025**	.029*	.010	.013*	.018+	.006	.024+	.007	.014	.009
T_{ij}	11.679**	10.811**	6.044**	7.275**	6.556**	4.963**	5.511**	5.085**	5.529**	2.433**	5.615**	4.859**

+Significant at 0.20 level.
*Significant at 0.10 level.
**Significant at 0.05 level.

Chapter Three

Residential Location and Local Public Services

Howard S. Bloom
H. James Brown
John E. Jackson

Considerable progress has been made in understanding the determinants of residential development and of public sector budgeting, but so far relatively little attention has been given to the integration of those two bodies of research. Researchers interested in the spatial form of urban residential growth are expanding the emphasis previously given to workplace accessibility and land availability to include the impact of neighborhood characteristics, local taxes and public services on residential location decisions.[1] At the same time researchers concerned with local fiscal decisions and the provision of public services explain intercommunity expenditure and tax differences on the basis of variations in towns' population characteristics and tax bases.[2] Undoubtedly in some, if not all, cases public fiscal decisions affect residence location decisions and residence location decisions affect local fiscal decisions. Still, it is important from the standpoint of metropolitan governance to know the relative importance of each effect and under what circumstances each is most apparent. Are the observed fiscal variations relatively fixed, and do they lead to a stratification of the metropolitan population based upon household demands for services and their ability to pay for them? Or are population changes the result of exogenous factors that lead then to political decisions affecting the type and level of local services?

People studying local expenditures and tax determination assume

This work has been partially supported by a grant from the National Science Foundation (RANN) to the Graduate School of Design, Harvard University, and a grant from Resources for the Future to Harvard University. We thank both institutions for their support and exonerate them from any responsibility for errors. We appreciate also the assistance given to the project by David Christensen, Seymour Neustein, and Lisa Trygg.

that variations in economic and social characteristics reflect variations in tastes and the ability to pay for public services. Town to town variations in level and type of service result as each individual votes for different referenda and for candidates proposing alternative public expenditures. How and why these people located in their respective communities is not discussed and is implicitly assumed to be independent of local fiscal policy issues. Questions of how to better satisfy people's needs and demands for public services naturally focus on changes in the political and in governmental institutions for answers.

The relationship between residential choice and local budgetary decisions was originally recognized by Tiebout.[3] He postulated that people had the option to "vote with their feet" on local public decisions as well as to "vote with their hands." Instead of actively working to get a school board to adopt some educational expenditure policy or to work for the election of an individual who advocates such a policy, it is conceivable and possibly easier for a person to move to a new community offering the type and amount of public education desired. Tiebout and others argue that if people exercise the move alternative, the result will closely approximate an efficient allocation of public goods, just as the private market does for other commodities. The proposition that public services are an important determinant of residential location and that the allocation of public goods can be accomplished by locational choice has become known in the literature as the "Tiebout hypothesis."[4]

The opportunity for people to choose public services by selecting their residence has its virtues. A problem facing all local governments is the need to satisfy opposing demands over appropriate public policies and to resolve the legitimate conflicts that exist among people over these policies. The problem arises because it is not possible for people in the same community to have different public school systems or recreation programs. Following the Tiebout reasoning, it is argued that instead of worrying about how local governments can better deal with the problem of resolving conflicting demands, we should take advantage of residential mobility and encourage people to select their own desired mixture of public services by selecting to reside in the appropriate community.

The Tiebout hypothesis has a number of implications for metropolitan governance. First, local governments must be constantly alert to the effect their expenditure and tax policies have on the socioeconomic characteristics of their population. Second, given that demands for public services are correlated with social, demographic, and economic characteristics, household residential locations based on the supply of public services is likely to lead to very homogeneous communities as well as stratification of metropolitan areas.

While the Tiebout hypothesis has been discussed extensively, and although some researchers recognize the simultaneous relationship between residential location choice and local budgetary decisions,[5] there are few attempts to integrate empirically the two explanations into a single model of urban residential development and local fiscal changes. Without such a model there can be no definitive test of the importance of public services in household location decisions, nor any determination of the relative importance of traditional political channels versus residential location choice as means for households to adjust their consumption of public services. This paper makes an initial attempt to provide such integration and reaches some tentative conclusions about the relative importance of each effect on the process of satisfying demands for public services and on the pattern of metropolitan development.

THE CONCEPTUAL MODEL

A simplified representation of the present synthesis of the residential location and fiscal determination model is shown in Figure 3-1. The interrelationships among the endogenous variables in the system are illustrated within the dashed lines. In addition, there are two major groups of exogenous or predetermined influences on the system. The first—external fiscal influences—are shown on the left side of Figure 3-1, and the second—exogenous metropolitan growth factors—are shown on the right side.

Population and housing characteristics and local fiscal decisions are simultaneously related to each other, as well as to their respective exogenous determinants. For example, according to the Tiebout hypothesis, public services and tax rates affect household location choices. At the same time, changes in the location and composition of metropolitan employment and the availability of vacant land lead to alterations in the characteristics of town populations. This change may affect demands for public services and thus influence subsequent fiscal decisions.

The complete model consists of eight equations describing the determination of fiscal, population, and housing characteristics in 65 communities in the Boston metropolitan area during the period 1960-70. For expositional purposes, these equations are discussed as three separate submodels.

Fiscal Decisions

This portion of the model consists of two equations. The first explains changes in public school expenditures per household and the second explains changes in equalized property tax rates. These equations are based on a budget allocation model where decisions are made about the size of the local public budget and how this budget is to be allocated among the different services provided by local government. Important influences on these decisions are the aggregate demand for different public services, the implicit price of these goods to individual citizens, and the availability of outside revenues. Thus the amount spent for any service, such as schools, depends upon the demand for that service, the price of that service, and the competing budgetary demands for other services.

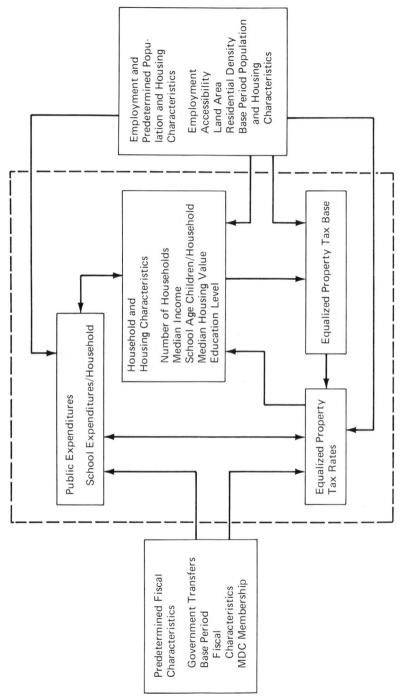

Figure 3-1. Metropolitan Development and Local Fiscal Decisions

The school expenditure equation contains demand, price, and transfer variables. Demand variables, represented by changes in income, education, and school age children per family, are expected to positively correlate with changes in school expenditures per household. By contrast, change in employment (which is assumed to measure demands for competing services) are expected to be negatively related to changes in school expenditures. The tax price variables[6] in this equation are the 1960 level and the change during the decade in the equalized valuation per household. Essentially, the higher the assessed valuation per household the lower the individual tax price and the greater the demand for public services. Finally, intergovernmental transfers are expected to lead to additional expenditures on public services. Some of these transfers may go toward reducing local property taxes, but the rest will be devoted to providing additional public services.

The first set of variables included in the property tax equation are hypothesized to relate to changes in the demand for public services. Demand variables include change in family income, change in local education levels, and change in local employment. It is expected that: (1) income is positively related to demand for public services and to education in particular, (2) changes in children per family and education levels are positively related to demand for educational expenditures, and (3) local employment reflects demands for competing noneducational services such as sanitation and police.

The second set of variables in the tax equation measures changes in the tax base and the availability of intergovernmental transfers. Increases in both of these are expected to lead to lower tax rates. For example, other things being equal, tax rates will be lower in communities with large tax bases. Also, intergovernmental transfers (primarily from the state), which are used to subsidize local public services, permit the substitution of state funds for local tax money. Consequently, increased transfers should result in lower tax rates. It should be noted that in order to estimate their differential impact, these transfers were subdivided into those specifically for education and those for all other purposes.

Housing Characteristics

This portion of the model consists of three equations that explain changes in housing values, rents, and the number of households in each community in the sample during the period 1960-70.

Traditional analyses of housing value have emphasized the importance of housing stock characteristics and accessibility to employment.[7] Empirical studies have found that people will pay more for larger new houses having more accessible locations. In addition, one of the arguments for the increasing suburbanization of our metropolitan areas is presumed to be a desire for residential communities without the burdens associated with the congestion, safety, and service problems associated with nonresidential land uses. If this is the case, people will pay more for housing in areas that do not have extensive nonresidential activities.

The major determinants of changes in rents and housing values are: (1) changes in a municipality's accessibility to employment, (2) the composition of the housing stock in 1960 and its subsequent changes over the following ten years (as measured by the average number of rooms per unit), (3) changes in the age of the stock (the proportion of the 1970 units built after 1960), and (4) alteration of community type (measured by the change in local employment).

A recent addition to the studies of housing value has been the analysis of the impact of differences in public services and tax rates among communities. Oates, for example, has shown that housing prices in northern New Jersey communities are higher in towns with larger school expenditures for given tax rates, and lower in towns with a higher tax rate for a given level of school expenditures.[8] This and other, similar results are advanced as one form of a test of the Tiebout hypothesis.[9] Presumably some households have demands for better schools and want to get those schools and/or low taxes through the selection of their residence. These households will be willing to pay more for housing in communities with good schools and/or low taxes. The result of this process will be higher housing prices in good school and low tax towns.

This analysis of the effect of local public expenditures and taxes on housing prices unfortunately confounds two quite different effects. First there is the traditional capitalization effect associated with permanent differences among communities that cannot be duplicated by other towns, such as workplace accessibility and/or availability to beaches and scenic views. Persistent differences in local tax rates, for a given level of service, will be capitalized. This tax differential results either from differences in the size and the composition of towns' tax bases or from efficiencies in producing public services. As a result of the differences certain towns will be able to supply a given level of services to their residents at lower per resident cost. To the extent that this tax price or efficiency difference persists over time, and other communities cannot duplicate or approximate this advantage, values and rents in the lower tax community will incorporate this advantage and will be permanently higher. Permanent tax differentials along with locational or geographical attributes, are capitalized into housing prices because of both household demands for them and the inability of other communities to duplicate them.

In order to test the extent of capitalization of this kind, it is necessary to have detailed information about the size and composition of the tax base and output measures to control for the quantity of services supplied. Unfortunately we have neither adequate tax base information nor measures of service output; therefore, it is not possible in this study to test for this kind of tax differential capitalization.

The second kind of capitalization, which is described as a test of the

Tiebout hypothesis, rests on the assumption that people will pay more for housing in communities with a more appropriate mix of public services. In this view the test of the importance of public services in the residential location choice is the extent to which public expenditures and tax packages have a significant effect on housing prices. It is our view that this test is inappropriate.

Whether or not households will pay a premium for housing with good schools depends in part on how difficult it is to find the desired housing and good schools in the same community. If there are a large number of communities offering the desired public services, no household is likely to pay a premium to live in one particular town. If there are relatively few communities with the desired public services, then housing prices will be bid up. This capitalization is exactly analogous to the quasi-rent on some physical housing characteristics and should be only temporary.[10]

Households who want good schools, but who are not able or willing to pay the necessary premium price to locate in a particular town, may locate in another town and over time vote to raise the level of schooling. It is easy over time for a town to raise taxes and provide better schools if that is what people want. When this happens in enough towns, the premium people will pay for housing in the first town will decline because of the competition from additional towns with good schools. Housing prices will only reflect service level differences for the period required for other towns to build up their schools and establish their educational reputations.

It is possible at any given time in a metropolitan area for there to be quasi-rents for various public services if there are temporary shortages of communities with good services. Consequently, we include the change in school expenditures per household as one of the determinants of the change in median housing values and in gross rents, along with changes in equalized tax rates. We do not believe, however, that the inclusion of fiscal variables in the price equations serves as an adequate test of the Tiebout hypothesis. It is our opinion that this hypothesis is more properly tested with the equations discussed below that estimate the changes in towns' population characteristics.

The final equation in the housing submodel estimates the change in the number of households in each town. This equation is included to complete the model of the housing market and because it is expected to influence tax bases and public service levels. Household change is expected to be negatively related to housing prices and the change in housing prices and positively related to changes in accessibility and the number of renter occupied units. The latter variable measures increased development density plus the conversion of single family units to multifamily units. Household changes are also expected to be positively related to the land capacity of a town. Land capacity simply measures the amount of vacant developable land in a community multiplied by the existing density of residential land. Assuming that a community does not radically alter its permissible land use patterns, this variable measures the number of additional households each town could absorb.

Population Characteristics

The most explicit implication of the Tiebout hypothesis, and the one with the strongest implications for metropolitan governance, is that people sort themselves among towns according to their preferences for public services and the services provided by each municipality. If people give much weight to public services in their location decisions, one should be able to relate changes in municipal population characteristics to changes in local public service bundles. Thus the last three equations in the model examine changes in the income, education level, and number of school age children per household of towns within the sample.

Each of these three population characteristics are hypothesized to be affected by similar forces. Changes in per household school expenditures and equalized tax rates are used as measures of the Tiebout effect. Also included is the change in the median value of owner occupied housing to represent changes in housing services.[11] The simple expectation is that people with higher income and education levels will locate in areas with greater housing services and thus with more expensive houses. Our expectations are not so clear with respect to the impact of housing prices on the number of school age children per household. However, we expect that larger families will need larger (and thus more expensive) dwellings, so that areas with larger homes will attract larger families.

The explanation for each of these population changes contains one or more additional variables felt to affect the metropolitan distribution of population attributes. In part, these additional variables are required because of the data used to estimate these equations. Available data describe changes in community populations between 1960 and 1970, but do not distinguish between changes attributable to migration of households and changes in the characteristics of nonmoving households. For example, with no migration, the number of school age children per family will change as the population ages during the ten years. As discussed in the next section, our measure of local family composition changes includes changes due both to this aging process and to migration. Consequently, we include as one explanation for increases or decreases in the number of children per household, the number of children per household between the age of 9 and 19 minus the number less than 5. This difference represents the expected natural change if no migration took place. The same problem exists for changes in median income. If incomes increased proportionately during the decade, towns with high median incomes in 1960 would show a larger absolute increase than towns with low median incomes, regardless of migration. Thus 1960 median income is included in the income equation to account for this effect.

There are other factors besides housing prices and public expenditures that might be expected to help explain changes in a community's population characteristics. The 1960 level of income and education are included in the income and education equations to serve as measures of neighborhood quality and of the tendency for households to locate in communities with populations having characteristics similar to their own. It is also expected that families with children have a greater demand for residences in less densely settled areas. Consequently, these households are expected to be found more frequently in communities with a high proportion of owner occupied or single family housing units and with more open space.

Finally, it should be noted that a community's education level is the one population characteristic most likely to be changed through migration. Families residing in a town in 1960 can easily alter both their incomes and their number of school age children during the decade. By contrast, it is much less likely that these families can or will change their formal education level. Thus most of the changes in the educational level in the communities should be attributable to household mobility and their location decisions.

In addition to the dependent variables of the eight preceding equations there are several variables that are treated endogenously but for which equations are not estimated. These variables include change in proportion renter, change in owner and renter rooms per unit, and change in equalized valuation per household. We recognize that these changes are an integral part of the development and growth of a metropolitan area but do not feel that they are directly affected by fiscal decisions. Because the purpose of this chapter is to examine the strongest links between fiscal decisions and residential development, we feel it unnecessary to estimate and discuss these equations.

A possible exception to this statement is change in equalized valuation. In theory, these changes are simply an accounting identity, which incorporates the value of new residential and nonresidential construction plus changes in the value of existing land and structures. In fact, these determinations are subject to the practices of local assessors as well as to the Commonwealth of Massachusetts, which establishes equalizing formulas; consequently, we are presently unable to specify a model explaining this phenomenon. However, the link between housing values, nonresidential development, and local tax bases should be clear without such an equation.

ESTIMATING THE MODEL

Estimation Procedure

A two-stage least squares procedure is used to estimate each of the equations in the model. This is necessary in order to account for the simultaneous interactions of the variables. Observations are weighted by 1970 population.

The Sample

Estimation of the model is based on the characteristics of 65 cities and towns in eastern Massachusetts during the period 1960-70. All these municipalities are included in the 1963 Eastern Massachusetts Regional Planning Project (EMRPP) study area (Figure 3-2). The central city areas of Boston, Chelsea, Cambridge, Somerville, and Revere are excluded. The sample cities have similar regional characteristics, thus enabling the study of metropolitan changes, controlling for regional and state influences. Although all municipalities in the

TOWNS NOT USED IN ANALYSIS

Figure 3-2.   Eastern Massachusetts

sample are located within a 40-mile radius of the Boston CBD, they represent a broad range of characteristics. For example, 1970 populations vary from under 4,000 to nearly 100,000 and gross population densities vary from 153 to 12,200 persons per square mile.

Various forms of local government are represented in the sample, including mayor-council city governments and traditional New England open town meetings. In addition, municipalities vary from suburban "bedroom" communities with almost no industrial or commercial development to more industrialized urban ring areas with nonresidential land use representing over two-thirds of the property tax bas. There is also a substantial variation in the growth experienced by municipalities during the period. Some cities exhibited virtually no growth in households and losses of employment during the 1960-70 decade, while some rapidly expanding towns grew by over 100 percent in population as well as gaining considerable employment during this same period.

A broad range of fiscal characteristics also exists within the sample. In terms of the magnitude of the public sector, 1970 municipal budgets vary from $1.3 million to $49.5 million. Alternatively, changes in school services in terms of additional school expenditures from 1960-70 range from less than $70 to almost $800 per household. In addition, increases in local tax burdens during the same period, as measured by equalized tax rates, ranged from 2 to 84 mills. To further illustrate the range of characteristics contained in the sample, Table 3-1 lists summary statistics describing the distribution of several important variables.

Data Sources

The primary source of fiscal information is Schedule A forms filed annually by each municipality with the Massachusetts Department of Corporations and Taxation. These forms provide a standardized accounting format that has been relatively consistent over the past several decades, facilitating both cross-sectional and time series analysis of budgetary decisions. Minor adjustments have been made with the assistance of Department of Corporations and Taxation personnel to assure that 1960 and 1970 budgetary information are comparable. Detailed information concerning the finances and operation of schools was obtained from Annual Reports of the Massachusetts Department of Education. With certain adjustments to account for revision of the budgeting system during the decade, these reports represent a consistent source of school expenditure information.

The major sources of population and housing data are the 1960 and 1970 U.S. Censuses of Population and Housing. Because of the manner in which 1960 data are reported it has been necessary to supplement material in the States and Small Areas Volume and SMSA Census Tract Reports with information prepared by the Eastern Massachusetts Regional Planning Project (EMRPP) from unpublished Census tables. The Census data are also missing some observa-

Table 3-1. Summary of Municipal Characteristics

Variable	Mean[a]	Standard Deviation	Minimum	Maximum
1. Change school exp./household ($)	197	100	66	778
2. Change number of households	1775	1461	214	6705
3. Change median family income ($)	1877	553	1034	4971
4. Change median housing value ($)	1833	1226	−768	7681
5. Change equalized valuation/household household ($00S)	−3202	2878	−20797	5498
6. Change total employment	1840	2048	−3590	8780
7. Change educational transfers/ household ($)	67	48	10	379
8. Change equalized tax rate (mills)	23	9	2	85
9. 1960 school exp./household ($)	257	72	141	568
10. 1960 median family income ($)	7260	1193	5285	12953
11. 1960 median housing value ($)	16527	4148	10500	31680
12. 1960 equalized valuation/ household ($)	20616	5675	10924	56093
13. 1960 equalized tax rate (mills)	24	5	8	35

[a]Weighted mean as described in text.

tions for 1960 median rooms per unit by tenure type for the smallest towns. Estimates for these missing values are based on values of the rooms per units variable for all housing units in each town missing this information.[12]

In order to control for the effects of inflation, the analysis has been conducted entirely in terms of 1960 dollars. Dollars were deflated according to the Boston SMSA consumer price index. These indices were obtained from local Bureau of Labor Statistics officials.

Land use data for each municipality are obtained from an aerial photographic study conducted for the EMRPP by Vogt-Ivers in 1963.[13] Although definitions of most of these variables are self-evident, one of them (land capacity) requires some explanation. This variable is defined as the product of net residential density times vacant developable land. Thus it is a measure of the number of additional households that could be accommodated in a municipality by developing existing (in 1963) vacant land at the then current densities. An update of the Vogt-Ivers study is currently being conducted by the Boston Metropolitan Area Planning Commission. However, the results have not been tabulated; thus it is only possible to use 1963 levels rather than changes in the values of these variables during the period.

Employment data for all cities and towns in the EMRPP area were obtained from the Massachusetts Department of Employment Security. Annual data for all municipalities in the state are available by two-digit SIC code.

Changes in total employment are subdivided into manufacturing and all other employment. It should be noted that employment figures represent only employees covered under the state unemployment compensation law. In general, this eliminates individual proprietors and institutional employees; however, covered employment includes the overriding majority of persons employed and thus is considered to be a good measure of towns' industrial and commercial development.

Accessibility to employment has been calculated according to a gravity model formulation.[14] According to this formulation, the accessibility of town *i* equals the sum of employment in municipalities throughout the region weighted by their respective travel times from town *i*. It should be noted that the accessibility index includes neighboring out-of-state commercial and industrial complexes. Employment data for these areas was obtained from the Rhode Island and New Hampshire Bureaus of Employment Security.

Unfortunately, change in accessibility is based solely on changes in employment levels, because travel time data are only available for 1963. Thus the change in accessibility of towns near major highways completed since 1963 is underestimated.

Data Problems

The biggest obstacle to estimating the model outlined above with the available data is the level of aggregation with which one must deal. This aggregation hinders the measurement of factors to which people are responding and obscures many important individual decisions. A number of the towns in the sample are composed of fairly diverse areas. For example, the proportion renter and the median value of owner occupied dwellings may vary considerably from one part of a town to another.

In making their location decisions, people are primarily motivated by the characteristics of their potential house and immediate neighborhood and secondarily by the characteristics of the town as a whole. Since our data deal only with characteristics of entire towns, the aggregate data may be hiding substantial geographic differences that may influence location choices. At the same time, highly aggregative data compound the natural collinearity that exists between income levels, housing consumption, and school expenditures in "good" versus "bad" neighborhoods. There are neighborhoods with high quality housing in towns with relatively poor schools, and vice versa. However, very few towns as a whole have both good housing and poor schools or the reverse. Greater variation in these intramunicipal attributes would substantially help in estimating the model.

The aggregate nature of the data hinders our ability to separate the characteristics of people moving into and out of our sample towns from changes that occurred to households which did not move. For example, the effect of fiscal differences between municipalities is expected to be most important for people choosing new residential locations. Unfortunately, the Census only reports net changes in local population characteristics, thus combining the effects of intrametropolitan migration with changes attributable to the aging of the nonmoving population. These latter changes are clearly unrelated to fiscal differences and thus complicate the assessment of fiscal impacts. The example of this problem with respect to changes in school age children per household and income changes was discussed previously. The only way to completely avoid this problem is to obtain a sample of recent movers and examine their location choices.

A conceptual problem that plagues virtually all studies of the present type is the inability to measure public services by anything other than expenditures per household. People are undoubtedly responding to some notion of school quality, not just money spent. School expenditures are only one of the elements required as input to good schools; in fact, some authors have suggested that money is not even the most important input.[15] An alternative might be based upon some form of standardized test scores, if they were available. The question then would be to what extent people's location decisions are based on these supposed output measures. We have partially dealt with this measurement problem by limiting the towns in our sample and excluding central city areas, which are the areas most likely to have school expenditures that far exceed the quality of their schools. Nonetheless, this is one area where substantial additional research is needed.

A more conventional data problem is the deficiency of measures of equalized valuation and tax rates. Equalized valuation is estimated biannually by the State Department of Corporations and Taxation, Bureau of Local Assessment, and is supposed to represent the true market value of taxable property in each municipality. However, because of the vagaries of appraisal techniques and possible political interference with these statistics (they are the basis for county assessments and some state grants and supposedly require approval by the legislature) they can only be considered rough estimates of property value. The resulting equalized tax rates based on these figures contain the same measurement errors. Any systematic bias to these equalization ratios would result in underestimates of local tax bases and hence overstatements of tax rates. A number of the towns totally reassessed during the decade, supposedly to full market value in compliance with state legislation. When this occurred, the ratio of the reassessed full market valuation to the state's estimate of equalized valuation at the time of reassessment was used to correct the 1960 equalized valuation and tax rate. However, this provides no guarantee of accurate measurement of the tax base and tax rate variables, even for these communities.

A final problem is the length of the period over which changes in the variables took place. Because appropriate data for many variables exists only at the beginning of each decade, ten years is the smallest time interval for which sufficient data are available. In the context of ten-year intervals many changes that are in reality sequential must be viewed as simultaneous. For example, over shorter periods the model postulates that changes in income cause changes in the bundle of local public services. In subsequent periods this change in public services results in further changes in local income as families relocate. Thus it would be highly desirable to analyze the lag structure of the interactions between these two variables. More frequently reported data would be necessary to carry out such an analysis, however.

THE ESTIMATED MODEL

The results of estimating the equations of the model present a fairly consistent picture of the reciprocal interactions between the forces of urban development and local fiscal decisions. The presentation of these results is organized according to the individual submodels described above, although it is clear that the models interact with each other, thus precluding any obvious starting point.

Fiscal Decisions

Table 3-2 summarizes the results of the two fiscal equations. However, before discussing specific results it is necessary to describe the information contained in the table. The top portion of the table includes the statistics for each regression equation; the bottom portion of the table provides a perspective for evaluating the impact of the various forces involved in local fiscal decisions. Comparisons based on estimates of the impact of a 10 percent increase in the average 1970 values of each variable are listed in the bottom of the table.

Take the effect of family income, for example: Table 3-1 shows that the 1970 median income (in 1960 prices) in the average community is $9,207. Thus a 10 percent increase would be $921 (column 1). Multiplying this amount by the coefficient in the school expenditure equation for change in family income yields an increase in per household school expenditures of $56 (column 4). This is a 12.3 percent increase over the 1970 level in the average town (column 5).

Comparison of the effects of a 10 percent increase in each of the other variables listed in the table thus yields a measure of the relative strength of their impact on school expenditures. Columns 2 and 3 compare a 10 percent change in each variable with the actual observed 1960-70 changes that occurred within the sample. For example, column 2 indicates that a 10 percent increase above the 1970 average family income is 48.5 percent of the actual average change in this variable during the decade and 23.2 percent of the maximum change in any one municipality during the period.

The educational expenditure equation indicates that population characteristics measuring demand for public education are the most important influence on the level of school expenditures. For example, as previously demonstrated, a 10 percent rise in family income would have resulted in a 12.3

Table 3-2.   Determinants of Fiscal Changes

Explanatory Variables	Dependent Variables	
	Change in School Exp. per Household ($1,000)	Change in Equalized Tax Rates (Mills)
Change in median income ($1,000)	0.061[a] (0.021)	3.57[a] (3.941)
Change in proportion with college education	0.72 (0.339)	103.14 (56.292)
Change in children/ household	0.464 (0.096)	42.83 (17.523)
Change in school transfers/ household ($1,000)	0.592 (0.181)	−23.71 (33.112)
Change in other transfers/ household ($1,000)	0.485 (0.121)	−26.42 (22.401)
Change in mfg. employment (1,000)	−0.011 (0.003)	0.69 (0.553)
Change in other employment (1,000)	0.003 (0.002)	0.84 (0.402)
Proportion change in equalized value/household	0.109 (0.061)	−85.50 (12.001)
1960 equalized value/ household ($1,000)		−0.91 (−.790)
Proportion change in households		−29.71 (11.304)
Intercept	−0.013 (0.031)	20.76 (5.232)
R^2	0.88	0.60

*Change in the Fiscal Variables for a
10% Change in the Explanatory Variables
from Their 1970 Levels*

Explanatory Variables	10 percent of 1970 Level			Resultant Change in School Expend./Household	Resultant Change in Total Revenue/Household
	Amt.[b]	% of Av. Δ	% of Max. Δ	As percent of 1970 Level	As percent of 1970 Level
Median income	0.921	48.5	23.2	12.3	6.9
Proptn. with college educ.	0.029	60.5	14.6	4.4	6.3
Children/ household	0.094	195.5	10.3	9.7	8.5
Educ. trans.	6.014	20.7	3.7	1.8	−0.7
Other trans.	0.003	100.0	0.6	0.3	−0.1
Mfg. emp.	0.557	−	12.2	−1.3	0.9
Other emp.	0.866	35.4	10.2	0.7	1.6
Proportional change equalized value/household	1.740	−	31.7	2.0	−6.9

[a]The standard error of the coefficient is contained in the parentheses under each coefficient.
[b]Units the same as shown above.

percent increase in school expenditures. If the average number of school children per household had been 10 percent higher, school expenditures per household would have been 9.7 percent higher than they were in 1970. Last, although the substantive meaning of a 10 percent rise in the proportion of college educated adults is somewhat ambiguous, such an increase would have resulted in a 4.4 percent rise in expenditures per household. Thus in each case a change in the population characteristics assumed to positively correlate with preferences for public education is estimated to lead to substantially increased public school expenditures.

Differences in the structure and incidence of the revenue sources for education expenditures also has important effects on the level of these expenditures. Larger tax bases and more transfers lead to higher per household expenditures. For example, if 1970 educational transfers had been 10 percent greater than they were, expenditures per household would have been 1.8 percent higher. A 10 percent rise in other transfer payments would have raised the school expenditure level by 0.3 percent. In terms of dollar amounts, local educational expenditures increase by \$0.59 and by \$0.49 for each additional dollar of educational and other transfers respectively. The only measure of local tax prices available for the present analysis is equalized valuation per household. To the extent that variations in this variable among towns are caused by variations in nonresidential property or the presence of a few highly valued homes, this variable is an indicator of the actual price an average household pays per dollar of additional public expenditures.

The lower the tax price (the greater the tax base per household) the greater the resulting public school expenditures. If the average 1970 tax base per household had been 10 percent higher, school expenditures per household would have been 2.0 percent higher. It should be noted that the relatively low estimate of the impact of tax price compared to Peterson's estimates may be due to the inability to separate changes in tax base per household due to increased nonresidential activity from residential property growth (see also Chapter Four).

Finally, the two employment variables included in the equation measure competing demands for local public funds. For example, given a public resource constraint in terms of a tax base and set of transfer payments, the more industrial and commercial development the greater the demand for noneducational public expenditures and the less funds available for schooling. In accord with this hypothesis, results indicate a −1.3 percent decline in school expenditures for a 10 percent increase in manufacturing employment. The results suggest school expenditures increase with nonmanufacturing employment, although this estimated effect is quite small.

The results explaining property tax rate changes are harder to present. The equation itself is estimated in terms of changes in tax rates, equalized for different assessing practices. The analysis indicates that property tax rates increase with increases in the demand for public services as measured by median income, percent having attended college, school age children per household, and employment levels. Tax rates decrease with increases in intergovernmental transfers, per household assessed valuations, and number of households. This last result may sound strange, but the equation includes a tax base per household term so that the negative coefficient measures the effect on tax rates of a percent change in the number of households, holding the tax base per household constant. In other words, if households are added and each household has the average tax base, then tax rates are decreased, leading to a decrease in expenditures per household.

To put these tax rate changes into perspective, the bottom part of Table 3-2 converts them into corresponding changes in total revenues for a community with the average 1970 tax base. For example, the 10 percent increase in income implies a 3.57 mill property tax increase. Converting this property tax increase into a revenue change (using the average assessed value in 1970 of $17,400 per household) results in a revenue increase of $57 per household, or a 6.9 percent increase over average 1970 property tax revenues per household.

One anomalous finding is that total revenues decrease with increases in local tax bases. This reduction occurs because the estimated reduction in tax rates for an increase in base more than offsets the increased revenues associated with the larger base. In this case we have probably overestimated the tax rate reduction associated with the base increase because of the difficulty in obtaining accurate equalized assessed values. Towns have a certain incentive to underestimate both their tax base and their equalization ratio and this increased during the 1960-70 decade. Consequently, our estimates of tax base changes will be too low (in fact our estimate is that tax base per household decreased in real terms during the decade), and the estimate of tax rate changes will be too high. The consequence would be a strong negative correlation between the errors in rate measurements and base measurements. This negative correlation leads to an overestimate of the effect of base changes on rate changes and our estimate that total revenues would decrease with increases in the tax base. Unfortunately, we know of no way to correct for such biases, as the only equalization ratios available are those published by the state.

The above discussion, which calls into question our measure of tax rate changes, means that any discussion of the precise impact of population composition changes on tax rates and total revenues could be misleading and certainly these estimates are imprecise at best. Consequently, we feel it would not be fruitful to go into a discussion of these results, other than to point out the computed effects, which are shown in Table 3-2.

Housing Characteristics

The second part of the model is comprised of three equations estimating the determinants of change in owner occupied housing values, gross housing rents, and the number of occupied housing units in each of the sample municipalities during the decade. Results of these equations are displayed in Table 3-3, which is organized in a manner similar to Table 3-2.

Table 3-3.   Determinants of Housing Prices and Residential Development

Explanatory Variables	Change in Housing Value ($1,000)	Change in Gross Rent ($)	Change in Number of Households (1,000)
Change in school expenditure/household ($1,000)	−0.051[a] (2.252)	26.614 (13.800)	
Change in equalized tax rate (mills)	0.010 (0.015)	0.019 (0.134)	
Change in median rooms/ unit[b]	1.482 (0.890)	−6.256 (8.543)	
Proportion new units	4.068 (2.190)	41.231 (16.333)	
Change in median housing value ($1,000)			0.003 (0.356)
Change in median gross rent ($)			−0.058 (0.042)
Change in proportion renter			19.752 (10.092)
Change in accessibility	0.109 (0.061)	1.751 (0.665)	0.255 (0.120)
Change in mfg. employment (1,000)	−0.019 (0.631)	−0.829 (0.506)	
Change in other employment (1,000)	−0.127 (0.059)	−0.831 (0.622)	
1960 rooms/unit[b]	2.102 (0.257)	−0.012 (3.419)	
1960 land capacity			0.113 (0.221)
1960 median housing value ($1,000)			0.078 (0.095)
Intercept	−12.22 (1.452)	−5.974 (15.531)	−1.597 (1.310)
R^2	0.74	0.60	0.41

Housing Price and Household Change for a 10% Change in Each Explanatory Variable from Their 1970 Level

Explanatory Variable	10 percent of 1970 Level			Resultant Change in Owner Value	Resultant Change in Rent	Resultant Change in Households
	Amt.[c]	% of Av. Δ	% of Max. Δ	As percent of 1970 Level	As percent of 1970 Level	As percent of 1970 Level
School exp./ household	0.045	22.8	5.8	−0.00	1.14	
Equalized tax rate	4.76	20.4	9.7	0.26	0.09	

Table 3-3 (cont.)

	10 percent of 1970 Level			Resultant Change in Owner Value	Resultant Change in Rent	Resultant Change in Households
	Housing Price and Household Change for a 10% Change in Each Explanatory Variable from Their 1970 Level					
Explanatory Variable	*Amt.*c	*% of Av. Δ*	*% of Max. Δ*	*As percent of 1970 Level*	*As percent of 1970 Level*	*As percent of 1970 Level*
Rooms/unit	0.62	723.4	59.5	5.00		
Percent new unit (owner)	0.10	74.3	19.6	2.21		
Percent new units (renter)	0.10	53.2	15.3	–	3.93	
Accessibility	4.43	91.8	36.6	2.63	7.41	10.25
Mfg. emp.	0.556	–	12.2	–0.06	–0.44	
Other emp.	0.866	35.4	10.2	–0.60	–0.69	
Land capacity	1.105	10.0	3.0			1.13
Change in housing value	1.84	100.2	23.9			0.04
Change in rent	10.53	66.9	18.9			–5.54
Change in proportion renter	0.037	140.7	27.6			6.63

aThe standard error of the coefficient is contained in the parentheses under each coefficient.
bFor owner and renter occupied units respectively.
cUnits are the same as shown above.

The important determinants of housing prices are accessibility, age, and size of the unit. All had substantial effects on housing prices and rents. A 10 percent increase in accessibility leads to a 7.4 percent and a 2.6 percent increase in rents and values respectively. For each 10 percent of the housing stock less than ten years old, rents and values increase by 3.9 percent and 2.2 percent respectively. For owner occupied units, a 10 percent increase in average number of rooms leads to a 5 percent increase in the median house value.

The exception to the results discussed above was the number of rooms for rental units. The results imply that median rents actually decreased if the average apartment size increased. This is surprising, but an explanation might well be that there are several "rental" markets with relatively large units (such as duplexes or even house rentals) that constitute one market, and smaller, one- and two-bedroom units that constitute another market. If demand for these smaller units grew faster than the supply during the decade, it would substantially increase the rent of these units and lead to a negative relationship between changes in average number of rooms and average gross rents. The owner housing market may be much more homogeneous, leading to the constant relationship between unit size and price.

Neighborhood characteristics as measured by the change in employment in the town influenced values and rents, with both decreasing in areas with large employment increases. Employment increases indicate that a town is becoming less residential and possibly more congested and less desirable from an environmental point of view, with the expected depressing effect on housing values.

The last factor included in the two equations, fiscal characteristics, has an almost imperceptible impact on housing values and rents. Three of the four coefficients associated with these two variables are quite small. These results indicate that differences in local expenditures and tax rates are not substantially capitalized into housing prices. As discussed in a previous section, there are two forms of capitalization. The first, related to efficiency differentials, we cannot measure because we have no way to accurately assess the production efficiency of a given town. The second form of capitalization is a quasi-rent based on a short run undersupply of towns with high expenditure levels and associated tax rates. The results here suggest that there is little systematic quasi-rent for public school expenditures.

The one exception to this conclusion is that increased education expenditures were associated with increased rents. This result is quite possibly due to the absence of towns with both large school expenditures and a large number of rental units. The simple correlation between 1960 per household school expenditures and percent renter was −0.76 and there were only eight towns in the sample that were above the median on both school expenditures and proportion renter. These eight towns did not offer much choice to renter families who wanted good schools. Two of the towns are on the periphery of the metropolitan area (they are outside the formal SMSA) and three are quite small towns generally considered to be fairly exclusive suburbs (Lincoln, Concord, and Cohasset). These towns have a large number of single family rental units and few more conventional apartments. The vast majority of apartment units are located in the more central city areas with reputations for inferior schools; consequently, it would have been quite difficult for families wanting to rent to find a unit in a town with acknowledged good schools. If there was an increase in the number of such families during the sixties, it would push up the price of rental units in those few "good school" towns. This would be a short run effect, however, unless developers could be prevented from constructing rental units in these towns.

The last equation in this portion of the model estimates the determinants of overall residential growth. Its results are strikingly consistent with traditional urban economic theories of urban growth. The two most significant variables in this equation are land capacity and change in accessibility to employment. Their coefficients indicate that the more room there is for potential development and the greater the increase in accessibility, the greater will be the increase in the number of housing units. An additional factor influencing the change in the number of housing units is the change in the proportion of these units that are rental. Increasing the proportion renter substantially increases the density of land use so that we would expect populations to grow more in areas increasing the density of their land use.

Population Characteristics

The last three equations in the model bear most directly upon the question of whether local fiscal conditions influence residential location decisions. They attempt to measure the impact of local public services on the types of households that locate within each municipality. Thus they are a more appropriate test of the Tiebout model than prior attempts at indirect empirical verification through estimates of the capitalization of local fiscal conditions into housing values. Results of this analysis are presented in Table 3-4, showing the estimated equation and the expected change in an average community's population from 10 percent changes in the explanatory variables.

Not surprisingly, housing values and the characteristics of the housing stock are important determinants of the composition of a town's population. Areas with more expensive housing—meaning larger, newer, and more accessible houses—attracted families with higher income and education levels. Median incomes increased by $100 and the proportion with college training by 1.3 percent for each thousand dollar increase in median house value. In percentage terms, a 10 percent increase in the median house value led to a 2 percent increase in the median income level and an 8 percent increase in the proportion having attended college. These results indicate that population composition is quite sensitive to the available housing.

Families with school age children are attracted to larger, less expensive owner occupied houses in towns with more open space. The coefficients on the change in housing price and rooms per unit variables suggest that they have important effects on the location decisions of larger families, although this is not statistically significant. The strong implication here is that these larger families demand larger homes, as measured by the number of rooms, but want them to be less expensive. These families are in effect giving up accessibility and new construction in order to get larger, less expensive homes. These families are also clearly looking for homes to purchase rather than to rent. This result, combined with the positive effect of the proportion open space in the community, indicates that families with children place a greater premium on lower density living than do other families.

More important from the standpoint of our examination of the Tiebout approach to local public service decisions, the level of school expenditures per household is important in attracting certain types of families. The

Table 3-4. Determinants of Changes in Population Characteristics

	Dependent Variables		
Explanatory Variables	*Change in Median Income ($1,000)*	*Change in Proportion with College Education*	*Change in Children/Household*
Change in school expenditure/household ($1,000)	2.817[a] (0.451)	0.086 (0.034)	0.317 (0.136)
Change in equalized tax rate (mills)	−0.006 (0.005)	−0.000 (0.000)	−0.0015 (0.0009)
Change in median housing value ($1,000)	0.104 (0.050)	0.013 (0.004)	−0.007 (0.008)
Change in proportion renter			−1.118 (0.351)
Change in median rooms/unit (owner)			0.047 (0.061)
1960 median income ($1,000)	0.117 (0.051)		
1960 proportion with college education		0.065 (0.041)	
1960 family structure			−0.120 (0.058)
1963 proportion open space			0.155 (0.048)
Intercept	0.432 (0.331)	−0.006 (0.010)	0.032 (0.041)
R^2	0.74	0.64	0.79

	Changes in Population Characteristics for 10% Change in Each Explanatory Variable from Their 1970 Level					
	10 percent of 1970 Level			*Change in Median Income*	*Change in College Educ.*	*Change in Child/Household*
Explanatory Variables	*Amt.[c]*	*% of Av. Δ*	*% of Max. Δ*	*As percent of 1970 Level*	*As percent of 1970 Level*	*As percent of 1970 Level*
School expenditure/ household	0.045	22.8	5.8	1.4	1.4	1.5
Equalized tax rate	4.761	20.4	9.7	−0.3	−0.1	−0.8
House value	1.840	100.2	23.9	2.1	8.3	−1.5
Proportion renter	0.037	140.7	27.6			−4.8
Change rooms/ unit	0.621	723.5	59.5			3.1
Open space	0.101	33.3	11.8			1.6

[a]The standard error of the coefficient is contained in the parentheses under each coefficient.

[b]Number of children ages 9-19 minus those younger than 6 in 1960.

[c]Same units as above.

larger the increase in education expenditures, the larger the increase in median income, proportion with college experience, and school age children per family. A 10 percent increase in per household school expenditures over the 1970 level would have resulted in a 1.5 percent increase over the 1970 level for each of these population characteristic variables. At the same time, all three types of households were attracted to towns with low tax rates for a given level of school expenditures. The small magnitude and statistical insignificance of these tax rate differences may be due to inaccuracies in the tax rate variable, and not to the insensitivity of homeowners to such differences.

These estimated equations are useful for comparing the relative impacts of fiscal and housing stock influences. One can infer from these figures that housing stock characteristics have a greater impact on residential location decisions than do fiscal conditions. This conclusion is borne out by all three equations. For example, a 10 percent variation in the 1970 level of the most important housing factor in each equation has from 1.5 to almost 6 times the impact on population characteristics as that of school expenditures. Variations in school expenditures do influence changes in population characteristics, though, and people appear willing to sacrifice some housing consumption or accessibility to locate in areas with good schools.

CONCLUSIONS

Our analysis shows the interaction between local fiscal decisions and the other forces such as accessibility and housing stock that cause and shape urban development. Additionally, the analysis provides some evidence of the relative importance of each of these factors. The underlying questions are the consequences of metropolitan development on local fiscal decisions and the importance of fiscal decisions in affecting the pattern of residential development. The answers to these questions are important in evaluating the feasibility of the Tiebout model as a means of providing people the desired level and type of public services, in ascertaining the constraints under which that model would operate, and the conditions necessary for it to function efficiently.

The traditional urban economics location model explaining housing prices and urban growth by variations in accessibility, land use, and housing stocks, and ignoring fiscal differences, is generally supported as a first approximation by our estimates. Population growth results from changes in accessibility to employment, the availability of developable land, and the conversion to denser land uses. Changes in housing prices and rents are most affected by changes in accessibility and physical characteristics of the housing unit such as size and age. Location decisions and the resulting changes in communities' population composition are largely determined by accessibility and housing stock changes, as measured by the change in housing prices. These results imply that the suburbanization and stratification of American metropolitan areas is more the result of the suburbanization of employment, changes in transportation networks, rising income, and the growth in the demand for larger and newer houses, than it is of fiscal disparities between inner cities and suburbs.

It would be wrong to ignore the effects of fiscal differences in households' location decisions, although the analysis suggests that these variations play a minor role. Our results show that higher school expenditures did attract families with school age children, higher incomes, and more education. Both our results and Mayo's (see Chapter Two) suggest that these households take public expenditure differences into account when selecting their residential location, although they do not seem to sacrifice much housing consumption to get higher school expenditures.

It follows from this analysis that in order for the Tiebout solution to be an effective means of providing local public services, there must be a full range of alternative fiscal packages and housing choices available throughout the metropolitan area. Even in the Boston metropolitan area, which has a relatively large number of local jurisdictions, there would not appear to be enough opportunity for adequate choice for all households. For example, it was extremely difficult for renters to find units in areas with good schools. The only way the Tiebout model would assure an efficient solution to the public services delivery problem would be if there were literally hundreds of local communities with different public services and a large variety of housing stocks at each location. The local decentralization required would be many times the amount of "balkanization" observed in metropolitan areas today.

The importance of having a wide range of housing options within each of the small communities cannot be overlooked. To the extent that demand for public services is not perfectly correlated with the demand for housing characteristics such as age and size, or amount of land and tenure type, there must be units available within each community to satisfy the range of housing demands. Obviously, if all the best school districts are in communities with large and expensive housing, households with modest income, or those desiring smaller units such as apartments, will be required to make housing selections far from their preferred type in order to choose their desired public service package.

Finally, the Tiebout solution requires that there be no imperfections in the housing market that restrict households and developers from making free choices. The most obvious restriction of this type is that which has been a result of housing market discrimination against nonwhite households. Zoning restrictions prohibiting developers from building denser, lower cost housing in certain towns is another commonly observed example. As long as such restrictions remain in the metropolitan housing market, we cannot expect the location approach to the allocation of public services to even approximate an efficient—let alone an equitable—solution.

The fiscal equations suggest that families are more likely to express their demands for public services through the political process in whatever community they happen to reside. Presumably this means voting for candidates and specific proposals that attempt to change service levels and taxes in the desired direction. We observed considerable variation in both the level and the change in these fiscal characteristics.

Changes in population composition had the greatest effects on the changes in school expenditures and tax rates. In addition, population changes had a greater effect on public expenditures than expenditures had on population changes. The implication here is that families with high demands for education and other services locate in towns and then proceed through the political process to alter the level of services to meet their needs. The solution to the public service allocation problem, then, is not being accomplished so much through the choice of a residential location as through voting procedures—as outlined by Peterson, Hanushek, and Jackson in this volume.

Chapter Four

Voter Demand for Public School Expenditures

George Peterson

Among the means open to households for expressing their demands for public services, perhaps the most direct is voting in local tax elections. At the national level, voting requires casting one's ballot for or against candidates who have taken positions on a multitude of issues, with the result that it is difficult to read into voter response a mandate for any particular spending policy. Local elections for political candidates pose some of the same difficulties of interpretation. A mayoral candidate typically runs for office on a platform containing many planks, and voter support for his candidacy may have more to do with his personality or campaign style than with his position on any of the issues. Still, the lesser span of issues raised at the local level, and the greater prominence accorded to public service questions, may make it possible to discern citizen "demand" for basic public services from the votes cast in a local general election. Elsewhere in this volume, John Jackson has essayed this type of analysis (see Chapter Six).

If our objective is to investigate specific hypotheses about the character of household demand for public services, however, the most direct route lies in analysis of single issue referenda, such as local tax elections. In a tax election the voter is asked to register his preference, "yes" or "no," concerning a specific proposal for raising (or continuing) the local tax rate in order to finance a designated public service. In many states a wide variety of tax and spending proposals are regularly submitted to the electorate. Local financing of mass transit and public housing construction, shifts in the tax system, as well as a miscellany of more esoteric issues ranging from fluoridation of water supplies to Sunday closing of movie theatres frequently must be approved at referendum.[1] Referendum voting may no longer possess the aura of democratic reform that it did during the Progressive era, but it continues to be a popular device for reaching local policy decisions and one that is peculiarly revealing of voter demands.

In the United States the most important and most frequent tax referenda deal with school finance.[2] During the last decade an average of 1,500 school bond elections were held annually in this country.[3] Tax elections on millage rates to pay for schools' current operating expenditures are even more frequent. A study of voting by Californians was able to compile fairly complete data on some 970 school tax elections held between 1966 and 1972.[4] Since education represents by far the largest expenditure item in local governments' budgets, and usually is identified by citizens as the most important local public service, the voluminous data on voting in school tax elections affords an unmatched opportunity to study the character of local public service demand.

The first section of this chapter compares citizen demand for public school spending with household demand for ordinary goods, and shows how a demand function can be derived that is in every respect analogous to the demand functions economists ordinarily treat. It also demonstrates that in principle this demand function for school spending can be estimated cross-sectionally by comparing spending levels in different school districts, or inferred from household voting on school tax referenda.

The second section presents several empirical estimates of the demand for public school spending, drawn from a variety of geographical areas, and employing individual household as well as aggregate school district data. These empirical estimates reveal a remarkably stable picture of household demand for school expenditures. The third section of the chapter investigates the practical meaning of the estimated demand functions. When households determine their willingness to support public education, do they look on publicly provided schooling as if it were just another private consumption item, or do they significantly adjust their expenditure demands out of concern for the public good, or what has been termed "public regardingness"?

The final section of the chapter explores the policy implications of the strong "tax-price" term contained in the household demand function. A number of tax relief and other policies recently undertaken by state and local governments have had the effect of altering the tax-price households must pay for public sector spending. Although undertaken purely as measures to redistribute tax burdens, these policies are likely to have a marked impact on overall demand for local public services through their effect on tax prices. The concluding portion of the chapter examines this issue in light of our empirical estimates of the demand for school spending.

Throughout, I have analyzed the demand for school spending. As is now amply clear, school expenditures are by no means a reliable proxy for school quality. In a complete examination of citizen demand for schooling, households might be better conceived of as demanding school quality as the final output, and demanding school expenditures as an input, demand for which would depend both upon consumer desires to acquire the final products of schooling and upon their judgments as to the efficacy of increased spending as a means of achieving this end. My reasons for abstracting from this process are simple: the production relationships in public schooling are immensely complex. The essentials of citizen demand seem more easily analyzed by treating dollars spent on pupils as if they were the direct object of household concern.

HOUSEHOLD DEMAND FOR SCHOOL EXPENDITURES

On a private market a family usually can buy as much of a good or service as it desires, at a constant price per unit. Given the customary postulates of rationality in household choice, the observed level of household spending on an item will represent its desired or optimum level, given the item's price and household income and tastes. For a public service like schooling, such a fine adjustment of actual consumption to desired levels is not possible. It is an important characteristic of public services that, at least to a good approximation, they are made available equally (in terms of dollars spent) to all qualifying citizens within a service district. For this reason, the level of service availability is unlikely to satisfy precisely the demands of more than a few members of the community. The rest of the population must accept a nonoptimal level of service supply or move elsewhere, to a service district that better satisfies its requirements. (The latter option has been discussed extensively in preceding chapters.)

The inability of households to fully adjust their public service consumption without moving raises a difficult question: how are we to estimate household demand for schooling if the vast majority of households are known to be out of equilibrium—that is, paying for a level of school services that is either greater or less than they would freely choose to consume? Two fundamental approaches have been suggested. One examines the level of local school district spending and relates this figure to the characteristics of the local population.

Typically, median household characteristics are used for this purpose, on the grounds that in an election setting actual spending will represent the preference held by the median voter, the one who stands in the middle as far as desired spending is concerned. Just how to characterize this median voter, when there are numerous characteristics relevant to voter preference, is a difficult question that in empirical work has been largely bypassed by assuming that a family with the median value of each relevant characteristic, taken individually, is close enough to "the" median voter to serve as a substitute.[5] The resulting equation relating observed local school expenditures to median household characteristics is interpreted as a household demand function for school spending.[6]

The second approach to demand estimation focuses more directly on voting. In a rough sort of way, the kinds of households that regularly vote in favor of greater public service outlays can be said to "demand" greater expenditures than those households that regularly vote against such proposals. The actual connection between voting and household demand is complicated by the fact that an affirmative vote for a tax and spending increase represents a vote in favor of an increment in public service provision. The meaning of such a vote can be adequately assessed only in relation to the original spending level. Voters in communities in A and B may have the same demand for school spending, yet voters in A may reject a proposed millage increase while voters in B may approve it, if the initial spending level is higher in A than it is in B. For this reason, no simple inference can be made from referendum voting to household demand functions. However it is apparent that household voting potentially can reveal much about the character of demand for schooling and other public services.

A Model of Household Demand

A systematic interpretation of household voting would begin with household utility functions. I have shown elsewhere[7] that on the assumption that households strive to maximize personal utility in deciding the levels of school expenditure they will support, a demand function for school spending can be formally derived that is in every respect analogous to demand for private goods. If we suppose that all local school revenues come from the property tax, the demand equation for school spending takes the form:

$$L_i = f(Y_i, \frac{H_i}{V}, S, n_i) \tag{1}$$

where:

L_i = household i's desired level of local school spending per pupil;

Y_i = household income;

H_i = the value of household i's property tax base (its house value);

V = the average property value per pupil in the school district;

S = the amount of state aid received per pupil by the district; and,

n = the number of public school children in household i.

All the terms contained in expression (1) appear to be self-explanatory, with the exception of $(\frac{H_i}{V})$, which I will call the tax-price. If local per pupil spending on schooling is to be raised by one dollar and financed exclusively from a uniform local property tax, household i will have to pay $(\frac{H_i}{V})$ dollars in increased tax liability. This tax-price term then is exactly analogous to the price variable which appears in ordinary household demand functions for private goods. It is the "price" the household must pay for one dollar of additional school spending per pupil. The tax-price term, $(\frac{H_i}{V})$, will vary across households, according to the value of residential property, H_i, which each family holds, and will vary across communities according to the level of taxable property per pupil, V, in each school district. School districts that possess large amounts of industrial wealth or high average values of residential property will be able to raise school monies at a lower tax rate (and hence lower total tax cost to families that own homes of a given value) than less wealthy districts.

Because the "tax-price" variable, specified in this way, is a somewhat novel term, it may be useful to convey a sense of its magnitude and variation. In California, $\frac{H}{V}$, the cost to the median household in a school district of raising a dollar of per pupil school spending varied in 1969-70 from a high of $1.02 in Madera to a low of 7¢ in Mojave. In Michigan, the tax-price in 1969-70 varied from $1.41 in Davison to 17¢ in River Rouge. In New Jersey the variation (1971-72) was from $1.49 in Mountain Lake to 6¢ in Wildwood, and in New York from $1.77 in Brentwood to 17¢ in Green Island. The variation in tax-prices across individual households, of course, is much greater since this encompasses the entire range of housing values, H_i, as well as per pupil tax bases, V.

While the exact form of the demand function for school spending cannot be deduced without further information regarding the nature of household utility functions, I shall assume that the demand relation can be rendered in simple constant elasticity form as:

$$L_i = a\, Y_i^{\alpha} \left[\frac{H_i}{V}\right]^{\beta} S^{\gamma} n_i^{\epsilon} \tag{2}$$

Equation (2) can be empirically estimated across school districts within a state by using school district values for L_i, V, and S and household median values for Y_i, H_i, and n_i.

A Model of Voting Behavior

According to our interpretation, the household version of expression (2) represents family i's desired level of local per pupil spending on public schools. Whether or not a community actually spends this amount, of course, will depend on the distribution of all household demands. When it comes to school tax elections, family i will do what it can to set school spending levels at the amount that it regards as privately optimal, but the family cannot simply "buy" the optimal amount of education, as it could on a fully competitive private market. The cross-sectional procedure used to fit (2), in fact, assumes that only the median voter's exact demand for school spending will be satisfied. Nonetheless, there is a direct link between household demand, as given by (2), and household voting.

In deciding how to vote in a local school tax election, the rational household will compare the present level of local school spending with its privately optimal level, as revealed by the demand function. If present spending lags behind the level that the household finds most desirable, it will vote for an increase in school taxes and expenditures; if school spending already exceeds the level the household finds privately optimal, it will vote against an increase. If we want to predict how a household will vote in a school tax election, we should calculate its private demand for schooling by inserting household values for the variables appearing in the demand function, and then compare the household's predicted optimal expenditure level with the actual level of local school spending. When this difference is greater than zero, we would predict a "yes" vote on a proposed tax increase; when it is less than zero, we would predict a "no" vote.

The above procedure suggests that it may be possible to independently estimate household demand for schooling from voting data. According to the theory, the demand function ought to be the most effective discriminant function for distinguishing the "yes" and "no" votes that households cast in school tax elections. Conversely, by fitting a discriminant function to household voting data it may be possible to estimate the original demand curve.

I have illustrated the process in two dimensions in Figure 4-1. For purposes of illustration, I have represented household demand for school expenditures in 1a as a function of family income only. The privately optimal level of local school spending for families of different incomes is drawn as the solid demand curve, DD. A household with income level Y_A will demand L_A of local school spending. A household with median family income Y_{MED} will demand L_{MED} of local school spending. Assume that we collect our household voting sample from a single school district, so that actual school spending is fixed at a common level, as indicated in the diagram by the horizontal dashed line. On the theory of median voter determination of spending levels, this dashed line will coincide with the level of spending preferred by the median household, or L_{MED}.

Now the household demand function, of course, is estimated with some error. This fact is illustrated in the diagram by the scatter points that surround the demand curve, DD. These scatter points correspond to the actual preferred spending levels of particular households. They will diverge from the predicted preference levels as given by the demand curve for a variety of reasons: probably the easiest to visualize is the fact that numerous "taste" variables have been omitted from the demand specification. These divergent "tastes" for schooling may be insignificant in the aggregate, but nonetheless be of great

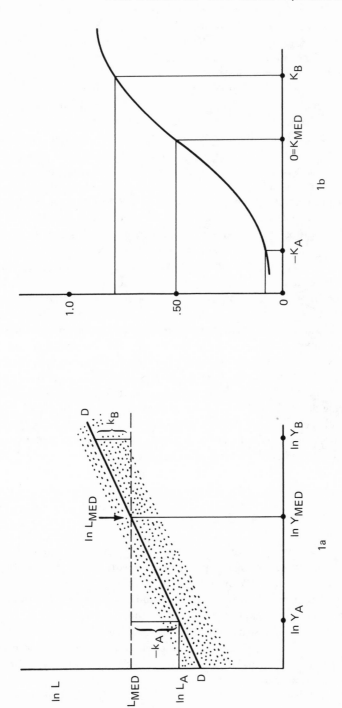

Figure 4-1. Probability of ''Yes'' Vote in Tax Election

importance in explaining an individual household's vote on a school tax proposal.

The probability that a household will vote in favor of a marginal school tax increase is equivalent to the probability that its true scatter point lies above the dashed horizontal line in 1a. The true location of the scatter point, of course, is unobservable. What is observable is its predicted location, given the observable characteristics of the household and the parameters of the demand function. For a household like A whose "predicted" spending preferences falls short of the actual level by k_A, the probability that its "true" spending demand will exceed the present level is very low. Hence, the probability of its voting "yes" on a proposal to increase school taxes is very low. This is shown by the near zero probability in 1b. The probability of a "yes" vote grows greater as the estimated demand level increases, until for a household like B with very high income, the probability of support for a tax increase approaches 1.

I have shown elsewhere that it is also possible to employ this argument in reverse. Given sufficient information about household voting, it is possible to estimate the nonlinear probability curve illustrated in 1b, and infer the underlying demand function, from which the probability function is transformed. The key data requirement is that we possess observations on household voting for at least two different tax and expenditure proposals in the same community. Given information on household characteristics and voting outcomes in two different tax elections within the same period, and given knowledge of the starting level of school spending, as well as an a priori specification of the form of the demand function, an exact estimation of the underlying demand function can be made. This function estimated from voting data should coincide with the estimates of (2) made from expenditure data. With information for a single tax election only, it is possible to estimate the relative magnitude of the coefficients in the demand function, but it is not possible to estimate their absolute values. The estimated coefficients in this case are defined only up to a linear transformation.

EMPIRICAL ESTIMATES OF DEMAND

In this section I report on several empirical estimates of the demand equation (2) made through cross-sectional expenditure comparisons and analysis of voting in school tax referenda. My purpose is, first of all, to determine whether the demand relationships derived from voting studies are consistent with the demand estimates based upon expenditure analysis, and, second, to identify the approximate magnitude and significance of the coefficients of the several variables appearing in the demand function for public school spending. In particular, I want to examine the importance of the tax-price term in determining demand for both homeowners and renters.

Table 4-1 summarizes the results of fitting equation (2) to school

Table 4-1. Estimated Demand Equations for School Expenditure

State	R^2	*Constant*	$+ \alpha \ln Y$	$+ \beta \ln \dfrac{H}{V}$	$+ \delta \ln S$	$+ \gamma$ *per Rent*
California	.81	1.04	.84	−.36	−.58	.33
(1969-70)		(0.7)	(7.9)	(6.2)	(5.6)	(2.5)
Michigan	.72	−4.24	+1.22	−.51	−.28	.33
(1969-70)		(2.7)	(9 9)	(6.5)	(3.2)	(2.2)
New Jersey	.75	−4.49	+1.23	−.25	−.16	+.29
(1971-72)		(5.7)	(16.0)	(7.5)	(7.5)	(3.8)
New York[a]	.74	−1.13	+1.35	−.55	−.87	+.41
(1968-69)		(0.7)	(12.5)	(9.1)	(4.8)	(2.9)
Kansas City						
SMSA	.71	−1.85	+1.10	−.70	−.49	b
(1970-71)		(0.8)	(4.9)	(6.4)	(4.3)	

[a]Estimated with dummy for New York City metropolitan area (Nassau, Suffolk, and Westchester Counties, and New York City). The dummy coefficient was 0.39 with t-statistic of 7.7.

[b]Data not available.

district data in the designated areas. To refresh the reader's memory: Y represents household income; $\dfrac{H}{V}$ is the tax-price term; and, S is state aid receipts.

The equation used to estimate the values in Table 4-1 differs from equation (2) in two respects. I was unable to obtain information on the number of public school pupils per household for smaller school districts and consequently was obliged to omit this variable from the demand specification.[8] Second, I have added the term, R, percentage of renters among the adult population, to represent the percent of households in the school district that rent, rather than own, their housing. The log-log specification of the demand function allows the estimated coefficients to be interpreted directly as elasticities. The sample size in each case is given in the footnote.[9]

As can be seen, the estimated coefficients show a high degree of stability, compared to customary estimates of demand functions for private goods. The income elasticity of demand in all states except California centers about the value 1.2. The estimated price elasticities show somewhat more variation, but are roughly of the magnitude −0.5. In calculating median house value, H, I have used a weighted average of the reported value for single family homes and the estimated value for rental units. The positive coefficient for "percent renter" in the demand equation, therefore, implies that renters of the same income level support higher levels of school expenditure than do other households, after control for the property tax burden on the property they occupy. Presumably this is so, because renters perceive themselves as bearing only a fraction of the tax liability.

Empirical Estimates from Voting Data

Table 4-2 compares the demand functions for school spending derived from analysis of voting in two local school tax referenda. As I pointed out above, only the relative values of the demand coefficients can be estimated from voting data for a single tax election. For purposes of comparison I have standardized the income elasticity at 1.0 and have adjusted the other estimated coefficients accordingly. The data in Table 4-2 thus permit a check on the relative magnitudes and statistical significance of the coefficients, although not on their absolute values.

The first row of Table 4-2 reports the results of fitting a nonlinear transformation of the demand function to precinct voting records in Ann Arbor, Michigan.[10] Most referendum studies by political scientists have analyzed such precinct voting records. As Hanushek demonstrates in Chapter Five, however, the aggregation of different types of families at the precinct level—especially renters and homeowners—creates a number of interpretive problems. Fortunately, the Ann Arbor data avoid many of these problems. Until May 1970 the State of Michigan was one of fourteen states in the union that restricted suffrage on local tax and expenditure referenda to owners of real property and their spouses. In May 1970, however, an Arizona court ruled that such voting restrictions were unconstitutional. Subsequently, this view has been upheld by the Supreme Court, with the result that local tax elections in all states are now open to all registered voters. In the interim, however, while the affected states were awaiting the resolution of their appeals, local voting officials were required to maintain dual voting records on tax referenda—one set for property owners and another set for renters. The existence of these dual records for an eight- or nine-month period affords an unusual opportunity to investigate precinct voting

Table 4-2.   Demand Functions for School Spending Estimated from Voting Data[a]

		(Coefficients have been standardized as noted in text)			
Precinct	R^2	$\alpha \ln Y$	$\beta \ln \dfrac{H}{V}$	αR	$\delta \ln$ *School Child*
Ann Arbor	.73	+1.0	−.83	+1.94	+.39
Precinct Data		(2.1)	(1.9)	(7.5)	(1.7)
Troy	82%[b]	+1.0	−.80	c	+.53
Household Data		(8.3)	(4.4)		(6.7)

[a]School Aid (S) is omitted from the demand function because there is no variation within a single school district.

[b]Percentage refers to percent of votes in sample predicted correctly on losses of felted demand equation.

[c]There were not enough renters in the Troy sample to estimate this coefficient.

behavior separately for the two classes of households. In fact, the prior impossibility of separating homeowner and renter returns would appear to invalidate much of the usual precinct level voting analysis.[11]

The choice of Ann Arbor as a study site also has certain drawbacks. The fact that university students dominate the voting lists in certain precincts almost certainly distorts the results. The rents that are paid by students living in university dormitories are determined independently of local tax and expenditure decisions. Under any and all theories of incidence, these persons are not required to bear the costs of the public expenditures they vote for. For this reason, I have eliminated from my sample the renter portion of the vote in the three precincts where university students constitute more than 50 percent of the eligible voter list. As might be expected, renters in these three precincts supported the proposal to increase taxes by a margin of more than eight to one.

The coefficients shown in the first row of Table 4-2 have the same signs as previously reported for the expenditure equations, although the t-statistics are lower. Moreover, the relative magnitude of the coefficients is quite comparable. (The renter term, R in the voting equation is a 0-1 variable; the coefficient needs to be divided by 100 to be put on the same footing as the coefficient for percentage renter, per Rent, in Table 4-1.) I interpret this as a general confirmation of the consistency of the expenditure and voting derivations of the school expenditure demand function.

The second row of Table 4-2 reports the results of fitting a demand function to individually reported household voting in a school tax election in Troy, Michigan. The findings are based on a special survey of 611 registered voters.[12] As can be seen, the estimated demand coefficients bear a close resemblance to those reported for the Ann Arbor voter sample, and again are comparable to the demand estimates based on expenditure analysis. It is important to emphasize, however, that the income elasticity of demand in Table 4-2 has been arbitrarily standardized at 1.0. Any linear transformation of the regression equations reported would serve equally well in discriminating between votes cast. The three-variable demand function estimated for Troy succeeds in classifying correctly 82 percent of the votes in Troy's school tax election.

Perhaps the one systematic difference between the demand functions for school spending estimated from expenditure data and the demand functions estimated from voting data lies in the relative magnitude of the price elasticity. In both of the referenda studies summarized in Table 4-2 the price elasticity of demand is considerably greater, relative to income elasticity, than was reported in the expenditure analyses of Table 4-1. I attribute this difference primarily to the omission of the variable "public school children" which imparted a downward bias to the estimated absolute value of the price elasticity in the expenditure functions.[13]

The consistently positive demand coefficient for renters suggests that renters do not perceive themselves as bearing the full costs of the property tax, and therefore are willing to impose higher school taxes than similarly situated owner occupants. The use of a dummy variable to designate renters is a highly imperfect approximation to the true effect that renting should have on household demand. Renter status should affect the demand for public services, if at all, by reducing the perceived tax-price that a family bears.

Elsewhere, I have shown that when renter status is treated in this fashion, the precision of the entire demand function is greatly improved.[14] The results obtained there imply that renters perceive themselves as absorbing only about 20 percent of any property tax increase. Whether this represents renters' implicit judgment as to the final incidence of the property tax, or merely reflects the rapid turnover in rental occupancy which, coupled with the lag in adjusting rental contracts, means that another set of renters will have to bear most of the costs of a property tax increase, I have been unable to determine. The evidence clearly indicates, however, that the rental population of a community provides a strong voting impetus for higher public service levels.

INTERPRETING THE DEMAND FUNCTION

The preceding sections demonstrate that a reasonably stable demand function for school spending can be derived on the assumption that households undertake to maximize private utility functions of the sort customarily attributed by economists to consumers of private goods. Does this mean that citizen demand for a public service like schooling is motivated solely by calculations of personal gain? Or to borrow the language of recent debate in political science: What light does our analysis shed on the role that "public regardingness," rather than private benefit, plays in household demand for school spending?

Two of the variables in our demand formulation are quite clear indices of purely private benefit calculations. The first is the tax-price term. The consistently negative tax-price coefficient implies that households will favor a lower level of school spending—or be less likely to vote for any given level of school expenditure—the more each dollar of school outlay costs the household in terms of tax payments. Unless households regularly took into account the size of the personal tax burden they would have to bear should a school spending proposal be passed, the tax-price term would not have this significant, negative sign.

Other evidence is also available as to the importance households attach to tax-prices when determining their position on school spending proposals. Jeffrey Smith has examined the willingness of voters in Oregon's Intermediate Education Districts (IEDs) to approve equalization taxes, whose sole purpose is to redistribute the tax burden associated with given levels of school district spending.[15] Each year voters in Oregon's IEDs have the opportunity to vote on proposals for redistributing school tax burdens from property rich school districts to property poor school districts. Smith found that voter support for such propositions rises steadily with the amount of tax relief that local residents stand to gain. His best fitting equation found the percentage "yes" vote to be: Percent "Yes" = $50 - 3.72 X$, where X is measured as the millage change in the effective local school tax rate. In other words, in cases where one district will save three mills on its school tax rate and another district will have its rate increased by three mills as the result of an equalization proposal, voter support for the measure will vary by approximately 61 percent to 39 percent.

The second term in our demand formulation that is consistent only with the private benefit explanation of voting is n_i, the number of public school children in a family. Private utility maximization does not predict any necessary overall relationship between the number of public school children in a family and the family's preferred level of school expenditure. Households with several school age children will "require" more of all goods, both public and private, than households without children. Whether demand for school spending grows with family size, then, will depend upon the nature of the trade-offs between private and public sector consumption. However, one straightforward prediction can be made: families who have no children in public schools derive no direct benefit from school expenditures and, on the private benefit theory, should be less supportive of school tax increases than families with public school children.

Table 4-3 indicates how citizens in our Troy, Michigan sample voted, according to the number of children currently enrolled in the Troy public schools. Families with children in the public schools voted more than two to one in favor of the school tax increase. Families without school children voted against the school tax proposal by a margin of 62 percent to 38 percent. By themselves, these figures understate the true split in voting. Many of the households listed as without public school children have preschool youngsters who over the long run are likely to benefit from increased school spending at least as much as those children now in the upper grades of the school system. A breakout of voting by families who either have children in Troy public schools

Table 4-3. Vote in Troy School Tax Election by Number of Public School Children

Children in Public Schools	Yes	No
0	84	139
1	72	39
2	67	36
3	41	19
4	24	6
5 or more	12	5

or have preschool children, compared to the rest of the sample population, reveals an even greater differential in voting behavior (this table is not shown).

The income term, Y, in the demand equation for school spending may be subjected to differing interpretations. The meaning I have assigned to it is a standard economic one. The coefficients estimated for Y imply an income elasticity of demand for school spending on the order of 1.2, which I have interpreted to mean that school expenditures are a superior good—that is, demand for public school spending (and, indirectly, school quality), viewed as a private consumption item, rises more than proportionately with income, just as does the demand for second homes, college education, and country club memberships. Banfield and Wilson,[16] however, have offered an alternative interpretation. They apparently regard support for increased public spending as in the public interest, and interpret the increased frequency of support for school tax proposals among the affluent as indicative of their greater concern for the public weal. This is a logically consistent interpretation, although one that requires a crucial intervening step (viz., a willingness to identify one response to the referendum question as more clearly associated with the public good than the other). Because of the possibility of interpreting the income term in a manner consistent with both the private-regarding and the public-regarding explanations of voter behavior, the statistically significant income term in the demand equation does not distinguish well between the two hypotheses.

In some respects, the best indication of the role self-interest plays in school tax voting can be gathered from a breakdown of votes by occupational classification. For the bulk of the occupations listed in Table 4-4, support for Troy's school tax proposal varies roughly in proportion to the expected income of an occupation. Support is high among highly paid professionals and managers. It is lower among less affluent workers. Two of the occupational groupings offer more interesting comparisons. Among those who identified themselves as

Table 4-4. Vote in Troy School Tax Election by Occupation of Head of Household

Occupation	For	Against
Teacher, principal, other education related	55	4
Professional and technical	118	68
Managers	34	27
Self-employed	7	6
Clerical and sales	46	36
Craftsman, laborer, operative	16	24
Service worker	11	19
Retired	6	41

teachers, principals or other employees of the public school system, or volunteered the fact that their spouses were so employed, support for the school tax proposal was overwhelming. Within this group the margin of support was 55-4. A large number of respondents in this category remarked that their salary levels or employment opportunities would be directly affected by the outcome of the tax election. Although I have no firm data on this point, it is my strong impression that the number of voters occupied in the teaching profession or married to teachers, in our random sample of Troy voters, far exceeds the proportion of all Troy adults fitting this classification. If so, the teaching profession was also much more diligent in getting to the polls than other citizens.

Among those who listed themselves as retired, and therefore members of a group that stood to gain no conceivable personal benefit from increased school spending, opposition to the school tax proposal was almost as clear as was support among teachers: retirees voted 41-6 against the tax increase.

I do not want to exaggerate the decisiveness of these data in distinguishing between private and public interest theories of public service demand. No one (least of all Banfield and Wilson) has maintained that citizens disregard private benefit altogether when deciding how to vote. Rather, it has been urged that a significant amount of observed behavior is left unexplained by concentrating solely on private gains. It is difficult to judge just what type of evidence would be deemed an adequate rebuttal of this hypothesis. When 38 percent of the voters who have no children in the local public school system nonetheless vote for a school tax increase, this may be judged to support the theory of significant public regardingness. Even the fact that four of 59 teachers and six of 47 retirees voted against their clearly defined private interest may be thought to constitute a "significant" showing of public regardingness. Several persons among our sample made clear that they voted as they did from their conception of public equity. In addition, most teachers affirmed that better schooling was essential to the community. Most retirees felt that the tax system for paying for schools was unfair.

In my judgment, the data in this paper justify only a limited conclusion. However significant the cases of clear-cut public regardingness may be (taken individually) as indices of the bonds that tie citizens to the polity, and however strongly families may believe that actions in their private interest serve the public interest (thus making the attribution of the "true" motive for voting almost impossible), if our objective is to explain public service demands in the most economical manner, or to make predictions regarding the character of future public service demands, it seems safe to assume that on balance voters cast their ballots in a manner consistent with self-interest. Treating household demand for public school spending as analogous to household demand for private services will not place us wide of the mark in predicting citizen behavior.

POLICY IMPLICATIONS OF THE TAX-PRICE TERM

I conclude this chapter by considering the practical importance of the tax-price term in the demand function for school spending.

Many proposals currently under consideration by state legislatures or state courts would change significantly the tax prices that households face when voting in school tax or other local public service elections. For example, what has been called "power equalization" of school district property tax bases would have the effect of equalizing the term, V, in the tax-price ($\frac{H}{V}$) for all school districts in a state. Power equalizing plans serve to erase distinctions in per pupil local property wealth among school districts. Virtually all households in a state would have their tax-prices for schooling altered by power equalization. Depending upon the level at which V was equalized, there might also be a preponderant shift—up or down—in the level of local tax prices.[17]

The equalization of school district tax bases has been discussed in the context of school finance reform, where it has been at least tacitly recognized that one direct effect of changing the per pupil property tax base would be to change local demands for school expenditure. In fact, it is often affirmed that one of the principal benefits of such a reform would be to increase local school tax spending in property poor school districts. Empirical estimates of the expenditure demand function such as presented in Table 4-1 could be used to predict the magnitude of spending changes that would result from any redefinition of local tax-prices.

Other public policies that alter ($\frac{H}{V}$) and hence have an impact on the demand for school spending are less obvious. A good illustration is to be found in "circuit-breaker" laws for limiting the property tax liability of low income households, some variant of which now has been adopted by all 50 states.[18] These laws operate by defining an upper limit to the percentage of family income that can go to pay for property taxes without being "excessive." If a family's property tax bill exceeds this limit, all or part of it will be remitted by the state. In Michigan, for example, 60 percent of a household's property tax bill in excess of 3.5 percent of income is remitted, up to a maximum of $500; for elderly households 100 percent of the excess tax burden is remitted.

Now it should be evident that circuit-breaker laws may substantially change the effective tax-price that voters confront. In the case of Michigan, elderly households whose current property tax burden exceeds 3.5 percent of income would face an incremental tax-price for school spending of zero (as long as the excess tax was less than $500). The entire additional tax burden resulting from imposition of a higher local school tax rate would be remitted by the state. To vote "yes" in a school tax proposal would cost such a household nothing. For similarly situated nonelderly families, the reduction in the effective tax-price would be 60 percent.

The sample of household voting in Troy, Michigan was designed in part to test the importance that a change in tax-prices due to circuit-breaker legislation could have on the outcomes of school tax referenda. Troy is in the unique position of having held two identical tax elections in the spring of 1973, within the space of six weeks. In early May, Troy voters rejected a proposed millage increase by a margin of 63 percent to 37 percent. In mid June, the same proposal was approved by a margin of 54 percent to 46 percent. Except for intensive campaigning by both partie: to the election dispute, the only intervening event to change the balance of citizens' support was passage of the state's circuit-breaker law.

School authorities made sage use of the new law. Tax kits were distributed to households, showing how their tax liability under the new law should be calculated. For key constituents, like the elderly, personal visits were made to demonstrate that the circuit-breaker legislation would greatly lower, if not remove, the personal tax cost resulting from a school tax increase.

From the school board's point of view, this campaign was eminently successful. Although I have not completed analysis of the vote changes, preliminary examination of our survey data indicates that almost all the vote switches in the May to June turnaround came from households whose incremental tax liability, or tax-price, had been reduced by the circuit-breaker law. Hopefully, this result could have been predicted from voting functions like those summarized in Table 4-2. As generous circuit-breaker laws come into more frequent use in other states, and as other tax shifts occur, the change in local tax-prices is likely to be substantial. The overall effect on public service demand may also be significant.

Appendix

REFERENCES

R. Barlow, "Efficiency Aspects of Local School Finance," *Journal of Political Economy* 78 (September/October 1970): 1028-1040.

J.L. Barr and Otto A. Davis, "An Elementary Political Economic Theory of the Expenditures of Local Governments," *Southern Economic Journal* 33 (October 1966): 149-165.

Y. Barzel, "Private Schools and Public School Finance," *Journal of Political Economy* 81 (January/February 1973): 174-186.

T.C. Bergstrom and R.P. Goodman, "Private Demands for Public Goods," *American Economic Review* 63 (3) (June 1973): 280-296.

Thomas E. Borcherding and Robert T. Deacon, "The Demand for the Services of Non-federal Governments," *American Economic Review* 62 (6) (December 1972): 891-901.

L. Bowman, D.S. Ippolito, and M.L. Levin, "Self-Interest and Referendum Support: The Case of a Rapid Transit Vote in Atlanta," in Harlan Hahn (Ed.) *People and Politics in Urban Society*, Urban Affairs Annual Reviews, Beverly Hills, Ca., Sage Publications, 1972.

D.F. Bradford and W.E. Oates, "Suburban Exploitation of Central Cities and Governmental Structure," in H. Hochman and G. Peterson (Eds.), *Redistribution through Public Choice* New York: Columbia University Press (1974).

H.E. Brazer, *City Expenditures in the United States*, National Bureau of Economic Research, 1959.

H.E. Brazer, J.S. Akin, G.E. Auten and C.G. Cross, "Fiscal Needs and Resources, Some Preliminary Findings: Second Interim Report to the New York State Commission on the Quality, Cost and Financing of Elementary and Secondary Education," Mimeo (April 1971).

James M. Buchanan, *Public Finance in a Democratic Process*, University of North Carolina, 1967.

Otto A. Davis, "Empirical Evidence of Political Influences Upon the Expenditure Policies of Public Schools," in Julius Margolis (Ed.) *The Public Economy of Urban Communities*, Baltimore: Johns Hopkins University Press, 1965.

Otto A. Davis and George H. Haines, Jr., "A Political Approach to a Theory of Public Expenditure: The Case of Municipalities," *National Tax Journal* (September 1966): 259-275.

F. DeLeeuw, "The Demand for Housing: A Review of Cross-Section Evidence," *The Review of Economics and Statistics* 53 (February 1971): 1-10.

Anthony Downs, *An Economic Theory of Democracy*, New York: Harper Bros., 1957.

Noel M. Edelson, "Budgetary Outcomes in a Referendum Setting," Discussion Paper No. 344, University of Pennsylvania, October 1972.

Noel M. Edelson, "Efficiency Aspects of Local School Finance—Comments and Extension," *Journal of Political Economy* 81 (January/February 1973): 158-173.

Rene Frey and L. Kohn, "An Economic Interpretation of Voting Behavior on Public Finance Issues," *Kyklos* 23 (1970): 792-805.

Harvey Galper, Edward Gramlich, Claudia Scott and Hartojo Wignjowijoto, "A Model of Central City Fiscal Behavior," Urban Institute Working Paper #506-2, October 1972.

A.K. Gustman and G.B. Pidot, "Interactions Between Educational Spending and Student Enrollment," *The Journal of Human Resources* 8 (Winter 1973): 3-23.

W.N. Grubb and S. Michelson, *Public School Finance in Contractual Societies*, forthcoming.

Harlan Hahn, "Ethos and Social Class," *Polity* (Spring 1970): 294-315.

Eric Hanushek, "The Demand for Local Public Services: An Exploratory Analysis," this volume.

James H. Henderson, "Local Government Expenditures: A Social Welfare Analysis," *The Review of Economics and Statistics* (May 1968): 156-163.

W.Z. Hirsch, "Income Elasticity of Public Education," *International Economic Review* (September 1961).

W.Z. Hirsch, "Determinants of Public Education Expenditures," *National Tax Journal* 13 (March 1960): 29-40.

Robert P. Inman, "Four Essays on Fiscal Federalism," unpublished Ph.D. Dissertation, Harvard University, June 1971.

H.T. James *et al., Determinants of Educational Expenditures in Large Cities of the United States* (Stanford School of Education, 1966).

J.C. Ohls and T.J. Wales, "Supply and Demand for State and Local Services," *The Review of Economics and Statistics* 54: 412-423.

G.E. Peterson, "An Economic Theory of Voting Behavior," Urban Institute Working Paper #1207-30, May 1973.

G.E. Peterson, "Household Voting on School Tax Referenda," Urban Institute Working Paper #1207-32, May 1973.

Brian Stipak, "An Analysis of the 1968 Rapid Transit Vote in Los Angeles," *Transportation* 2 (1973): 71-86.

G.R. Wilensky, *State Aid and Educational Opportunity*, Beverly Hills, Ca.: Sage Publications, 1970.

J.Q. Wilson and E.C. Banfield, "Public-Regardingness as a Value Premise in Voting Behavior" *American Political Science Review* 58 (1964): 476-487.

Chapter Five

The Demand for Local Public Services: An Exploratory Analysis

Eric A. Hanushek

Local governments serve an important role as a choice mechanism. They decide what goods and services to provide collectively, how these services should be produced (publicly or privately), and how the purchases should be financed. Clearly each of these decisions is important in the efficient provision of public goods, but, in a fundamental sense, the decision of what goods and services to supply is the key to the whole process. Efficient provision of the "wrong" bundle of community services cannot be considered exemplary behavior by a local government. Unfortunately, deriving a coherent and accurate set of community preferences or community demands is the most difficult facet of the governmental decision process.

If we look at either the governmental production decision or financing decision, we find that the conceptual basis for making the decision is well worked out. One need only adapt aspects of the economic theory of firm behavior or theoretical discussions of public finance to form a conceptual basis for these decisions. Further, the data required to make intelligent decisions in these areas are often readily available or at least can be approximated. Not so in the case of ascertaining community preferences for publicly provided goods and services: in that case the conceptual basis has not been as thoroughly developed, and the data required are generally unavailable.

Conceptual models related to demands for public goods are all very abstract in character. There are general theoretical models that discuss the optimal purchases of public goods, given a community preference schedule or social welfare function; but these assume that somehow the preferences are already known. Further, these discussions give few insights into how the preference function might be ascertained or even what data are relevant in considering the issue.

This research was partially supported by The Urban Institute. Considerable assistance in the empirical sections was supplied by Paul G. Evans.

The very nature of public goods precludes public officials from directly observing the preferences of individuals in the community. In the case of private goods consumed by individuals, it is possible to surmise individual preferences by observing the consumption pattern of individuals; market choices reflect individual choices at given prices and incomes. However, public goods, jointly consumed by members of the community, do not pass through a market where individuals express their preferences. Moreover, individuals may be reluctant to express their true preferences for public goods. An individual potentially increases his personal cost for a public good or service if he expresses his true preferences and if the public goods are financed by charges related to preferences; by masking his true preferences he can participate in the consumption of all public goods that have been provided without risking increasing his payments.

This all implies that local governments must use indirect means to ascertain community preferences and to develop a social welfare function to use in making public decisions. There are, of course, numerous ways in which partial information about community preferences becomes available: elections (primary, general, and recall), surveys and opinion polls, subjective data from community contacts (individuals, community organizations, news media, etc.), moving behavior of the population, and voting on issue referenda.

Each of these sources has some obvious strengths and weaknesses. Elections, while regular, are seldom single issue expressions of choice for public services; moving behavior involves much more than service preferences; surveys and polls are direct information but are also quite expensive; and so forth. Nevertheless, lacking even the hope of being able to decipher community preferences completely, it is necessary to rely upon such incomplete and possibly biased information.

In this regard it is useful to understand the information content of these different sources—that is, what can be learned about community preferences from the analysis of the indirect expressions that are available. There have been some studies that attempt to do just that, and a number of these are included in this volume. This particular study follows one of the relatively neglected lines of analysis—the study of the community preferences implied by voting on referenda.[1]

With each of these information sources, two issues must be examined. First, whose preferences are being considered. Each of the information sources implies a different weighting scheme for the preferences of individual members of the community, and thus any aggregate statement of demands from the individual sources pays differing attention to specific individuals. Second, what are the preferences for community services expressed in each instance?

The specific thrust of this analysis is understanding how characteristics of proposed public expenditures (price, nature of the expenditure item, and "using population") interact with characteristics of the population (incomes, age, background, and tastes) to determine both who expresses a preference and what the expressed preferences are. This is pursued by analyzing voting behavior (turnout and choice) for two different 1960 referendum ballots in Cleveland. For each referendum, two models are estimated: 1) the probability of voting is estimated as a function of the characteristics of the individual; and, 2) the probability of favoring an expenditure increase is estimated as a function of the cost to the individual, his income, and a series of taste and issue related demand characteristics.

The study can be considered a prototype investigation. One of the purposes is to ascertain what problems arise in this type of analysis and what inferences can be made from such studies.

SAMPLE DESIGN AND DATA

In order to focus upon the public choice mechanism involved in referendum voting, a limited number of public service issues within a single political jurisdiction were considered. In particular, this study investigates the expressed public expenditure preferences contained in two separate 1960 referendum votes on expenditure increases in Cleveland: a zoo levy and a welfare levy.

Both the expenditures analyzed and the choice of location of voting are convenient and interesting within the context of this study. First, the Ohio Constitution requires cities with tax rates over a fixed level to gain voter approval for a wide range of expenditure issues—both capital and operating. Most large cities in Ohio are already at the maximum permissible property tax rate, and in order to increase tax rates and expenditures, they must hold a referendum vote on the issue. This implies that the government must frequently raise the issue of community preferences.

Second, these referendum votes involved increases in the property tax rate to support the expenditure. The specific price of the added services thus depends upon housing assessed value. To the extent that assessed values vary within income classes, price effects can be separated from income effects. Such a separation is not feasible when an expenditure is financed from general revenues which are raised by sales or income taxes.

Third, by Ohio law, the precise increase in the tax rate is specified on the ballot. This lessens any possibility that the individuals are operating under incorrect information about the actual individual cost of a given public expenditure. (As noted below, however, it does not eliminate the problem of imperfect information when renters also vote on the issue. With renters, there are two problems: 1) the tax may not be completely passed on to them; and, 2) they may incorrectly perceive how much of the tax is passed on.)

Finally, the zoo and welfare levies were chosen to provide views of the preference patterns for different services where different specific demand factors would presumably be important. Thus, it is hoped that general support for public programs can be separated from specific issue support.

The principle advantage of using referendum voting to ascertain community preferences is that this is an explicit statement of individual preferences. However, there are also disadvantages in that voting is accomplished by secret ballot. As a result, it is not possible to relate characteristics of an individual to his actual vote. It is nevertheless possible to match aggregate voting behavior of groups to the characteristics of those groups. Since, as we discuss below, voting behavior and population characteristics are known for relatively small geographic areas, it is possible to make inferences about community preferences on the basis of aggregate behavior.

(An alternative method—which does allow the use of individual data—would be to survey individuals to ascertain how they would vote on different public expenditure choices. This has two drawbacks: it is very expensive, and there are significant questions about the validity of the responses in terms of true, underlying preferences.)

The sample was constructed by merging data on voting at the precinct level with 1960 Census of Population data to provide the data base. The map of voting precincts was overlayed on the Census tract map, and precincts were added together to approximate the Census tracts. A few Census tracts were also combined in places where precincts fell across tracts. A total of 140 observations for the city of Cleveland was available for analysis. (A separate sample of suburban areas was also constructed but is not presented here.)

The Census provides considerable information about the characteristics of the population within each of the voting districts created. From this source, data are available about incomes, valuation of housing (to ascertain the costs of a property tax increase), age composition, ethnic composition, and other "demand related" characteristics.

Table 5-1 displays means and standard deviations for variables used within the analysis. One important feature implied by Table 5-1 is the fact that there exists considerable variation across the districts in the sample. For example, districts range from 0 to 100 percent nonwhite; from 9 to 97 percent owner occupied housing; from 1.5 to 37 percent with some college education; and from $2,800 to $9,800 in median family income.

On the voting itself, on average half of the voters voted for the zoo levy; but this ranged from a low of 29 percent in one district to a high of 74 percent in another. For the welfare levy, 57 percent voted for the increased expenditures, but this varied by district from 23 percent to 86 percent. The variation among these aggregate voting districts is important when attempts are made to estimate models from these samples.

VOTER TURNOUT: WHO GETS LISTENED TO

There is no set manner in which the preferences of individuals should be aggregated to arrive at community preferences. In fact, there is no requirement that

Table 5-1. Variable Definitions, Means, and Standard Deviations

Variable	Mean	Standard Deviation	Definition
Welfare	56.5	14.0	Percent voting for welfare levy
Zoo	49.9	10.5	Percent voting for zoo levy
YMED	$5,831	1061	Median income
YHI	12.0	6.8	Percent income greater than $10,000
YLO	26.1	12.0	Percent income less than $4,000
Value	$122.8	2.7	Value of owner occupied dwelling (hundreds of $)
Rent	$80.1	13.6	Gross rent for renter occupied
Homeown	50.8	20.2	Percent homes owner occupied
Nonwht	24.7	37.1	Percent population nonwhite
German	3.6	2.7	Percent population German
Polish	5.5	8.4	Percent population Polish
Czech	4.1	4.3	Percent population Czechoslovakian
Hung	3.1	5.4	Percent population Hungarian
Ital	3.2	4.9	Percent population Italian
$E < 5$	10.8	5.8	Percent with less than five years of education
$E > 12$	8.6	6.3	Percent with greater than high school education
Age 21-34	30.3	6.2	Percent age 21-34 years of population over 21
Age 45+	47.7	8.7	Percent of population over 21 that is age 45 or above

the implicit community preference function, or social welfare function, that is used by local community decision makers represents any simple average of the preference functions of the individuals in the sample.

Different methods of gathering information about individuals' preferences do imply different methods of aggregating individual choices. A random survey of community opinions quite probably differs from opinions gathered on the editorial page of newspapers or from opinions of confidants to the local decision maker. In most cases it is difficult to infer whose opinions count, let alone how they are aggregated. This is not the case, however, with referenda votes. In that case, each voter gets equal weight. The key, however, is that all members of the community do not vote. In the first place, where registration is required, only registered voters' preferences can be considered. Second, these preferences are recorded only if those registered actually do vote—thus, even referendum voting does not represent a simple averaging of community preferences. However, referendum voting is interesting because it is possible to make some inferences about whose preferences are being recorded.

While it is not known which precise individuals did vote on any particular referendum, it is possible to gain some insights into this by looking at the pattern of voter turnout across the sample districts. In this regard, the specific referenda chosen for analysis offer an interesting contrast. The levy to increase expenditures for the public zoo was voted upon during the November 1960 general election, while the welfare levy came during the May 1960 primary election. Since November 1960 was a presidential election also, one might expect a different pattern of voter turnout than is found in the vote for the welfare levy. As seen from Table 5-2, there were significant differences in the level and distribution of voter turnout: almost twice as many eligible voters voted on the zoo referendum as compared to the welfare referendum.

The analysis of voter turnout relies upon estimating a regression model in which the dependent variable is the percentage of eligible voters (persons over 21) who actually vote, and the exogenous variables, which include the age, education, and income characteristics of the zones along with the ethnic distribution. The estimated voter turnout models are displayed in Table 5-3. Columns (1) and (2) are alternative versions of the turnout model for the welfare levy (held with the primary election of 1960); columns (3) and (4) are alternative versions of the turnout model for the zoo levy (held with the general election of 1960).

The models indicate the likelihood of voting in the referendum based upon the characteristics of the individual.[2] Positive coefficients imply increased probability of voting, while negative coefficients indicate lower

Table 5-2.   Level and Distribution of Voter Turnout

Referendum (date)	Mean Turnout[a] (percent)	Standard Deviation	Minimum (percent)	Maximum (percent)
Welfare (5/60)	22.9	5.4	11.1	43.8
Zoo (11/60)	42.8	10.6	20.2	80.7

[a]Mean turnout is votes cast as a percent of the estimated population over 21 years of age. Each of the entries in this table refer to the sample districts described in the text.

Table 5-3. Estimated Voter Turnout Models

| | Referendum | | | |
| | Welfare | | Zoo | |
Variable	(1)	(2)	(3)	(4)
YMED	.001[a]	.003[b]	.004[b]	.004[b]
E < 5	.281[b]	.325[b]	−.008	−.016
E > 12	.346[b]	.225[b]	.297[b]	.358
Age 21-34	−.697[b]	−.500[b]	−.275[a]	−.537[b]
Age 45+	−.524[b]	−.346[b]	−.213[a]	−.475[b]
Homeown	.085[b]	.067[b]	.185[b]	.137[b]
Nonwht		.050[b]		−.002
German		−.033		.330
Polish		−.074[a]		−.060
Czech		.206[b]		.240[a]
Hung		−.067		−.303
Ital		.002		.228[a]
Intercept	52.81	28.79	25.94	47.53
R²	.47	.54	.62	.63

[a]t-statistic greater than 1.0.

[b]t-statistic greater than 1.67.

All estimates are calculated by weighted regression using the total population over 21 years old in each tract as the weight.

probabilities of voting. The R^2 values mean that the models explain from 47 to 63 percent of the variation among sample tracts in voter turnout. In terms of explained variance, the models for the general election (zoo levy) appear to do better. However, as is discussed below, the individual parameter estimates for the zoo model are not as good as for the welfare model.

The alternative formulation for the zoo and for the welfare levy includes a series of racial and ethnic composition variables. These variables test the proposition that different groups in the population tend to express themselves through the electoral process more than other groups. If this were the case, the preferences expressed in the referendum vote would tend to match the preferences of these high vote groups more than other groups. Looking at columns (2) and (4), we find some weak support for this proposition in the welfare vote and virtually no support for it in the zoo vote.

In terms of individual coefficient significance, only nonwhites and Czechs have coefficients with t-statistics greater than 1.67 (significantly different from zero at the 10 percent level), and then only in the welfare vote. According to these estimates, both groups tend to vote more readily than other groups (mainly the white population not in the named ethnic groups). Particularly the nonwhite results may imply that groups that are restricted economically and in terms of residential location find the electoral process to be their best chance of satisfying their public service demands.[3] Nevertheless, this hypothesis is not supported in the zoo vote. Further, on the basis of an F-test for the joint hypothesis that there are no differences in voting behavior among racial and ethnic groups, we cannot reject this hypothesis of no difference in the zoo vote but can in the welfare case at the 2.5 percent level.[4]

There are a number of results that are consistent across all the estimated models. Income levels have a strong, positive effect on voter turnout: individuals with higher incomes tend to have a higher probability of voting than individuals with lower incomes. This estimated effect also holds in models (not presented) using measures of the distribution of income within tracts—i.e., the percent with high and low incomes. In terms of the elasticity at the point of means, the elasticity of turnout with respect to income (approximately .5) is consistently greater than the elasticity estimates for the other variables.[5] Thus referendum outcomes tend to be biased toward the preferences of higher income members of the community.

More educated members of the community also tend to vote more frequently. However, somewhat surprisingly, the models indicate that in the welfare vote, individuals with less than five years of schooling (other things being equal) tend to vote with a higher probability than individuals with five to twelve years schooling. This finding does not hold in the zoo voter turnout. Since income and age—other major factors affecting welfare eligibility—are accounted for in the model, it is not possible to interpret this schooling variable as reflecting a desire to vote for increased expenditures that would directly benefit the individual. The age variables indicate that voting behavior tends to peak between age 35 and age 44. Young voters vote least, and voter turnout falls off after age 45, yet does not return to the level of voters under age 35.

Homeowners tend to vote more readily than nonhomeowners. There are two competing explanations of this. Homeowners may have a greater community identity; for psychological or monetary reasons, homeowners may be more reluctant than renters to move to different communities if their preferences are not satisfied. This would lead to a heavier reliance upon making their preferences known—in this case, voting. Alternatively, home ownership may simply reflect increased stability and increased probability that the individual is registered to vote.[6] From these data it is not possible to distinguish between these two competing hypotheses.

As a general statement, these results indicate that educated, higher income, middle-aged homeowners tend to make their preferences on referendum expenditures known more than other groups. By voting more frequently, they also have a higher probability of satisfying their preferences for public goods. The results are mixed, but possibly Czechs and blacks also participate more frequently in this form of the public choice process. Since these votes coincided with national elections, it may be possible that referenda held at special elections or strictly local elections display a different pattern. Nevertheless, the results on these two different elections seem quite consistent.

INDIVIDUAL PREFERENCES

Conceptual Considerations

We can now turn to analyzing what the voting data for selected referenda tell us about the preferences of individuals. The conceptual framework is built upon the theory of demand. Based upon his utility function, each individual attempts to maximize his satisfaction. Given his income and the prices for different goods, the individual chooses that set of goods which leads to a maximum level of utility. This model can be easily extended to the consideration of public goods and services.

In its simplest form, suppose there is only one public good and one private good. Suppose further that the consumer has made his selection of the optimal mix of public and private purchases.[7] If the price of the public good goes up, we would generally expect less of the public good to be desired. Similarly, if the individual's income decreases, we would expect less of the public good to be desired. In other words, the standard demand model for private goods can be transferred to these considerations. However, when we leave the case of an individual's demand and go to the notion of the market demand for public goods, we must modify the model somewhat. In particular, we must allow for some special aspects of public goods.

With public goods, other considerations are also hypothesized to enter into the demand decision process. First (and related to private demand considerations), the demand for public goods would be expected to follow a pattern dependent upon the life cycle of the individual and the type of specific services under consideration. Thus the age of the individual would, ceteris paribus, exert an influence on the preference for a given public good, although the exact effect would depend upon the specific good and the "life cycle" of consumption for that particular good—for example, the demand for services to the elderly is probably an increasing function of age.

In addition, some consideration must be given to the behavior of individuals when assessing their preferences for public goods that may not be relevant to them personally. For example, why would an upper income individual support the expansion of a local welfare system? Several explanations have been offered for this phenomenon (which has been observed).

Clearly, if it is not possible to choose individual public goods, there would generally be an incentive to support the expansion of other, "nonrelevant" programs if it would help in gaining relevant programs. This is true if coalitions are needed to develop public expenditure programs. This type of behavior would generally be important when there is no individual choice on specific public goods, and the only choice available to individuals is the choice of a bundle—as when there are a limited number of candidates or a limited number of jurisdictions—and individuals generally choose their bundle of public goods by moving.

But even in observing single issue preferences, there are reasons for individuals to support "nonrelevant" public goods, or ones for which their direct benefits are slight or less than their direct costs. Even when individuals express their opinions and preferences on single issues—say with school bond referendums—they might tend to act in a manner similar to the multiissue behavior expressed above. They might attempt to act as a coalition in order to assure favorable action on issues they are more directly concerned with. Thus, even with single issue preference setting, there might be some informal "logrolling."

Alternatively, if there are external benefits to a public good, all individuals could receive some benefit from the public good, even though only a portion of the individuals receive direct benefits. Take, for example, support of public schools. A person with no children in school might support public schools because of external benefits from having a more informed community, from reductions in crime rates, and so forth. If these external benefits are large enough, they might cover the individual's cost of the public good, and therefore it may be to his advantage on a simple benefit-cost calculation to support a public expenditure that has small direct benefit for him.

There are also hypotheses which suggest that individuals may have preferences that lead to supporting some public expenditures even though narrow benefit-cost analyses indicate that it is against their interests to do so. One such hypothesis postulates interdependent utility functions for individuals such that the consumption and utility of one individual affects the utility of other individuals.[8] If this were the case, individuals would tend to demand more public expenditures than those justified on the basis of direct benefits or external benefits.

Another hypothesis that postulates a public expenditure demand larger than that dictated by individual interests is the "public regardedness" hypothesis.[9] According to this theory, some individuals have inclinations to support public expenditures above those indicated by their own private interests. Further, this public regardedness is linked to their heritage, and particularly to their ethnic background: some nationalities will tend to support public expenditures more than other nationalities.

Taking these factors together, the demand for public goods and services can be thought of as a function of several factors: community tastes, the price of services to the individuals, incomes, life cycle characteristics of individuals, and a set of other factors involving nondirect benefits of the expenditure to the individual. There are, of course, a series of very difficult measurement problems involved in actually estimating such a relationship. The next section describes some of the efforts to measure these concepts.

Initial Empirical Attempts

The estimation of demand, or preference, models from referenda data calls for some modifications to the basic conceptual model outlined above. One key difference between the conceptual model and the actual empirical application is the unit of analysis.

The conceptual model refers to individuals and makes inferences about the preferences of the community by looking at the individuals' preferences. However, the data available do not give information about the votes and characteristics of individuals—only about aggregations of individuals. Nevertheless, if the model holds for all the individuals in the sampled zones, the model can still be accurately estimated, based upon the average characteristics in the zones. (When going to aggregate units, some modifications of variable definitions are required, and these are discussed below.)

The most important modification involves the measurement of the preference variable itself. The theory suggests that one should analyze the quantity of a public good or service that is desired at a given set of incomes, prices, and so forth. However, with a referendum vote we observe individuals who either vote for or against a given quantity of public services—that quantity being set by the decision maker who initiates the referendum. When looking at the yes/no choices of individuals, we are really ascertaining the probability that an individual (with a given set of preferences and income, and facing a given set of prices) will choose the fixed amount of public expenditure that is proposed. The individual votes for and against are aggregated for each sample observation so that the dependent variable is the proportion voting for the increased expenditures of the referendum.

The appropriate definitions for most of the exogenous variables follow directly from the conceptual model except for the price variable for the services being considered. The referendum itself contains an explicit statement of the increase in mill levy for the property tax that will result from the adoption of the referendum. Thus, the price that any individual has to pay is proportional to the value of his dwelling in the case of owner occupied properties.[10] With owner occupied dwelling units, the estimated effect of price for public services could be found by estimating the relationship between voting for the referendum and the value of housing units.

However, all housing units are not owner occupied. Within the Cleveland sample, almost half the families lived in rented housing. There are two reasons to believe that the estimated relationship between value of unit and preferences might be different between owners and renters. First, if the property tax is not completely passed on to renters, the value of the unit for renters no longer has the same proportion to actual cost of the public service as that for owners. Second, renters may not perceive the costs as being the same even if the tax is fully passed on to the renters. Both suggest that different estimates of price effects should be made for owners and renters.

Assume that the individual model is the one depicted in equation (1). If there are H homeowners and R renters and we sum the equation over the $(H+R)$ households in a given district and then average, we have equation (2).

$$FOR_i = B_0 + B_1\ VALUE_i + B_2\ RENT_i \tag{1}$$

Where:

FOR_i = 0 if ith individual votes against referendum;

  = 1 if ith individual votes for referendum,

$VALUE_i$ = assessed value of home if owner occupied;

  = 0 if not owner occupied,

$RENT_i$ = proportional assessed value of dwelling unit if renter occupied.

  = 0 if not renter occupied.

$$\frac{\Sigma\ FOR_i}{(H+R)} = B_0 + B_1\ \frac{\Sigma\ VALUE}{(H+R)} + B_2\ \frac{\Sigma\ RENT_i}{(H+R)} \tag{2}$$

If we multiply the value term by H/H and the rent term by R/R, we see that the appropriate variables for the aggregate models are the average value of owner occupied homes times the proportion owner occupied within the district and the average value of renter occupied dwellings times the proportion of renters in the district. This is intuitively reasonable: the average zone in the sample has 1,700 dwellings; if all save one are renter occupied, even the price effect of a $500,000 home cannot involve more than two votes (husband and wife). Thus, in this hypothetical case, the average home value of owner occupied units ($500,000) must be adjusted to reflect the "vote pool" for which it is relevant. The formulation of (1) as a stochastic equation or the inclusion of other variables clearly does not affect the preceding development. If it is believed that the intercept as well as the slope of the price term differs between owners and renters, the aggregate model should also include a variable for the proportion of owner occupied (or renter occupied) units.

Table 5-4 and Table 5-5 display some preliminary estimates of the preference models estimated for the Cleveland referenda. These tables present alternative forms of the same basic preference model. In each case, columns (1) and (2) represent the simplest preference model: the probability of voting for increased expenditures is a function of income and costs (home ownership and value of dwelling or rent). Columns (3) and (4) add race and ethnicity to this

Table 5-4.   Regression Estimates—Probability of Voting for
Zoo Levy

Variable	(1)	(2)	(3)	(4)
YMED	−.0048[b]		−.0002	
YHI		−.0840		.2014[b]
YLO		.4516[b]		.2619[b]
Value*homeown	.0031[b]	.0024[b]	.0015[b]	.0010[b]
Rent*(100-homeown)	.0054[b]	.0049[b]	.0017[b]	.0021[b]
Homeown	−.2883[b]	−.1753[b]	−.3804[b]	−.1872[b]
Nonwht			.0920[b]	.0659[b]
German			.5600[b]	.4589[b]
Polish			−.3505[b]	−.3555[b]
Czech			−.2156[b]	−.3508[b]
Hung			−.0528	−.0481
Ital			.0472	.0700
Intercept	51.45	13.22	51.80	35.67
R^2	.74	.76	.84	.86

[a]t-statistic greater than 1.0.

[b]t-statistic greater than 1.67.

All estimates are calculated by weighted regression using the total vote in each sample tract as the weight.

basic model. Income is measured by either median income in the tract (columns (1) and (3)) or by the percentage of the population in the upper and lower tails of the income distribution (columns (2) and (4)).[11]

As a general observation, these models all explain a high proportion of the variation in preferences; all have R^2's of over .70. However, the overall explanatory power of the models does not tell the entire story. The estimated models are not consistent with the conceptual model that was sketched previously.

The most significant divergence of the estimated models from the conceptual ideas is the relationship between income and costs and preferences. The income estimates in all but one case (YHI in column (4) of the zoo estimates) are the opposite of the predicted relationship. The estimated models imply the individuals with higher incomes prefer less expenditure on these items. This holds in the case where median income is used to measure income and the case where the percentages at the high and low end are used.

At the same time, the effect of housing value also has the opposite sign of that expected. The models imply that higher housing values—and thus higher property tax costs of the added expenditures—imply higher probabilities of voting for the increased expenditures. While the housing value and rent

Table 5-5.   Regression Estimates—Probability of Voting for Welfare Levy

Variable	(1)	(2)	(3)	(4)
YMED	−.0112^b		−.0016^a	
YHI		−.6847^b		−.0452
YLO		.6442^b		.1547^b
Value*homeown	.0452^b	.0040^b	.0017^b	.0014^b
Rent*(100-homeown)	.0088^b	.0082^b	.0018^b	.0018^b
Homeown	−.0948	−.0557	−.2778^b	−.2234^b
Nonwht			.1494^b	.1460^b
German			.4104^a	.3990^a
Polish			−.5603^b	−.5544^b
Czech			−.5233^b	−.5626^b
Hung			−.2914^b	−.2929^b
Ital			−.0361	−.0220
Intercept	63.07	−6.49	63.28	49.43
R^2	.73	.71	.90	.90

^{a}t-statistic greater than 1.0.

^{b}t-statistic greater than 1.67.

All estimates are calculated by weighted regression using the total vote in each sample tract as the weight.

variables have an unexpected positive effect on voting, the percentage of homeowners in the tract has a significant negative effect on voting. Everything else being equal, homeowners tend to be significantly less inclined toward the public expenditures than are renters. This is consistent with either the renter perception model that property taxes aren't fully passed on to renters or with the case where the incidence of the property tax is partially on landlords.[1 2]

It might be possible to argue that welfare expenditures are not normal goods, in that people with higher incomes do not demand increased expenditures on welfare. In such a world, the estimated income signs would be correct. However, the consistency of the income estimates between the zoo and the welfare models suggests that this is at least not the whole explanation. In fact, part of the explanation may lie in the inability to separate the effects on voting of income and property value. Multicollinearity—the high correlation among independent variables—appears fairly severe in this case. As seen in Table 5-6, income and the housing variables are all very correlated. It is not possible to ascertain the effects of this correlation on the estimates without looking at other data that have different patterns of intercorrelations.

Strangely, variables measuring explicit demand considerations did not prove significant. For the welfare measure, variables relating to children

Table 5-6. Simple Correlations Among Income and Housing Variables

	Median Income	*Value*[a]	*Rent*[b]	*Home Ownership*
Median income	1.00	.80	−.48	.20
Value[a]		1.00	−.79	.92
Rent[b]			1.00	−.91
Homeownership				1.00

[a]Value is the median value of owner occupied units (in hundreds of dollars) times the percent owner occupied units in the tract.

[b]Rent is the median monthly rent of renter occupied units times the percent renter occupied units in the tract.

without a male head of family and to the elderly population had no significant influence on expressed preferences. For the zoo levy, the distribution of children or age of the family head had no bearing on expressed preferences.

On both expenditure issues, the racial and ethnic distribution show significant strength in the estimated preferences. This finding, previously noted by Banfield and Wilson, remains difficult to explain. To be more useful, it would be desirable to know whether this reflected some underlying differences in preferences or whether it is mirroring some unmeasured population differences such as geographic distribution or ability to influence the distribution of public goods and services.

There are enough discrepancies between the estimated models and what was expected to consider more fundamental problems with the estimates. In particular, combining what was learned about voter turnout with the attempts to estimate the community preferences themselves, it is necessary to question the adequacy of the statistical techniques used in the preference estimation. There are reasons to suspect that the models may give misleading views about community preferences because of statistical problems which fall under the general heading of "errors in variables."

ERRORS IN VARIABLES

We previously analyzed the voter turnout models from the perspective of whose preferences get counted. However, these models have other implications for the analysis of community preferences. A minority of the eligible population (23 percent for the welfare levy and 43 percent for the zoo levy) actually cast votes. Further, the voters were a systematic subset of the eligible population—i.e., the income, age, and so forth of a person affected the probability that he would vote. This has serious implications for statistical analysis of community preferences.

The sample of data for the analyses here was collected and constructed by merging precinct voting information with Census tract information about the characteristics of the population. The Census data, however, refer to the entire population in the tract, not just the voters. If the individuals who vote are systematic in terms of the characteristics that also relate to preferences (income, ethnicity, etc.), the independent variables pertaining to the entire tract population will be measured with error. For example, we have noted that higher income people tend to vote more frequently. This implies that the median income in a tract understates the income of the individuals who actually vote.

When the independent variables are measured with error, regression analysis yields biased estimates of the effects of each of the characteristics on preferences.[13] A number of corrective procedures have been proposed for errors in variables; however, these methods usually rely upon an assumption that the errors in measurement are random. In the case here, the errors are systematically related to the size of the variables. While this precludes most standard corrective actions, it does provide some hope that a statistical technique can be tailored to this type of problem.[14] The types of corrective procedures possible are beyond the scope of this paper, and here it is only noted that they seem feasible.

CONCLUSIONS

There are continued cries for the need to make local government responsive to the people. In large measure, the "responsive" discussions are concerned with the form of government—the use of local city halls, the development of metropolitan areawide government, the choice between a city manager form of government and a mayorality, and so on. One of the major shortcomings of these discussions, however, and of analyses into these issues appears to be the nonexistence of any ways of comparing individuals' preferences to the governmental services that are provided. This results largely from our inability to study systematically the community preferences for public goods.

As things stand now, we do not have a good understanding of whose preferences for public goods are currently being satisfied; of how people attempt to fulfill their preferences; or of how the system of metropolitan governance could be changed to accommodate public preferences better. This study delves into what information about public preferences can be gleaned from referendum voting. Referendum voting is one of the few times in which community members make explicit statements about their demands for public goods and services.

There are two aspects to the study: first, whose preferences are listened to; second, what are the underlying preferences of the members of the community. In terms of results, the analysis of voter turnout (the first issue) was more successful than the analysis of the underlying preferences. This differential success resulted from the significant statistical problems encountered in looking at the preference or demand models. Since it was necessary to merge voting data with Census data, and since all members of the community did not vote, serious measurement errors with respect to the independent variables (costs, income, tastes, etc.) were introduced. This condition led to biased estimates in the statistical models and made the preference results somewhat suspicious.

Nevertheless, there are several important analytical conclusions arising from these efforts. First, the evidence here and that presented by Peterson in Chapter Four indicate that there is much to be learned from studying the expressed preferences of community members. Second, considerable care must be taken in addressing the statistical questions that are raised through the merging of different data sources. Third, the statistical problems seem manageable, and the complete formulation of the errors in variables techniques for the systematic error case should be developed. Finally, the importance of understanding community preferences and the public choice problem dictates further research into referendum voting.

Chapter Six

Elections and Local Fiscal Policy

The existence of a link between the policies of incumbent elected officials and voters' decisions in subsequent elections is a critical consideration in our evaluation of public decision processes. An earlier study examined municipal expenditure and revenue decisions in Cleveland, Ohio and demonstrated that Cleveland's different mayors pursued different policies with regard to the size of the municipal budget, the use of property taxes, and user charges to raise the necessary revenues, and the allocation of revenues to the different service departments and agencies.[1]

It is obvious that elections are the reasons for changes in administrations. If the outcome of these elections is related to the policies of the incumbent mayor, and to the proposals of a challenger, then we have established the basis for a strong link between individual preferences and the provision of public services—the link being the electoral process. The existence of this link means that we must consider carefully the structure of the electoral process, how this structure affects policy decisions, and how well it aggregates people's differing demands for public services.

This paper relies on experiences in Boston, Massachusetts to provide evidence in support of this important linkage. Budget data collected for the period from the mid fifties to the early seventies further indicate that different mayors follow different fiscal policies. In particular, John Collins, who was mayor from January 1960 to December 1967, emphasized considerable restraint

This research was supported by grants to Harvard University from Resources for the Future and the Ford Foundation. I wish to express my appreciation to Professors James Q. Wilson and Edward C. Banfield for their Boston Homeowners Survey; to Mr. Theodore Anzalone of the City of Boston Assessor's Office for help in collecting some of the data; and to John Kain for his helpful comments. Of course, I accept all responsibility for the analyses and interpretations in this paper.

on increases in the property tax and set spending priorities on large scale urban redevelopment and possibly the city hospital at the expense of public safety, sanitation, and other services.

Collins's political career was abruptly terminated when he lost the Democratic primary for the U.S. Senate to ex-governor Endicott Peabody in 1966. In that election Collins received only 40 percent of the votes cast in Boston and managed to carry only one of the city's 22 wards. This chapter presents evidence to support the argument that Collins's poor showing in that election is the result of both the fiscal policies he followed and the voters' evaluations of those policies.

The revenue and expenditure decisions made during the Collins administration are first examined and compared to the decisions made by previous and subsequent mayors. This analysis gives a picture of Collins's fiscal priorities. From these priorities, hypotheses about which voters will most favor or most oppose Collins are developed based on the incidence of those decisions. For example, it is expected that owners of larger homes will be more inclined towards policies that keep property taxes low than other voters. Two different data sets are then used to examine and test these propositions and to relate people's attitudes and votes to the policies of the Collins administration. The first data set is a survey of Boston homeowners obtained during the last half of 1966.

Although not representative of Boston residents, the information in the homeowners survey will allow us to test in explicit detail the attitudes of a group of voters towards Collins and their evaluations of the public services they were receiving. The results of this analysis will establish a strong link between these attitudes, individual social and economic characteristics, and the policies of the Collins administration. The survey does not deal with the primary election directly, however. The only information about how people voted in the primary—which is the precise relationship necessary for the linkage in our model—must come from the aggregate election statistics. What we will show is that the pattern of aggregate voting results follows both the pattern hypothesized on the basis of our knowledge of Collins's policies and the pattern of attitudes towards Collins found among homeowners in the survey. The high correspondence between Collins's policies, people's evaluation of public services and their attitudes towards Collins, and the results in the election are very consistent with the existence of a strong link between public policies and electoral decisions evaluating those policies.

COLLINS'S FISCAL PRIORITIES

The most notable of Collins's priorities was his zeal to keep property taxes low. The property tax rate was decreased in five of Collins's eight years and rose only a total of 16.6 dollars per thousand during the entire eight-year period. This compares to an increase of 38.4 dollars per thousand during the previous eight years and 56.7 dollars per thousand during the first four years of the succeeding administration.[2] This record is not explained by large increases in the tax base. Total property tax revenues also increased in only three of his eight years, and the total increase in his eight years was $32M or 22 percent. In real terms this increase amounts to only 5 percent in eight years, which is a very small increase in the size of the public sector. Given these observations it is not hard to detect Collins's strategy with respect to the property tax, and thereby his opinion of the value of local public services.

The consequence of this tax policy was the provision of little in the way of additional public services that could not be financed by intergovernmental transfers. Collins's expenditure priorities are evident from changes in budget shares of various activities during his tenure, the growth rate of different departments in this period, and the distribution of capital expenditures. This information for several activities for selected years of the Collins administration and for years prior to and following his terms are shown in Tables 6-1 and 6-2.

The most enlightening comparisons are the capital expenditures. Public health and hospitals, urban development, and general administration are the only areas that received increased capital expenditures during Collins's last four years. The large general administration account covers the capital cost of the new city hall, which as part of the new Government Center redevelopment was an essential part of his redevelopment strategy. The remaining activities all had smaller capital expenditures in real terms in the last four years of the Collins administration than they did in the four years preceding his election.

The same pattern is evident in the distribution of current expenditures and budget shares. The only activities that received a larger share of the budget were health and hospitals, general administration, and welfare. The indicated increase in the welfare share is misleading since all the increase occurred in 1967, when changes in eligibility were mandated by the state and the welfare department took over financing of the medical care for the aged program. Welfare's share of the 1966 budget was only 5.6 percent and real welfare expenditures had decreased by 4.0 percent between 1959 to 1966; consequently it is hard to argue that welfare expenditures were a high priority item.

The figures in Table 6-2 exclude intergovernmental transfers for specific programs. The programs most affected by this convention are welfare and education expenditures, whose support from state and federal programs increased substantially during the 1960s. If these transfers are included in the department accounts and in the total budget, the share going to welfare and education rose substantially during the Collins years. With these transfers included, education and welfare expenditures both increased by over 60 percent in real terms between 1959 and 1967; these are the only two departments to show increase in budget share during this period.

Table 6-1. Capital Expenditures by Period and Department

	Amounts[a]				Percent of Total Capital Outlay				1964-67 as percent of 1956-59
	1956-59	1960-63	1964-67	1968-70	1956-59	1960-63	1964-67	1968-70	
Public safety	2.0	0.0	1.0	5.0	2.9	0.0	1.0	4.1	50.
Health & hospitals	2.0	3.0	7.0	9.0	2.9	5.4	6.7	7.3	350.
Sanitation	11.0	5.0	6.0	3.0	16.0	8.9	5.7	2.4	55.
Gen'l. admin.	6.0	8.0	39.0	22.0	8.7	14.3	37.1	17.9	650.
Urban development	9.0	16.0	25.0	29.0	13.0	28.6	23.8	23.6	278.
Education	12.0	6.0	9.0	35.0	17.4	10.7	8.6	28.4	75.
Highways	26.0	16.0	17.0	19.0	37.7	28.6	16.2	15.4	65.

Data from "Municipal Expenditures in the City of Boston," prepared by Alex Ganz, Boston Redevelopment Authority.

[a]Dollars in millions of 1970 dollars.

Table 6-2. Budget Shares and Growth Rates of Departments' Current Expenditures

Department	Including Welfare				Excluding Welfare[a]					Percent Growth[b]
	1956	1959	1963	1967	1956	1959	1963	1967	1970	1959-67
Public safety	16.9	17.8	16.8	16.2	18.2	19.0	17.9	18.2	17.9	8.6
Health & hospitals	11.5	11.2	11.5	11.8	12.3	12.0	12.2	13.2	14.1	25.6
Sanitation	7.3	6.6	7.7	5.2	7.8	7.1	8.2	5.8	8.5	−7.0
Gen'l. admin.	36.4	39.6	35.6	38.4	39.0	42.4	37.8	43.0	40.5	15.1
Urban development	0.2	0.5	0.3	0.4	0.2	0.5	0.4	0.4	0.3	0.0
Education	17.6	16.2	18.8	12.5	18.8	17.4	19.9	14.0	14.7	−8.3
Welfare	6.7	6.6	5.8	10.7[c]						92.6[d]

Data from "Municipal Expenditures in the City of Boston," prepared by Alex Ganz, Boston Redevelopment Authority.

[a]The welfare program was taken over by the state in 1968. Consequently budget shares have been computed with and without the welfare expenditures for comparative purposes.

[b]This growth rate is computed in real terms using 1970 GNP Deflator.

[c]All of this increase came in 1967 and is related to state determined policies. In 1966, welfare expenditures, exclusive of special grants, comprised only 5.6% of the local budget and had decreased by 4% in real terms between 1959 and 1966.

Based on these data it seems fair to characterize Collins's priorities as a combination of low property tax rate and meager increases, if any, for all expenditures other than those that could be supported by intergovernmental grants (except possibly health and hospitals). It is difficult to associate any changes in current educational expenditures with the mayor, however, because the education budget is administered by a separate and independently elected school committee. The only control the mayor can exert over this body is through public statements aimed at bringing pressure on the committee, since he may increase but not decrease the budget presented to him by the school committee. He does control the school capital budget however, which shows much lower expenditures during Collins's administration than under preceding and succeeding mayors. Likewise many of the welfare decisions during this period were strongly influenced by state requirements and thus out of Collins's control. The services neglected were quite clearly police, fire, and sanitation. This quick survey of Collins's priorities forms the basis for our analysis of citizen attitudes and electoral behavior.

CITIZEN EVALUATION OF SERVICES

The proper way to assess the impact of Collins's policies on electoral results is to determine the structure of voters' demands for public services, and to compare these demands to Collins's policies, then to voters' evaluations of him, and finally to their subsequent votes. The information needed for such an analysis of people's attitudes, evaluations, and voting decisions is not available. However, it is possible to obtain a fragmentary view of this process and test some of the expected relationships with a survey of Boston homeowners conducted by Banfield and Wilson in 1966 and the aggregate election returns from the 1966 primary.[3] The survey covers only a limited and unrepresentative segment of the Boston population and does not ask about intended primary votes, so its results cannot be generalized to either the entire electorate or the primary election.[4]

The advantage of using the survey is that it does ask this group of citizens for their evaluation of certain public services and their attitude towards the incumbent mayor, John Collins. From the homeowners' responses to these questions we can ascertain if their evaluations and attitudes conform to the ones anticipated, given Collins's policies and priorities. If these citizens' attitudes reflect the expected effects of Collins's decisions, we may be confident that homeowners at least are responsive to local policies. There is no compelling reason, then, to believe that renters, as a large group, behave so differently as to be unresponsive to these policies if homeowners are responsive. The results obtained from this analysis, which relates citizens' evaluations and attitudes to the characteristics of the individual, also provides important information on how to specify the aggregate voting analysis. If the characteristics that explain people's evaluations and attitudes then explain the distribution of Collins's primary votes, we have a stronger case for believing in the link between policy and voting.

Homeowner Evaluation of Three Activities

Three specific areas of local policy are examined: (1) demands for additional public hospital expenditures, (2) attitudes towards the Boston Redevelopment Authority (BRA), and (3) homeowners' evaluations of whether they are getting adequate police protection. Responses to questions on these three subjects are assumed to reflect both people's demands for these activities and their evaluations of the performance of the Collins administration in providing them. The demands and evaluations expressed by these responses should be related to the characteristics of the individual respondent and to the area of the city in which the person resides. These characteristics are selected to measure the individual's desire for certain services and the cost to the individual of these services.

The following three questions are included in the Wilson and Banfield survey:

1. "Do you think we should spend more on the Boston City Hospital, used by low income people, even if it costs more in property taxes?"
2. "Has the city done anything in this part of town or failed to do something which has hurt you personally or which you didn't like? . . . Police protection?"
3. "I'd like to ask you about different city officials—how good a job you feel they are doing . . . The Boston Redevelopment Authority (the BRA). They deal with Urban Renewal?"

The responses to the questions about City Hospital and police protection are coded simply as 1 for those not opposed to spending more on the hospital and for those who felt they were not getting adequate police protection and 0 for people opposed to hospital spending and those satisfied with their police protection. The responses to the question about the BRA—categorized as Very Good, Good, Fair, and Poor—were assigned the categorical values 4, 3, 2, and 1 respectively.

The individual characteristics used to explain homeowners' responses to these questions are the person's race and ethnic background, education, and income. Variables characterizing the area of the city in which people lived—and which presumably relate to the need for services and possibly differences in the distribution of services within the city—are residence in a ghetto area (defined as a Census tract with over 50 percent black in the 1970 Census), distance from the ghetto, and median income in the tract. These latter variables are expected to be particularly related to the need for and evaluation of police services.

Finally, a variable measuring the assessed valuation of the respondent's residence is included. This information was not included in the original survey, but was obtained subsequently by the author from the city assessor's records using the addresses on the original questionnaires. Recent analysis of the demand for public services has treated the incidence of the property tax as a pricing variable in which people with more expensive homes in any specific jurisdiction face a higher price for public services than those with lower valued homes.[5]

This higher price implies that people with higher valued homes will be less sympathetic to increases in the level of public services or in this survey to additional hospital expenditures. They are also likely to be more favorable towards large scale urban renewal because it is promoted as enlarging the property tax base and reducing the price of services. The effect of assessed valuations on the evaluations of police protection is less clear. The question does not ask about additional expenditures, but simply the adequacy of current services. At the same time it may be hard to separate the price and demand effects for police services of homeowners, because the benefits from increased protection of personal property are more likely to accrue to the owners of more expensive homes.

Findings

The relationships between homeowners' evaluations and the individual and neighborhood characteristics are shown in Table 6-3. While the Wilson and Banfield survey included 1,059 respondents, only 823 individuals are used in this study, since a number of these interviews were conducted in early 1968 after Collins left office and more than a year after the election. Also, a number of questionnaires could not be located to code the assessed valuation data and had to be deleted.

The results, though not striking in their explanatory power, have some important implications. (All variables not dichotomous are expressed in logarithmic form.) Assessed valuation is the only variable which is related to demand for city hospital expenditures. The coefficient means that support for this activity decreases by 0.06 for each additional thousand dollars of assessed valuation and thus support is inversely related to the individual's share of the cost. Education is the only other characteristic at all related to the demand for hospital expenditures, suggesting that demand for city hospital services decreases as education level increases up to the college level, college graduates being more likely to support this program than high school graduates. However, neither of these coefficients is statistically significant enough to warrant much reliance on this implication. The lack of results may be reflecting the absence of much real information on demand for public health services: only 20 percent of those surveyed indicated that they opposed such expenditures, which seems like an underestimate of how much opposition would exist if people were asked to give up other services or private consumption for city hospital expenditures.

Table 6-3. Attitude Towards Public Activities

Group	Pay More for City Hospital	Received Poor Police Service	Attitude towards B.R.A.[a]
Black	−0.023 (−0.46)	−0.042 (−0.80)	0.052 (0.97)
Irish	0.034 (0.69)	−0.012 (−0.29)	0.015 (0.27)
Italian	−0.041 (−0.84)	−0.013 (−0.30)	0.082 (1.47)
Age in tens of years[a]	−0.008 (−0.74)		
Education in years[a]	−0.057 (−1.09)	0.018 (0.42)	−0.032 (−0.57)
College degree	0.037 (0.74)	0.011 (0.25)	0.228 (4.17)
Income (thousands)[a]	−0.002 (0.40)	0.010 (0.42)	−0.021 (−0.71)
Distance from ghetto[a] (thousands of feet)		−0.022 (−1.38)	
Residence in ghetto		0.096 (1.24)	
Residence in Wards 4, 9			−0.186 (−2.38)
Assessed valuation[a]	−0.063 (−1.94)	0.002 (0.06)	0.101 (3.02)
Median income in tract[a]	−0.012 (−0.16)	0.255 (3.14)	
Constant	0.946 (6.02)	0.139 (1.19)	0.893 (6.48)
R^2	0.01	0.05	0.07

(t-statistics)

[a]Variable is expressed in log form.

Responses to questions about the adequacy of police protection exhibited many of the same problems as the analysis of the demand for hospital expenditures. Again, only a small percentage (15 percent) said they were not satisfied. These negative responses, however, depended strongly on where the respondent lived. Residents of wealthier areas were much less satisfied with the protection they received, and the dissatisfaction decreased with increasing distance from the ghetto, which in Boston would be considered the high crime areas. For example, the combined ghetto residence and distance effects are statistically significant and indicate that the likelihood of a ghetto resident's being dissatisfied with police services is 0.10 higher than a similar person living immediately adjacent to the ghetto, and 0.15 and 0.16 higher than comparable people two and four miles from the ghetto respectively. Since crime statistics are not available for tracts, it is not possible to relate these responses directly to crime rates. None of the remaining variables, which referred to the characteristics of the individual respondent, were even weakly related to evaluations of police protection.

Attitudes towards the Boston Redevelopment Authority exhibit the strongest relationship with individual characteristics. Approval of urban renewal is much higher among people with a college education. Because the BRA attitude variable is expressed as the log of the categorical scale used to code the responses, the coefficient of 0.23 on the college education variable indicates that having a college degree raises a person's attitude towards the Authority by an amount equal to the difference between a Good and a Very Good response, or over half the difference between a Fair and a Good Response. Homeowners in Wards 4 and 9 were much less favorably disposed towards the BRA. This is not surprising because one of the more controversial redevelopment proposals was located in these wards.

Finally, the owners of more expensive homes were far more likely to approve of the Authority. This result is expected because BRA policies benefit them in two ways. First, Collins and others promoted the idea that the BRA's extensive renewal activities would revitalize downtown and expand the city's tax base, thereby further reducing the local property tax rate and making public services less expensive to homeowners. At the same time, by eliminating supposedly blighted areas, the renewal efforts might have the effect of raising property values throughout the city, if one supposes that people will pay more for housing in a "New Boston." Although both effects presumably are operating, I strongly suspect the anticipated effect of renewal on property taxes largely accounts for the strong relationship between assessed valuation and support for the BRA.

ATTITUDES TOWARD COLLINS AND
ELECTORAL BEHAVIOR

The final and most important relationships in our model are those between people's evaluations of an incumbent administration's policies, their attitudes towards that administration, and their voting decisions. The homeowners survey can help establish whether people's attitudes toward Collins are related to expressions of satisfaction or dissatisfaction with Collins's policies. The link with voting behavior can then be examined with the aggregate election returns from the 1966 primary. These returns include both homeowners and renters and thus constitute a better reflection of the support and opposition generated by Collins and his various policies. However, the interpretation of these results is aided considerably by the survey analysis, which provides specific information about people's evaluations and attitudes.

Homeowners' Attitudes Toward Collins

Homeowners' assessments of the delivery of different public services, as measured by the three variables analyzed above, should be important determinants of people's attitudes toward Collins. The brief analysis of his budgets strongly suggests that the people who most support Collins will be those who favored urban renewal, or at least approved of the BRA's aggressive policies towards downtown renewal; those who have more expensive homes and therefore must pay more for any additional services and who benefit the most from reduced or low property taxes; and possibly people who want more public health services. We expect less support for Collins among people who have a need for additional public services such as police protection and who felt that their needs were not being met, and among those who have less valued homes.

In addition to the expected effects of Collins's fiscal policies, our analysis of attitudes toward Collins must include some of the local political effects associated with any Boston political figure. These effects are derived from the very ethnic character of the city and the residual feelings from past campaigns in which any politician has been involved.

Boston is very rich in these traditions and cleavages and their impacts clearly remain from one election to the next. The most salient of these considerations—besides the fact that Collins is Irish (as are most Boston politicians)—is Collins's first campaign for mayor when he ran as the "good government" candidate against one of the Boston "pols," as Collins referred to him.[6] This opponent was John Powers, president of the Massachusetts Senate, who had had a long career in Boston and Massachusetts state house politics. This stance of Collins and the image he tried to project, along with his very close associations with the upper levels of the Boston financial and business community, strongly suggests that part of Collins's appeal was to the better educated and upper income groups.

Factors often included in analyses of Boston politics are ethnicity and a friends-and-neighbors effect. Presumably candidates for office always do better among "their people" and the residents of "their" ward. Consequently, variables measuring both Irish, Italian, and black ethnic backgrounds are included in the Collins equations as well as a variable indicating if the person resides in Ward 10, which is Collins's ward.

The specific question ascertaining people's attitudes toward Collins is the question asking for people's evaluations of public officials. This is the same question used to analyze attitudes toward the BRA only the words "the mayor" are used instead of the "Boston Redevelopment Authority." Thus the question does not refer to Collins specifically, but only to the mayor. The responses are in the same four categories as the responses to the question about the BRA and are coded for statistical analysis the same as the BRA question. The results of relating these evaluations of Collins to the opinions of specific services, individual assessed valuations, and the characteristics of the individual and the residential neighborhood are shown in Table 6-4.

Table 6-4. Attitudes Toward Collins

Pay more for City Hospital	0.077
	(2.26)
Attitude towards BRA[a]	0.152
	(5.12)
Dissatisfied with police service	−0.056
	(−1.41)
Irish	0.070
	(1.49)
Italian	−0.065
	(−1.35)
Black	0.003
	(0.06)
Residence in Ward 10	−0.110
	(−0.79)
Education in years[a]	0.155
	(3.20)
College degree	0.125
	(2.67)
Income[a]	−0.017
	(−0.68)
Distance from ghetto[a]	0.050
(thousands of feet)	(2.95)
Residence in ghetto	0.099
	(1.14)
Assessed valuation[a]	0.060
	(2.06)
Constant	0.203
	(1.50)
R^2	0.14

(t-statistic)

[a]Variable expressed in logarithmic form.

Homeowners' evaluations of Collins as mayor were strongly influenced by their attitudes toward public services, their evaluation of the delivery of these services, and the incidence of the property tax. The effects of these evaluations are as expected: people who wanted additional hospital expenditures and who approved of the BRA expressed more support for Collins, while people who felt that the city was not providing sufficient police protection were less likely to give the mayor a high rating. At the same time, the higher the assessed valuation of the person's house, the higher the rating they were likely to give Collins. Again this is expected, given Collins's conservative approach to increasing the tax rate to provide services.

The variables included to represent the ongoing effects of traditional Boston politics and the appeals of Collins's previous campaigns performed as expected, with the exception of his own ward: approval of Collins increased with education and was much higher among people with a college education. This is consistent with Collins's previous campaigns and appeal as a good government administrator as opposed to a "Massachusetts pol" and his ties to the Boston establishment. The observed ethnic loyalties were also as expected, with Collins receiving more support from the Irish and less support from the Italians. Race had no appreciable effect on homeowners' evaluations of Collins.

Collins's Defeat in the 1966 Primary Election

The real test of our model is whether Collins's policies can be linked to electoral results and used to account for his defeat in the 1966 Democratic senatorial primary. Ideally, we would like to analyze a contest between Collins and a challenger in the 1967 mayoral race. However, after his 1966 defeat Collins did not seek reelection in 1967 and retired from public office. His opponent in the primary was Endicott Peabody from Cambridge, a former governor of the Commonwealth who had been defeated by his Lt. Governor, Francis Bellotti, in a 1964 primary fight.

With due caution, the primary results in Boston can be both interpreted as a referendum on Collins's performance as mayor and assumed to reflect people's evaluations of Collins's policies. The principal factors permitting this interpretation are that (1) only 6 percent of Boston voters were registered as Republicans, (2) Independents are permitted to vote in the Democratic primary if they desire, and (3) there was no Republican primary in 1966 to attract their attention. Thus, only 6 percent of Boston's registered voters were legally excluded from voting in this primary election, and since 50 percent of the registered voters actually voted we will assume that they are as representative of Boston citizens as is turnout in any election.

It is necessary to assume, of course, that the Boston residents who voted in the primary were more influenced by Collins's performance as mayor than by their evaluations of Peabody. There is no direct way to test this assumption; one simply has to formulate an electoral model for this primary on the assumption that people's votes were influenced by Collins's policies, along with the other factors likely to be present in such an election. If the characteristics that explained people's evaluations of Collins and his policies are also strongly related to the voting results, it at least provides a consistent argument for why people voted for or against Collins.

Collins's support in the primary is measured by his proportion of the votes cast in each of the city's census tracts. The returns from individual precincts are combined to obtain this measure.[7] The explanatory variables are the characteristics of each tract as described in the Census. This procedure provides accurate measures of each explanatory variable while admitting some random error into the measure of Collins support. These random errors will reduce the correlations between the vote and the explanatory variables, but will not affect our estimates of the effects of these variables on the vote.

The most important consideration in specifying our analysis of the Collins vote is to include measures of all the factors associated with systematic influences on the voting decisions. These influences will be of two types: those related to people's evaluations of Collins's policies and their attitudes of him as mayor, and those factors such as ethnicity, education, and Collins's home ward that are traditionally related to voting in Boston. The variables needed to measure people's evaluations of Collins are the ones identified in the survey analysis as being related to people's evaluations of the services they were receiving, or as being directly related to their attitudes towards Collins. These variables include median income in the tract, the tract's distance from the ghetto, and whether the tract is part of the ghetto. All these variables relate to people's determination that they were not receiving adequate police protection, which was then negatively related to attitudes towards Collins.

The proportion of the over-25 population with a college degree or some college experience, and whether the tract is in Ward 4 or 9, are included to partially represent people's favorable attitudes toward urban renewal. The education variable will also be strongly related to Collins's vote because of his reputation with the upper class, good government group. Finally, the median value of owner occupied dwellings is included. This variable is multiplied by the proportion of owner occupied dwellings in the tract to take account of the fact that we expect the effect of increasing home values on Collins's vote to be much stronger in tracts with a high percentage of homeowners.

To illustrate: picture the effect of increasing home values in two different types of tracts, one with a very small proportion of owner occupied dwellings, the other with virtually all owner occupied units. In the first case, even if all homeowners switch to Collins, it will have only a small impact on his proportion of the vote in that tract. In the second tract, however, increasing values will result in much larger increases in Collins's vote because of the greater proportion of homeowners. The value of a person's home was directly related to his evaluation of Collins's performance as mayor and to a favorable attitude towards the work of the Redevelopment Authority. The variables percent Irish, percent Italian, and location in Ward 10 are included to represent the remaining aspects of Boston's politics likely to affect the voting decisions.

The results of estimating this electoral model are shown in Table 6-5. The results shown are for the equation with Collins's percentage of the vote as the dependent variable and all the explanatory variables in logarithmic form except the ward and ghetto dummy variables. Other equations with the vote variable expressed both in log form and in logit form were also used, with virtually no difference in results. With one exception, the results are quite consistent with our expectations derived from the discussion of Collins's fiscal policies and the analysis of the Wilson and Banfield homeowners survey. Collins's vote was much lower in ghetto areas and in areas with higher median incomes, which is where people were most dissatisfied with police protection.

Table 6-5. The Collins Vote in the 1966 Primary

Tract in Wards 4 or 9	−0.040 (−1.13)
Percent Irish[a]	0.006 (1.22)
Percent Italian[a]	0.021 (3.36)
Tract in Ward 10	0.103 (4.91)
Percent with some college[a]	0.039 (3.50)
Median income[a]	−0.075 (−1.76)
Distance from ghetto[a] (thousands of feet)	−0.006 (−0.87)
Tract in ghetto	−0.097 (−3.95)
Home value * percent owner occupied[a]	0.028 (3.52)
Constant	0.692 (6.18)
R^2	0.52

(t-statistic)

[a]Variable expressed in logarithmic form.

In the survey, dissatisfaction with the police had been highest in the ghetto and declined with distance from there, while support for Collins followed the opposite pattern. In the electoral analysis, Collins's vote was much lower in the ghetto, but did not rise from the edge of the ghetto to outlying areas. In fact, if there was any change in Collins's vote as tracts get further from the ghetto it was a decline in support, rather than an increase. Although this seems contrary to our expectation, the coefficient on the distance variable is so small and so far from statistical significance that there is virtually no difference in Collins's vote between areas adjacent to the ghetto and areas which are the maximum distance away, but his vote is much lower inside the ghetto (defined as tracts with over 50 percent black).

For example, Collins's vote declined by 1.4 and 1.6 percent relative to the edge of the ghetto as one gets two miles and four miles respectively from the ghetto edge and was 9.7 percent lower in the ghetto. Collins's vote was also higher in tracts with a greater proportion of the over-25 population attending college, as implied by the analysis of attitudes toward renewal and towards Collins himself. Collins's vote was lower in tracts in Wards 4 and 9, as predicted by the urban renewal equation. Finally, in terms of our initial model, Collins's vote was substantially higher in tracts with a greater proportion of homeowners and owners of more expensive homes.

The Boston politics variables had the expected coefficients, with the exception of the percent Italian variable. Collins's vote was higher in areas identified as Irish, in tracts located in his ward, and in areas with higher education levels, which also measures approval of the mayor for his urban renewal efforts. The positive coefficient on the proportion Italian variable is hard to explain, especially considering the fact that it is quite statistically significant. One possible explanation is that the Italian vote is anti-Peabody rather than pro-Collins. The 1964 gubernatorial primary, which Peabody lost to Bellotti, was a very bitter affair that many say caused irreparable harm to the state Democratic party, as evidenced by the fact that Bellotti lost the race for governor to the Republican John Volpe in the year that Lyndon Johnson and Ted Kennedy were sweeping the state. The fact that Bellotti was closely identified with the Italian community in Massachusetts may have led Italians to dislike and possibly vote against Peabody.

FISCAL POLITICS

There are two points to be drawn from these analyses, one broad and one narrow in their application. The first concerns the links between public policy decisions and electoral behavior and the role of elections in achieving some conformity between policy and citizen interests. The more narrow implication is further evidence of the importance of tax incidence in establishing these citizen interests and how one goes about viewing the effects of different taxes in this context.

The analyses both of the homeowners survey and the election results imply a very strong link between the policies of the incumbent administration, voters' evaluations of that administration, and their subsequent voting behavior. Collins gave great priority to keeping the property tax rate down and promoting urban renewal, at the expense of other services. We then found that homeowners who supported the urban renewal agency, who were not concerned about the lack of police services, and who owned expensive homes were much more inclined to evaluate Collins favorably. Finally, voting in the senatorial primary closely paralled the homeowners' evaluations. This leaves the very strong impression that people are evaluating incumbent administrations on their performance and policy decisions, and that these evaluations are important factors in people's voting decisions. From this we can draw the conclusion that people do attempt to use the voting booth as a means to express these preferences and influence the type of public services available.

The argument that people do express their demands for public services through the electoral process, and try to evaluate incumbents (and quite possibly challengers) on the basis of the decisions and fiscal policies being followed or advocated, has important implications for how we consider and evaluate the political process. It lends considerable support to the notion put forth in the earlier study of municipal budgeting that even though individual administrations may make decisions in an incremental fashion, and may largely reflect the interests of particular bureaucrats, that over time as administrations change (presumably through the electoral process) priorities will change, and different mayors will favor different increments and will reward different bureaucrats.

This process of changing administrations has the effect of introducing different priorities into the budgetary process, which alters the pattern of allocations among activities over time, even though the process may look quite stable during one administration. The evidence here, which argues that these electoral choices depend upon voters' evaluations of the fiscal decisions made by incumbent mayors, argues that these shifts in administration will occur when the policies of that administration deviate from the collective demands of the voting populace. Furthermore, this also argues that if mayors want to hang onto their jobs—or as in the case of Collins, if they aspire to higher office—they had best take into account these individual demands when they are making their fiscal decisions and not lapse into some arbitrary incremental pattern or become the captive of the bureaucratic structure.

In fact, the analysis of the budgetary process in Cleveland found that the annual decisions about both revenues and departmental expenditures were not purely bureaucratic, but did respond to changes in the economic and social environment in the city. The argument was made there, and is further supported here, that social and economic changes correspond to changes in the demands of citizens for different services (or to at least the aggregate pattern of demand) as a city's population changes, and that changes in the budget occur as the mayor tries to meet or satisfy these shifting demands.

If the above observations and arguments seem to hold in an old, large, central city such as Boston, or Cleveland, with their long histories of ethnic and personal cleavages and political structures that many have seen as dominating the political process, then the impact of policy decisions on voting and electoral decisions in other cities should be at least as important, and the process outlined here at least as evident. The less important nonpolicy related considerations become, the more effective the political process becomes as a way for people to express, and hopefully accommodate, their demands for public services. It also means that the structure of the political process—namely what gets voted on, and by whom—becomes important in considering how effective the political process is, or can be, in responding to people's needs and demands and in determining whose demands get satisfied.

The narrower application of these results is further reinforcement for the argument put forth by others that the direct incidence of the taxes used to finance public services (in this case the property tax) functions as a pricing variable and influences people's demands for public services, just as prices influence demand for private goods. The obvious effect of this pricing variable is that the people who pay a larger share of the cost of public services, everything else being equal, are more likely to want to restrict the size of the public sector and to support candidates who hold down taxes, even at the cost of public services.

In terms of building support for public services, or alternatively, for evaluating the effects of a shift from one tax to another, one must consider the impact of the tax structure on people's demands for public services and how this will influence their voting behavior. For example, the shift from a property tax to a local wage or sales tax will shift the cost of public services among different groups in the community. By this analysis it will alter the support that members of these groups have for different public expenditure programs, and thus their voting behavior, when provided an opportunity to express those preferences. Analyses that relate the incidence of taxes to the pricing of public services and to people's demands, and to this their voting behavior (to which this particular study lends some support) are important steps in our understanding of tax effects and decisions about public resource allocation decisions.

When the two points made here are combined they make a persuasive argument about the role of local politics in making decisions about the allocation of resources to and among public activities, and conversely about the importance of these allocation decisions in the political process. Once it is recognized that the local political process, and primarily elections, are one of the important means people have of expressing their needs and demands for services that cannot be obtained privately, we can begin making the appropriate and necessary evaluations of how well different political structures and processes perform this function.

At the same time, once we recognize that people have these demands, that they will be influenced by both their own characteristics and by the incidence of public tax policies, and that they are an important determinant of voting and presumably of other forms of political behavior, we will then have made considerable progress in our understanding of the political process and, hopefully, how it relates to other aspects of urban development.

Chapter Seven

The Municipal Service Equalization Suit: A Case of Action in Quest of A Forum

Daniel Wm. Fessler
Christopher N. May

Though by no means conclusive, the posture of the United States Supreme Court assumed over the past 40 months suggests that the tide of judicial activism has abated. Among the vessels likely to be marooned on the shores of these receding waters is the municipal service equalization suit. Two factors, beyond the inconclusive nature of this premise, suggest that the topic of service equalization efforts pursued via the processes of litigation deserve contemporary interdisciplinary consideration by students of metropolitan governance.

First, the client pressure for reform of those conditions that reference the "right" from the "wrong" side of the tracks will, notwithstanding the trends of macro legal development, continue to mount. Second, the fundamental change accomplished within the past decade in distributing for the first time litigating and counselling armaments to the urban have-nots, renders almost certain of fulfillment the prediction that assaults upon the status quo will supplement if not supplant the more traditional (and traditionally ineffective) forms of political action.

It is the purpose of this chapter to make a tentative assessment of the nature and strength of these potential combatants; to survey the front for indications of impending attack; to assess at least the short term probabilities of success or failure of such tactics; and to draw upon our direct experience for some lessons of potentially general application regarding the impact upon the personnel and institutions of metropolitan governance of first the threat and then the reality of a civil suit.

THE "NEIGHBORHOOD LAW OFFICE" vs.
CITY HALL

Two factors presage this potential clash; neither has influenced the governance scheme in the past. On the one hand we have as a nation completed two solid decades in which the judiciary has shown marked tendency to depart from the stereotyped "passive coordinate branch" and assumed an activist role in sharpening for debate, and then attempting to resolve, macro social problems. The publicity that attended the "Warren Court," and the local reaction to the school desegregation, voting rights, and free speech litigation, demonstrated beyond the ability of even the least perceptive to forget that the courthouse was the eye of a social storm. Though perhaps belatedly owing to a general lack of sophistication, that message has now crossed the tracks and has excited the expectations of the politically neglected and socially disadvantaged.

Skeptics may note that episodes of judicial activism, though on an admittedly lesser scale, have obtained in the past, and yet the law reports do not bear witness to a wave of litigation aimed at engaging the forces of local government. This leads to an appreciation of the second phenomenon. Until this hour the economically deprived have lacked the ability to bring their grievances to the judicial forum for the sufficient reason that they were unable to command the services of an advocate. Today such an enforced muteness emphatically no longer obtains. As many incumbent mayors have already discovered, city hall in Anytown, U.S.A. is confronted by the potentially dynamic fusion of social expectations increasingly assuming a prayer for judge ordered reform combined with a yearly more numerous segment of the bar resident in and committed to righting the wrong side of the tracks. It cannot be overstressed that this combination is absolutely unprecedented in the experience of the Republic.

THE COMBATANTS

Should a monument ever be erected to the "Poverty Law Movement," it will doubtless commemorate the date 1965. In that year, with the inclusion of comprehensive civil legal services as one of the Community Action Programs of the Office of Economic Opportunity, financial resources in heretofore undreamed dimension were placed at the disposal of the chronically starved "legal aid" concept. The idea that legal assistance would benefit—and, for that reason, ought to be rendered to—the economically disadvantaged was not new. Beginning in the 1870s, there had slowly spread among the nation's urban centers a charitable effort under the auspices of which those few attorneys who seriously held the ideals of their profession might undertake a one-to-one relationship with nonfee paying clients questing for relief from individual problems.

While some legal aid offices were manned by salaried staff, most functioned with parttime volunteers. With little coordination or continuation, these ad hoc efforts were incapable of generating a vision of the problems, let alone innovating in the direction of solutions for the disadvantaged as a client class. It is no detraction from the record of accomplishment of this period to conclude that it was physically, temperamentally, and financially incapable of any reform effort aimed at the conversion of policies and practices that had evolved into de facto or de jure institutions.

The impact of the post-1965 OEO programs has been (1) a tenfold increase in the level of financial support; (2) a restructuring and standardization of the service delivery vehicle; and (3) a redefinition of the goals of legal assistance from a one-to-one treatment of the symptoms of socioeconomic deprivation to a reform effort aimed at restructuring those institutions and conditions that habitually oppress the economically deprived as a class. "Legal Aid" has undergone a metamorphosis and emerged as "Legal Services."

A further description of the nature and mission of the new service delivery vehicle will suggest that an eventual confrontation with city hall was inevitable. Perceiving the inherent weakness of the unstructured legal aid effort, OEO funds were awarded only to those grantees who, by contract, agreed to provide the following:

1. Projects were required to decentralize their operations and to open permanent and easily accessible *neighborhood law offices* in areas of client residential concentration.

2. Projects were required to subscribe to the mandate to engage in a broad program aimed at reforming both civil and administrative practices that adversely affected the poor.

3. Regarding the representation of individual clients, the traditional model of the lawyer-client relationship was, insofar as it was possible, to be retained.

4. The grantee project was charged with the development of a law reform effort that would contribute to the economic development of the community served by the provision of legal skill to community enterprises.

5. The total services program was to include efforts at preventative legal education.

6. In order to preserve the integrity of the neighborhood community, the OEO funded legal services project was specifically empowered to provide advice and representation to organized groups in the community served.

Thus from their inception these requirements have envisioned a community based, neighborhood promoting services project destined to sharpen a perception of grievances shared within a defined economic stratum and geographic concentration. Nearly a decade later, amid a loud chorus of complaint by state and local officials, it would appear that this initial vision has been fulfilled. Notwithstanding the express provision for a traditional lawyer-client representation of the individual, the mission to seek broad ranging reform of the causes of common complaint has produced a preference for class actions wherein representative clients seek wholesale judicial relief on behalf of all persons similarly situated within the community.

The cumulative impact of these developments has produced a new area of legal specialization—poverty law. Interest has spread beyond the range of government sponsored programs to influence the curricular offerings and emphasis of the contemporary law school and to reshape the activities and interest of the private bar.[1] The emergence of alternative sources of representation indicates no departure from one central factor. The presence of zealous advocates has summoned an expectation from within the populace resident on the wrong side of the tracks that reform is possible. The pressures so harnessed in turn become the motivation of attorneys who are skilled at but one capacity—seeking relief through the threat of and ultimate reality of litigation.

Arrayed in opposition to this gathering momentum are those lawyers who serve as "corporation counsel" or "city attorneys." While holding the initial advantage of organization and an established posture within the governance framework, the typical office of the corporation counsel is unprepared for a strenuous litigation campaign. Finding that his time is consumed with ordinance drafting, contract negotiations, and an occasional eminent domain dispute, the routine demands upon the time and talents of the city attorney do not include substantial trial experience. Rarely, if ever, will his official duties have taken him to a federal court. With his staff deployed in the discharge of established functions, a significant number of "law reform" cases have caught counsel for the defense armed with little more than the substantial advantage of institutional inertia that forms a natural barrier to assaults upon the status quo.

MUNICIPAL SERVICES THE MOST LIKELY TARGET

In 1972, Resources for the Future published the second in a series of collected monographs produced by a Study Group in the Governance of Metropolitan Regions. Documented in that volume is an assertion that we can all affirm by substantial suspicion: to wit, that the politically powerless and economically disadvantaged bear the most oppressive burden of blighted housing, inadequate transportation, substandard schools, and inferior governmental services.

Given the now completed deployment of a litigating capacity, in theory any of these grievances can form the basis of a "law reform" suit. In practice, city hall can anticipate that it offers the most vulnerable target when sued over disparities in both the quantitative and qualitative rendition of direct governmental services. When the complaint centers upon discrimination in such basics as sanitary sewerage, potable water, street lighting, traffic control, or garbage collection, the responsibility of the municipal government is primary. Neither federal nor state policies or funds can be substantially implicated, and their absence as codefendants greatly simplifies the scope of the litigation. Given these practical considerations, and acknowledging the need to structure the following theoretical discussion of "the law," we have centered this portion of our analysis around the general model of a municipal services equalization suit.

THE SERVICE EQUALIZATION SUIT

Both commentators and litigation strategists agree on the end to be sought: a mandate for a meaningful measure of equality in qualitative and quantitative distribution of existing municipal services.[2] Prominent among such services, though by no means an exhaustive list, are the following: (1) paving, surfacing, and maintenance of streets; (2) curb and gutter installation and maintenance; (3) street lighting and traffic control; (4) recreational facilities; (5) garbage collection; (6) water for domestic consumption and fire protection; (7) domestic utilities; (8) fire fighting services; and (9) police patrols.

The Theoretical Approaches to Reform and Relief

There are three candidate theories that historical experience and contemporary preference suggest as potential vehicles for an equalization effort. Two of them involve federal constitutional claims; the third is a state law approach. Within the context of federal constitutional law we consider both the Equal Protection and Due Process Clauses of the Fourteenth Amendment, with the Equal Protection Clause receiving the major emphasis. In the area of state law, we examine the potential utility of state constitutional claims and the relatively unnoticed and nearly forgotten doctrine, the so-called "common law duty of equal and adequate services." Finally, in assessing the probable chances for success or failure of the law reform effort, we note some problems of forum selection and touch briefly upon questions of federal jurisdiction, pendant jurisdiction over state law claims, and the abstention doctrine.

Federal Constitutional Law Claims

Jurisdiction. It must first be recognized that any claim for relief predicated upon an alleged violation of the Federal Constitution can be asserted before either a state or federal court. However, the selection of a federal constitutional claim is usually an indication of preference for a federal forum. If such a tactic is adopted by the litigating attorney, the first task is to secure federal jurisdiction over what at first glance seems to be the essence of a "local" dispute. Jurisdiction will normally be asserted on the theory that the cause of action is a "civil rights case."[3] A plaintiff proceeding under the terms of these provisions may seek relief both at law and in equity. Furthermore, jurisdiction cannot be defeated upon a showing that the plaintiff has failed to exhaust available local remedies before commencing the federal litigation.[4]

The Equal Protection Theory. The essence of an equal protection claim can be easily summarized. If one can demonstrate the fact of substantial disparity in either the quality or quantity of municipal services provided to identifiable classes of citizens (such as by neighborhood) within the same community by either the municipal government or its assign, a potentially viable equal protection claim can be established. Thus plaintiffs can be expected to allege that the municipal corporation, acting through its elected and appointed officials, had practiced—and under local custom or usage continued to practice—discrimination in the provision of municipal facilities and services based on the economic status and geographic location of its citizens.[5]

To such a complaint, the municipality can be expected to reply either that there is no inequality since neighborhood needs differ; or, as is more likely the case, that such inequality as does exist is the unintended consequence of a need to establish local priorities in the expenditure and conservation of insufficient resources. Plaintiffs can further anticipate that this "business judgment" defense will be buttressed by the allegation that in the "master plan" for community development it is necessary to begin at some point, and that a temporary disparity between the services in these initially improved areas and the rest of the community is reasonable, if not unavoidable.

Faced with this type of defense, the viability of an equalization suit will vary in direct ratio to the stringency of the standard utilized by the reviewing court. It is in the formulation or adoption of this standard that the most critical phase of the litigation occurs. At this juncture, the court assumes either a passive or aggressive posture, and adopts or rejects a historical pattern of presumptions favoring the regularity of governmental actions and their constitutionality. If the plaintiffs can qualify their service equalization suit for an application of the "strict review" standard, their chances of ultimate success are excellent.

There are two avenues. A pattern of discrimination, which either is predicated upon a "suspect classification"—*McDonald v. Board of Election Commissioners of Chicago*, 394 U.S. 802, 807 (1969)—or trenches upon a "fundamental personal interest" of the disfavored citizens—*Reynolds v. Sims*, 377 U.S. 533, 561-62 (1964)—is "invidious"; and a violation of the Equal Protection Clause is established unless the defendant can justify its conduct through the vindication of a "compelling governmental interest." *Shapiro v. Thompson*, 394 U.S. 618, 634 (1969). A failure to qualify for the strict review standard will nearly always prove fatal to this type of litigation.

Absent the "new equal protection" (the strict review standard), recourse is made to the traditional standard under which a reviewing court will sustain a governmental practice if it can be rationally related to any (even speculative or imagined) legitimate governmental purpose.[6] In *Shapiro*, the Court specifically held that conservation of the local fisc was not a "compelling governmental interest," although it was assuredly legitimate.[7] Since the conservation of chronically insufficient public funds will be the major theme in nearly every answer to a municipal service equalization complaint,[8] it should not require the perception of the greatly experienced to realize that the question of selecting the standard of review is a conclusive, not a preliminary, stage of equal protection litigation.

The posture of a service equalization case vis-à-vis the already established criteria for attaining the strict review standard is not encouraging. It seems doubtful that the Court, which has expressly refused to find in public assistance benefits (which it had previously recognized as constituting the "very means to subsist, food, shelter, and other necessities of life,") a fundamental personal interest,[9] will be willing to sweep the enumerated municipal services into this rather ad hoc category.[10] In *Dandridge v. Williams*, 397 U.S. 471, 484-85 (1970), the majority expressly equated the constitutional status of "social welfare" legislation and substantive regulation with that of "state regulation of business or industry." *Id.* As such, Maryland's maximum grant regulations for recipients of Aid to Families with Dependent Children (AFDC) were to be reviewed under the "old" or "passive" standard, by the terms of which " '[a] statutory discrimination [would] . . . not be set aside if any state of facts reasonably may be conceived to justify it.' "[11]

As the dissent of Mr. Justice Marshall indicates, the state's only justification for this classification in the trial below was the conservation of its limited resources. However, the majority of the Court approved another rationale, which the state had wisely added on appeal: "It is enough that a solid foundation for the regulation can be found in the State's legitimate interest in encouraging employment and in avoiding discrimination between families of the working poor." *Id.* at 486. Therefore, it should be anticipated that a governmental unit that urges in a municipal services suit justifications other than conservation of the public fisc—e.g., special geographical or topographical problems of the blighted area, special traffic patterns, or long range planning considerations—may well be rewarded for its efforts. For as the Supreme Court has stated: "The problems of government are practical ones and may justify, if they do not require, rough accommodations—illogical, it may be, and unscientific."[12]

Superficially, the "suspect classification" route would appear more promising. If the disparity in the provision of municipal services coincides with the racial composition of the favored and disfavored neighborhoods, a classically sanctioned application of the most stringent reviewing standard is in order. Indeed, from the vantage point of theory, we will suggest that only in the presence of clearly demonstrable racial discrimination would we encourage the use of a federal constitutional theory and a federal forum to resolve a service equalization suit.[13] Yet reform litigation, if it is to be successful, must survive the passage from theory to a workable judicial hypothesis—the transition from law reviews to law reports.

Before discussing the current attempts to effect this passage, a general observation seems appropriate. The prosecution of municipal service equalization suits as variants of a racial discrimination pattern limits the effective scope of this litigation to only those communities wherein demonstrably segregated housing patterns can be isolated and the respective levels of service provision compared in a particularized evidentiary showing. The problem, however, is far more universal than the incidence of either de facto or de jure racial discrimination. Equal protection, if it can get us no farther than this, cannot offer a potential for relief coextensive with the dimension of the problem.

Finally, there is the fact that in its most recent Terms the Supreme Court has turned aside what were at least colorable bids for the suspect criteria routes to the strict review standard. While it is probably too early for grounded speculation, it is obvious that a refusal to recognize a particular evidentiary showing as being sufficient to warrant the new equal protection permits the Court to decline further active law reform involvement without the embarrassment of repudiating the recent history of intervention on a variety of sociopolitical fronts.[14]

Perceiving the limited utility of racial discrimination, proponents of equal protection strategies have suggested that future litigation place primary reliance upon classifications drawn along lines of economic wealth as an alternative suspect criterion. Such a strategy in service equalization litigation offers a substantial advantage, in that economic discrimination will permeate the record of nearly every case that documents the history of disparity in the rendition of municipal services on the wrong side of the tracks. This advantage of potential universality must be discounted by a realization that wealth has not incurred the same degree of infamy as an inherently suspect basis of classification.[15] True, the Court has declared that "... a careful examination [of the disparity in the respective levels of treatment] is especially warranted where lines are drawn on the basis of wealth *or* race ... two factors which would *independently* render a classification highly suspect and thereby demand a more exacting judicial scrutiny."[16]

Asserted in a dictum, such a broad statement is a departure from solid precedent. The statement by Chief Justice Warren in *McDonald* cannot overcome the fact that in no case has the Court ever found in the fact of economic discrimination, standing alone, an invidious classification. The concept that a citizen's race should be an absolute constitutional irrelevancy not only harmonizes with the Court's recognition of the main purpose of the Fourteenth

Amendment, but also seems eminently sound.[17] To contend for the same degree of condemnation each time the government takes account of a citizen's economic position is to assume a posture that cannot be sustained on either hard judicial precedent or long established sociopolitical assumptions.

This is not to say that access to those fundamental interests which depend upon the state for their protection and provision ought ever to be conditioned on the respective ability of a citizen to pay for a "fair trial" or the "right to vote." Such seems to have been the conclusion of the Supreme Court of California which, after a long discussion of the status of "wealth as a suspect classification," declared that: "Until the present time, wealth classifications have been invalidated only in conjunction with a limited number of fundamental interests—rights of defendants in criminal cases (citations omitted) and voting rights (citations omitted)." *Serrano v. Priest*, 487 P.2d 1241, 1255 (1971). Beyond the absence of judicial precedent, there is the fact that some economic considerations that enjoy official government sanction (such as approved tariff regulations) qualify or burden the exercise of the "fundamental personal right of interstate travel." This will be so until the principle of capitalistic provision is eliminated from society—a development not likely to result from any judicial mandate.

Analysis of the rationale that has motivated the Supreme Court to hold wealth a suspect criterion vis-à-vis the machinery of criminal justice and the franchise would seem to suggest a perception that inherent in these two areas are functional means to the achievement or preservation of constitutionally protected rights of "life, liberty, and property." An attempt to qualify municipal services as partaking of a comparably fundamental nature should succeed only if it can be demonstrated that they serve the same functional role in preserving the individual against unacceptable encroachments by the collective society in general and the government in particular. Ranked in terms of this function, municipal services would span a continuum ranging from police and fire protection as practical equivalents to the more esthetic interests in a municipal band shell or public landscaping project.[18]

Given the context of a municipal service equalization suit, there is no question but that the citizen must depend upon the government for provision. The fact of direct governmental provision, or the alternative system of provision by an assign enjoying a de jure monopoly, marks a basic departure from reliance upon a free market economy. It is equally certain that discrimination in the provision of municipal services can be attacked in a civil rights suit, and as such is subject to review under the Equal Protection Clause of the Fourteenth Amendment. The major obstacle to widespread utility of this theory is, as noted, the apparent unavailability of the strict review standard, without which the assertion of a denial of equal protection is effectively emasculated.[19]

The judicial developments reviewed thus far could be termed by some future historian as evidencing the rise and fall of the new equal protection.

It would appear to be the unfortunate fate of municipal service litigation to have emerged at a period when the doctrine is in a state of decline. One further development must be noted before leaving the topic of equal protection, and that is the possibility that the Court may be in the process of creating a third standard with which to gauge the propriety of judicial intervention.

In November 1971 the Court was faced with a challenge by Mrs. Sally M. Reed. The gravamen of Mrs. Reed's complaint was that the substantive law of Idaho discriminated against women citizens in a statutory provision which declared that as between persons equally qualified to administer estates, males must be preferred to females. In seeking judicial intervention, Mrs. Reed took the position that "sex" was a "suspect" criteria as invidious as race or religion. The State of Idaho denied this proposition and asserted that the challenge mounted by Mrs. Reed ought to be turned aside under the noninterventionist or "traditional" standard of equal protection analysis. In the state's view, the statutory preference for male executors could be tied to the legitimate governmental goal of simplifying the matters of probate procedure within the Idaho courts. This rationale was found persuasive by the Supreme Court of Idaho, which dismissed Mrs. Reed's claim.[20]

On appeal, the United States Supreme Court, speaking through Mr. Chief Justice Burger, reversed.[21] The Burger opinion found it unnecessary to decide the broad ranging question of whether or not "sex" is an inherently "suspect" basis for legislative classification. While it made no observation on the point, the Court was obviously aware of the vast implications inherent in adding "sex" to the very short list of criteria which, with only one exception, have mandated that the government can never prevail.[22] Seeking to avoid the lockstep determinant of standard selection, the Burger opinion places the Idaho statute under the traditional analysis, but then goes on to grant relief.

If a third standard has arisen in the resolution of *Reed v. Reed*, it was accomplished by amending what has struck some as the most offensive aspect of the noninterventionist approach: that of sustaining a state classification if it could be rationally linked to any, even hypothetical, legitimate governmental interest or goal. As redefined by the Chief Justice, the Fourteenth Amendment denies states the power to

> . . . legislate that different treatment be accorded to persons placed by a statute into different classes on the basis of criteria wholly unrelated to the object of that statute. . . . A classification must be reasonable, not arbitrary, and must rest upon some ground of difference having a fair and substantial relation to the object of the legislation, so that all persons similarly circumstanced shall be treated alike.[23]

The Idaho probate classification fell because, in the Court's opinion, the state had failed to demonstrate a "fair and substantial relation" to the legitimate governmental goal of reducing the complexity of judicial process.[24]

Whether *Reed v. Reed* signals the emergence of a third standard, and whether such a standard would advance or retard the success of municipal service equalization suits grounded upon an alleged deprivation of equal protection, remains an object of speculation. The Court's subsequent decisions in *Rodriguez* and *Lindsey* suggest that analysis continues to respond to plaintiffs' attempt to gain the "new equal protection." In both cases there is no evidence that plaintiffs' lawyers had the opportunity to avail themselves at trial of contentions predicated on the then too recent decision in *Reed*. All that can be stated with certainty is that in neither *Rodriguez* nor *Lindsey* did the Court volunteer an analysis under the "fair and substantial relation" test.

Due Process

A constitutional law theory, free from any question of classification or standard selection, is the concept of due process. Again, the essentials of such an action are easily conceptualized. If a particular service is rendered in neighborhood A, but not in neighborhood B, and if the residents of neighborhood A pay no compensatory user charges for their privileged status, then the taxpayers in neighborhood B are in a position to contend that they are not receiving a fair return on their taxes. Assuming that the service in question is provided out of the municipality's general fund, the claims of the nonserved residents look quite appealing. The matter is not that simple. Aside from the formidable question of *standing* to bring a taxpayer's suit, the city might meet the claim on the merits.[25]

A defendant municipality might answer a services suit brought on behalf of the economically disadvantaged by pointing out the fact that the favored neighborhood (A) consists of very substantial dwelling units that provide the bulk of the property tax revenues raised by the municipality, whereas the residences or improvements in neighborhood B have little assessed valuation and thus yield only a minor input into the general fund. If the service in question is city supported landscaping of parkways that divide main residential streets, the case would be further complicated if all such parkways are found in neighborhood A and none in neighborhood B.

While we might wish that this defense—if it is to be accepted at all—be limited to luxury services, on the plateau of due process the "you get what you pay for" psychology is difficult to avoid.[26] The question of what would be a "fair market return" to the residents of neighborhood B, given the amount of their tax input into the service supporting fund, will seldom yield an "equalizing" answer when the comparison is between the substantial and prosperous neighborhoods of a municipality and the decayed or ghetto areas of that same entity. The goal of qualitative and quantitative equality, to the extent that it requires a functional redistribution of goods and services, will achieve only limited actualization through any contemporary notion of due process.

Implicit in these remarks is the opinion that where the residents of the apparently favored neighborhood actually do pay compensatory user charges for the admittedly higher level of municipal services provided in their privileged enclave, a due process action pursued by a class of nonassessed and nonserved residents will not be successful. A closer question would be presented if the complainants had been given no opportunity to purchase the service. This would sound more in the area of a denial of a "liberty to participate" than in the deprivation of the complainants' "property" without due process. In addition, it should be noted that actions claiming a deprivation of due process exacted through a disproportionately small return on taxes levied have a history of little success. One suspects that the visceral hostility to such a complaint is the desire to avoid the "supermarket" concept of individual service selection all at the expense of the commonwealth norm.

Finally, and perhaps most important, there is the question of a remedy that would most naturally comport with a due process theory. It would not seem to be an extension of existing services, but rather a remedy of tax abatement or territorial detachment. Tax abatement may yield very little direct return for residents of the wrong side of the tracks; territorial detachment, in the context of municipal service equalization suits, is the exact opposite of a desirable result.

THE INITIAL EQUALIZATION EXPERIENCE

Sweeping pronouncements regarding the likely fate of attempts to employ litigation as a means to reorder local practice and policies in the rendition of governmental services are of little value. The desire for a certain forecast is hopelessly at odds with the evolutionary process whereby judge made law is spun out and posited. Nevertheless, initial results are now a matter of public record, and through an understanding of these developments we may gain a measure of insight regarding the factual contexts and litigation strategies most conducive to judicial intervention.

First, some general observations. Civil rights suits designed to secure a judicially ordered equalization of existing municipal services have, to date, been inaugurated before federal courts in Mississippi, Alabama, Tennessee, New York, and South Dakota.[27] In each instance the judgment of a United States District Court was solicited on the theory that the qualitative and quantitative inequality in the rendition of municipal services was but another manifestation of constitutionally forbidden racial discrimination, violative of the Equal Protection Clause of the Fourteenth Amendment.[28]

A further common factor is that each was filed as a class action, wherein relief was sought not only for the named plaintiffs but for "all other persons similarly situated" within the defendant's territorial jurisdiction. A distinguishing strategy of potential importance will be observed in that while some of these suits attempted to assail alleged inequality in a broad range of local services, others singled out a particular service as a discrete target for judicial relief.[29] Finally, while it is true that communities of relatively small populations have attracted a majority of the existing equalization suits, both Chattanooga and New York City have become sites of vigorous contests.

Because it was the first case to survive appellate scrutiny, *Hawkins v. Town of Shaw* enjoys current primacy in the annals of service equalization efforts. A contrast between the reception given by the United States District Court for the Northern District of Mississippi, where the suit was dismissed with prejudice, and the reversal of that judgment by the Court of Appeals for the Fifth Circuit, is instructive of the attitudinal and doctrinal limitations that inhere in a federal constitutional approach. In company with other named plaintiffs, Andrew Hawkins asserted a class action on behalf of disadvantaged black citizens of Shaw, Mississippi. Plaintiffs' case consisted of an allegation that there existed in Shaw a long standing practice, custom, and usage according to which black and white residents, who lived in patterns of clear-cut housing segregation, received a grossly disparate treatment in the rendition of city supplied services. With the exception of police and fire protection, nearly every service was covered by the complaint.

To these allegations, plaintiffs added an elaborate series of statistics that documented the objective facts of disparity in both the levels and varieties of services available to Shaw's black and white citizens. A bid for the strict standard of federal equal protection analysis was predicated upon the issue of statistical disparity, which plaintiffs alleged could only be rationalized on a theory of de facto racial discrimination. No effort was expended in contending that the services represented any sort of fundamental citizens' interest. In the District Court the *Shaw* case was effectively lost when this bid for the strict standard was rejected by the trial judge.[30]

Given the tenor of plaintiffs' pleadings and proofs respecting the presence of discrimination based upon race, the decision of the trial judge to apply the noninterventionist standard of equal protection analysis was palpable error, and the Court of Appeals has now twice so held.[31] Writing for the original panel, Judge Tuttle concluded that the evidentiary showing presented to the trial court, standing in the absence of direct confrontation by the defendant, was of sufficient probative strength to enable the Court of Appeals, itself, to proceed to an application of the strict review standard. Thus scrutinized, the failure of the defendants to make out the presence of some compelling governmental interest served by the pattern of racial discrimination required the court to enter a broad ranging equalization decree. As framed by Judge Tuttle, that decree required the Town of Shaw to present for approval by a federal judge a plan designed to "equalize" both the quantitative and qualitative rendition of its municipal services.[32] Following reargumentation before all sixteen judges, this order was affirmed en banc.[33] No appeal to the United States Supreme Court was attempted.

Prior to the reversal of *Hawkins*, the net result of three municipal services suits, after full evidentiary trials, was the decree desegregating a jail and courthouse restroom facility in Belzoni, Mississippi,[34] and the court ordered expenditure of municipal funds to equalize the facilities and equipment in one small park.[35] Thus not a single governmental "service" has been successfully attacked. The tendency of the federal trial judiciary was to restrict relief to the occupation and enjoyment of community facilities on the strength of an analogy to public schools.

Three lines of defense accounted for plaintiffs' sparse success. The municipal officials in both Shaw and Belzoni, Mississippi, contended that an evidentiary demonstration of the fact of disparity in the levels of service provided black and white residents was insufficient to make out a violation of the Equal Protection Clause, absent a further showing of "bad faith." Both trial courts agreed and, upon receipt of sworn denials that racial discrimination had been intended, used this factor as a basis for dismissal.[36] A second line of defense was to admit that past practices had resulted in discriminatory patterns of service provision, but to allege that such practices had been recently abandoned in favor of good faith, though as yet unsuccessful, efforts to administer municipal services on a colorblind basis.

Such a defense was successful for the officials of Prattville, Alabama. Judicial acceptance of such a proposition regarding the provision of street lighting led to a denial of relief notwithstanding the explicit concession by all parties that contemporary levels of service as between black and white residents were not equal. A good faith effort to attain that goal was accepted as constitutionally sufficient.[37] Finally, the Prattville litigation revealed the first encounter with the defense that the services in question were not financed out of general tax revenues, but were allocated under a scheme of betterment assessments and user fees.[38] Upon this rationale the court was able to conclude that differences in consumer preference, rather than racial discrimination, accounted for the uncontroverted statistical disparity in the levels of service as between black and white neighborhoods.

The fate of these defensive positions following reversal of the judgment in *Hawkins* is of primary significance. The first defense, the one that sought to inject an issue of defendants' motive as an element of plaintiffs' case, has been ruled irrelevant to any constitutional issue. Where racial discrimination is the alleged result, the *Hawkins* appeal has held any issue of motive on the part of the defendants immaterial.[39] The fate of the second defense (that of the good faith effort), and of the third (that general tax revenues do not support the service in question) remains clouded. Influenced by the *Hawkins* reversal, the most recent federal litigation in Alabama has held the absence of present discriminatory practices not to constitute a defense to an equalization suit where the impact of past discrimination remains uncorrected.[40]

Yet in the same year a federal judge in South Dakota dismissed an action brought on behalf of the native American residents of "Indian Town" that sought injunctive relief and monetary damages for alleged racial discrimination in the provision of numerous municipal services. In a variation of the second defense, the defendant municipality contended that since the inception of the litigation various steps had been "voluntarily" taken, which had the effect of mooting the controversy since they had corrected the deficiencies.[41] This nonsouthern case also provides strong evidence of the continued vitality of the third defense—that the services in question are not provided out of an expenditure of general tax revenues but are rendered in response to citizen initiation and special financing assessments.

Without offering any definition of the term, the court distinguished between those services that were governmental and those "improvements associated with property ownership."[42] Like the pre-*Hawkins* decision regarding the City of Prattville, the municipal fathers in Winner, South Dakota, were rewarded for their assertion that certain of the services included in plaintiffs' complaint were provided in response to citizen initiation and special assessment or betterment fees. The presence of such a financing scheme detracts from the prima facie showing that racial discrimination is the explanation accounting for the disparate levels of service. While the court did not reach the point, absent the presence of a showing of racial discrimination the strict review standard of equal protection analysis was unavailable to plaintiffs. Dismissal was inevitable.

Issues of finance and public expenditure dominated a fourth discernible line of defense, which became prominent in the only nonsouthern services equalization suit to gain appellate review. Put in a sentence, the issue in *Beal v. Lindsay* was a working definition of "equality."[43] Plaintiffs, black and Puerto Rican residents of the Crotona Park neighborhood in New York City, commenced a class action seeking declaratory and injunctive relief predicated upon allegedly inferior equipment, facilities, services, and repairs in their park when contrasted with the park facilities maintained by defendant in predominantly white neighborhoods. The city did not deny that the "output" or results of its effort to maintain the Crotona Park left it in a condition inferior to that of those parks to which plaintiffs referred. But defendants contended that on the "input" or expenditure side they had obligated equal, if not greater, sums of public monies on Crotona Park and that such input equality satisfied the dimension of their constitutional duty.

The admitted output disparity was explained with reference to the high crime and vandalism factor, which substantially diminished the benign product of the city's efforts. In affirming the District Court's dismissal of the complaint, the Second Circuit Court of Appeals justified its satisfaction with input equality in the face of proof of output disparity in the levels of service available to classes of citizens on pragmatic grounds. "In these early days of developing the implications of *Town of Shaw*, it seems wiser, particularly in view of the difficult problems with respect to remedy, generally not to go beyond requiring equality of input. . . ."[44]

From this survey of the federal judicial response to these initial class action complaints further generalizations seem warranted. Thus:

While in theory any service for which the defendant bears governmental responsibility may be included in a complaint, the greatest chance for judicial intervention obtains where a single service is targeted rather than a wholesale assault on the service package. Reasons both evidentiary and attitudinal support this result. First, if the case is limited to a single service such as public park facilities or street paving, the proofs are correspondingly limited and rendered susceptible of manageable documentation. Second, the enforcement task of a willing court is rendered much easier if the decree need cover but a single service rather than assuming jurisdiction over the entire service function of the municipal government.

Regarding the nature of the services themselves, we detect a greater willingness to remedy disparity in the provision of physical services where the per unit allocation can be statistically documented. Included in such a list would be street paving, lighting, traffic control apparatus, sewerage, etc. Since the constitutional command is for "equality" rather than "adequacy," the reviewing court can utilize numerical tests both in passing upon the merits of the complaint and in framing a decree for relief.[45] Soft services such as police and fire protection are most difficult to document with statistical evidence. *Maye v. Lindsay* underscores this point.[46] Again, the defendant was the City of New York. The class action assailed a claimed racial discrimination in the level of fire protection accorded plaintiffs' neighborhood when contrasted with the protection given white areas.

Although the case has not yet reached a final disposition, plaintiffs' motion for a preliminary injunction to restrain defendants from certain announced reorganizational moves within the fire department was refused. The federal judge underscored his belief that plaintiffs had failed to discharge their burden of proof that disparity in effort to protect was in fact present. While conceding that plaintiffs were able to allege a greater incidence of fire loss in their neighborhood, the court remained skeptical that from this fact alone there could be deduced the critical conclusion of racial discrimination. Unlike the street paving record presented in *Selmont*, the court could not determine on a unit by unit basis the physical disparities.

Provision of services in response to betterment assessments or user fees confers limited immunity against equalization decrees. The fact that the services of which complaint is made are not provided out of general tax revenues but are apportioned on the basis of special assessments has two debilitating effects upon plaintiffs' claim. First, it offers an alternative rationale to explain the statistical fact of disparity in the levels and kinds of services received by different neighborhoods within the same community. As such it can defeat attainment of the prima facie case of racial discrimination upon which the strict review standard is dependent. Second, since the claim is for "equality," it would seem that the constitutional burden is discharged when the municipal government stands ready to offer the service upon tender of the requisite fee or fusion of the minimum number of users.

Uncertain is the fate of such a defense where the original services to the advantaged neighborhoods were made out of general tax revenues, while in recent years the municipality has shifted to a requirement of dedications or special assessments to cope with the problems of physical expansion. In *Selmont* the court ordered an expenditure from general tax revenues to correct the disparity resulting from past discrimination. Thus if the complainants are residents of a neighborhood that was in existence at the time of the initial provision of service and that was then neglected, *Selmont* suggests strongly that a subsequent switch to a user financing scheme is not a defense, and that equalization efforts will be ordered out of general tax funds (see *infra*). If the plaintiffs reside in an area constructed or annexed since the changeover in fiscal policy, their right to provision out of general tax monies is to be doubted.

Consonant with their preference for facility of proof and simplicity of a remedy, the federal judiciary can be expected to settle for input equality as constituting a satisfactory discharge of the constitutional obligation not to discriminate. Requiring an equality of "output" or result is too difficult to attain and is viewed as involving burdens of supervision and control inimical to the long range interests of either federal/local comity or the already burdened workload of the national judiciary.

Passing from these more specific observations to the broader question of the judicial climate for a confrontation between the poverty law movement and city hall, what conclusion can be advanced from this record of less than warm receptivity to equal protection claims in quest of an equalization of municipal services? We can suggest but tentative answers. Viewed from the vantage point of a federal district judge, efforts to make a "federal constitutional case" out of street lighting or sewerage maintenance practices of a given community encounter both conscious and unconscious natural resistance.

Surely the experience with school desegregation is at least partially responsible for a noticeable judicial reluctance to further exacerbate what are perceived as already strained federal-state relations in the South. Indeed, those familiar with the early school desegregation cases will perceive shadows of that experience in the reception given those seeking judicially mandated equality in the rendition of municipal services. Even with the absolute mandate from the

Supreme Court in the *Brown* cases that educational segregation was unconstitutional, the federal district courts acting as courts of equity were loath to place school districts under injunctions.[47] Until corrected upon appeal, district judges required of black plaintiffs a showing of "bad faith" on the part of the governmental unit as a condition precedent to justiciability. In the Dallas litigation alone it took four separate remand orders from the Fifth Circuit Court of Appeals before the first injunction was entered in 1960.[48] Furthermore, all the administrative difficulties encountered in restructuring educational facilities after a century of discrimination spelled continuing jurisdiction and judicial supervision until the transition was finally complete.

The considerations that militated against judicial enthusiasm for scrutinizing local programs and effectuating school desegregation are all present in municipal services equalization suits. First there is the cardinal rule of federal equitable jurisdiction, that federal-state-local friction is to be minimized by weighing the private rights of the individual with the public interest before wielding the ultimate and extraordinary sanction of the injunction.[49] Certainly an equalization suit appears to be the essence of a "local matter." The enforcement of a decree seems to pose the unsettling prospect of the court's attempt to act as a receiver for a plethora of decisions it has neither the expertise nor the inclination to assume. There is the spectre of the endless host of such cases. Not only is the political water chilly, but at this juncture one cannot even plumb its depth.

Although initial judicial reluctance to entertain school desegregation cases was overborne, one cannot predict with any decent odds that the same fate will be shared by service equalization efforts. There is no Supreme Court mandate in these cases, nor is there likely to be if current ideology is projected. Without such an imprimatur, it is a better bet that district courts will avoid wholesale involvement with a condition that stretches into nearly every city and town in the land. All these attitudinal difficulties can apparently be overborne if the factual record in a given case yields to no other conclusion but that the disparities fall with regular and greatly disproportionate harm upon members of one race. Two decades of involvement with school desegregation and allied causes have brought the federal judiciary to the point wherein the "invidious" nature of these de facto classifications cannot be doubted. If the letter of this rule cannot be questioned, the high Court's attitude in *Jefferson* and *Rodriguez* indicates that its spirit may be eroded by simply refusing to recognize or lend credence to evidence that suggests that in fact a racial classification has been the result.[50]

Yet the federal courts will continue to play a critical role in future municipal services equalization suits. Judicial reluctance to play the part, particularly at the district court level, hardly warrants concluding that the drama has ended. New remedies are available to plaintiffs in their encounter with city hall, remedies that may strongly encourage municipalities to equalize their services rather than risk battle in the courts. Moreover, if the federal forum proves a reluctant host to all save the complaints of blatant racial discrimination, it does not follow that the poverty law movement is stymied, or that city hall is safe. Demonstration of this point carries us to our next topic.

RAISING THE STAKES IN MUNICIPAL SERVICES LITIGATION

The eight municipal services cases that have been reported to date[51] were all filed in federal court, and all sought declaratory and injunctive relief against particular legal practices alleged to be unconstitutional. However, in one case, *Fire v. City of Winner*[52], the plaintiffs were more ambitious: in addition to seeking declaratory and injunctive relief, they sued the city and its officers for damages in excess of $12,000.

Though the plaintiffs in *Fire* were unsuccessful in their bid for damages[53], the presence of the damages claim had an interesting effect upon the litigation. As the court found, the defendants made many substantial improvements in the plaintiffs' part of town

> ... subsequent to the commencement of this lawsuit. . . . [W]hile there may have been some neglect on the part of the City of Winner with respect to those improvements normally financed by the city's general fund, namely, adequate culverts and drainage ditches, street lights and fire hydrants, the deficiencies were corrected prior to the trial of this matter. . . .[54]

Thus, in order to moot the controversy—and to reduce the likelihood that damages would be awarded against them—the city officials voluntarily complied with the vast majority of plaintiffs' demands, and did so within a relatively short period of time.[55] While the court's decision is silent as to the cost of making the various improvements, their very nature suggests that the cost must have been substantial.

Of equal significance is the fact that the suit against the City of Winner was not a class action and was not based upon claims of racial discrimination.[56] Rather, the suit claimed simply that the services provided in "Indian Town" were inferior and unequal to those available in the rest of the city. We have noted earlier that, to date, the courts have been much more receptive to equalization suits founded upon racial discrimination than to those based simply upon a denial of equal protection. The pure equal protection case, however, is far from dead. The *Fire* litigation indicates that at least one municipality, when faced with a damages claim of more than $12,000, was unwilling to risk a trial in a straight equal protection case, and instead found it expedient to improve all the general fund services that were challenged.

Fire v. City of Winner may well be a harbinger of things to come.

The groundwork for municipal services equalization suits was laid by a handful of cases that attempted no more than to halt patterns and practices of inequality. The successes—particularly *Hawkins v. Town of Shaw*[57]—have paved the way for future suits that will significantly increase the stakes for the defendant governmental entities while challenging inequalities much less visible than those involving racial discrimination.

Moreover, the growing tendency of the courts to assess losing defendants with plaintiffs' attorneys' fees in suits to vindicate federal rights will greatly improve the ability of disgruntled citizens to bring suit against governmental entities, while at the same time substantially increasing the risks of suit for the defendant public entities. Though all the reported municipal services equalization suits have been brought in federal court, it can be anticipated that as the potential for damages actions is expanded, more and more such cases will be filed in state courts to avoid jurisdictional and class action restrictions, which are applicable only in the federal forum.

The Award of Attorneys' Fees as Incentive to Sue and Incentive to Settle

By definition, municipal services equalization litigation involves a class of citizens who live in a part of town where the quantity and quality of governmental services are inferior to those provided elsewhere. Excepting those eccentric millionaires who deliberately choose to "slum it," the citizens who live in these underserviced areas are the poor and the lower middle class; often they consist largely of racial and ethnic minorities.

The ability of these indigent citizens to bring legal action against local governmental entities is severely impaired by their limited access to legal services. Private attorneys are generally unwilling and unable to handle major litigation without some assurance that they will be compensated for their time. Publicly funded legal services attorneys, while available on a nationwide basis to the poor and while willing to handle cases that are not fee generating, are often too busy and understaffed to handle major affirmative litigation. Thus it is not surprising that since 1969 there have been only eight reported municipal services equalization suits in the entire United States.[58]

Recently, however, the courts have begun awarding attorneys' fees to successful plaintiffs in suits brought to vindicate constitutional and statutory rights.[59] The courts have held that such fees, which must be paid to plaintiffs' counsel by the losing defendant, may be awarded to OEO funded legal services attorneys and to private "public interest" attorneys, even though they do not charge their clients for their services.[60]

Moreover, the courts have required the payment of attorneys' fees even in situations where there is no applicable statute authorizing such an award. The courts have justified such awards on the theory that plaintiffs, by vindicating the rights of a large number of persons other than themselves, have acted as "private attorneys general" in effecting important congressional and public policies.[61] The private attorney general rationale is particularly applicable in the context of municipal services equalization suits, where the action is founded upon the Constitution and the Civil Rights Act, and where there is seldom statutory authorization for the award of attorneys' fees.

While it does not appear that attorneys' fees have been awarded in any of the municipal services suits brought to date, in none of those cases did plaintiffs seek such an award. This may have been due to the fact that the right to attorneys' fees in such cases has only recently matured, as well as to a reluctance on the part of plaintiffs to ask the court for too much at a time when the legal basis for the equalization suit was itself uncertain. There can be little doubt that in future services equalization suits, the courts will award attorneys' fees to successful plaintiffs who request them, for courts have awarded such fees against public bodies in numerous cases—the fees in some instances exceeding $50,000.[62]

The significance of these recent decisions awarding attorneys' fees in public interest cases is threefold. First, and most important, the availability of attorneys' fees will enable private attorneys to litigate municipal services equalization claims on behalf of poor and low income clients who are themselves unable to pay counsel. As the government funded legal services movement risks emasculation or extinction at the hands of Congress, it is of vital significance that a new pool of lawyers, not dependent upon the government for their survival, now have a financial incentive to move into the field. To the extent that the legal services program does survive, the availability of attorneys' fees will help offset the substantial cost of preparing and litigating a municipal services equalization suit, thus making the handling of such cases considerably more attractive.[63]

Second, the prospect that a court will award successful plaintiffs generous attorneys' fees should operate as a deterrent to illegal conduct by state and local governmental bodies. The availability of attorneys' fees not only increases the likelihood that illegal conduct will be judicially challenged, but that if successfully challenged, that the governmental entity will be liable for a substantial fee in addition to whatever other monetary and injunctive relief the court may order. Indeed, the courts have recognized that the award of attorneys' fees to plaintiffs in actions vindicating federal statutory and constitutional rights is partially punitive in nature.[64]

Finally, the availability of attorneys' fees, like the threat of damages in *Fire v. City of Winner,*[65] should provide the defendant governmental entity with a powerful incentive to settle the case rather than await the outcome of contested litigation. An important factor that the courts have considered in awarding attorneys' fees is the extent to which the defendant has opposed the action; thus a vigorous but unsuccessful defense may be cited by the court as the principal ground for its decision to award plaintiff generous attorneys' fees. This is particularly true where the state of the law has become settled and defendants should therefore have known that their practices were illegal. For example, in *Gates v. Collier*,[66] a suit challenging unconstitutional practices in the Mississippi State Penitentiary at Parchman, the court stated:

> [W]e have no difficulty in finding that defendants' actions were unreasonable and obdurately obstinate. From commencement of the suit . . ., defendants staunchly denied the existence of unconstitutional practices and conditions at Parchman. . . . The position thus consistently maintained by defendants compelled plaintiffs' attorney to expend time and expenses which otherwise would not have been incurred. . . . [T]his suit was necessary only because of defendants' unreasonable refusal to comply with accepted constitutional principles. We are further convinced that the unnecessary delay, extraordinary efforts, and burdensome expenses incurred incident to the resolution of this case were occasioned because of defendants' maintenance of their defense in an obdurately obstinate manner. Thus, plaintiffs' attorney is entitled to reasonable fees and expenses [of $52,736.05].[67]

The constitutional parameters of municipal service equalization suits are now well established. Municipalities and local governmental entities have been put on notice that the Constitution requires equal distribution and availability of publicly offered services. In future equalization suits, the courts, even if they do not award damages, are more than likely to assess defendant governmental entities a substantial sum for plaintiffs' attorneys' fees.[68] In many cases, the costs of complying with plaintiffs' demands may be far less than the cost of unsuccessfully defending a lawsuit.

The Award of Damages Against
Local Governments

The municipal services equalization cases that have been reported as of this writing all involved federal court actions brought pursuant to the Civil Rights Act, 42 U.S.C. § 1983.[69] Although § 1983 allows a plaintiff to recover damages for a violation of constitutional rights,[70] none of the equalization cases sought monetary relief under this provision.[71]

The failure to seek money damages was undoubtedly due in part to the Supreme Court decision in *Monroe v. Pape*[72], which held that a municipality may not be sued for damages under § 1983. However, even under § 1983, as we shall discuss below, damages may be obtained against local governmental officials for violation of plaintiffs' constitutional rights. In addition, recent developments suggest that damages are also available in such cases under principles of state law, as well as directly under the Constitution itself.

There is little doubt that the availability of damages in municipal services equalization litigation will exert a strong deterrent effect upon local governments in the provision of services. In addition, as with attorneys' fees, the chance that damages may be awarded to a successful plaintiff will provide defendant governmental entities with a major incentive to settle claims of alleged constitutional inequality rather than risk a trial on the merits.

42 U.S.C. § 1983

The Supreme Court has severely restricted the applicability of 42 U.S.C. § 1983 in suits involving local governmental entities. As noted, the court has held a municipality is not a "person" within the meaning of § 1983 for purposes of a suit for damages. More recently, the court held that a municipality is similarly exempt from suit under § 1983 where only declaratory and injunctive relief are sought.[73] For a time, it appeared that these exemptions might be narrowly restricted to municipalities, allowing § 1983 damage actions to proceed against other nonmunicipal public entities.[74] However, in *Moor v. County of Alameda*,[75] the Supreme Court made it clear that even a county is not a "person" within the meaning of § 1983, and held that a county cannot be sued under that section even though under state law it is vicariously liable for the wrongs of its employees.

Insofar as declaratory and injunctive relief are concerned, the effect of these recent Supreme Court decisions will be merely cosmetic: instead of suing the governmental body[76], it will be necessary for plaintiffs to bring the action against the public officials themselves.[77] An injunction is equally effective whether it is directed to the city or to its officers and employees.[78]

The impact of these decisions with respect to damages claims, however, is far more substantial. If plaintiffs have been harmed by the unconstitutional conduct of local governmental entities, they are far less likely to obtain financial redress if their only choice is to sue the individual officials rather than entities themselves. As a practical matter, public employees and officers will often be judgment proof.[79] In addition, the deterrent effect of damages is probably much more effective when the entity itself is liable, rather than its employees; for the entity has the power to assure that similar violations will not recur.

Nevertheless, if the damages sustained are not astronomical, plaintiffs in many cases may be able to obtain effective relief by suing the individual officers and employees who are directly responsible for the unconstitutional discrimination involved. The courts have held that plaintiffs in such cases may recover both nominal and punitive damages, even if no actual damages have been sustained—i.e., plaintiffs need not show that they have suffered pecuniary harm as a result of defendants' conduct in order to recover money damages.[80]

While local officials are not immune from suit under § 1983, they may enjoy a "qualified privilege" that will protect them from liability in certain limited situations. The question of immunity and privilege is determined by federal common law; state statutes and state common law governing such matters are not controlling.[81] The courts have held that some state and local officials are not liable for discretionary acts undertaken in good faith.[82] However, this is a very limited discretionary immunity and does not protect an official who has abused his discretion or acted in an arbitrary, capricious, or unreasonable manner.[83] The immunity is one that the courts have held should be "applied sparingly."[84] Moreover, the Supreme Court has indicated that the "qualified immunity" that officers of the executive branch of government enjoy is one that varies "dependent upon the scope of discretion and responsibilities of the office. . . ."[85] Officials at the municipal level of government are thus likely to enjoy much less immunity than their state counterparts.

In a recent municipal services equalization suit, one federal court rejected a claim of good faith action and qualified immunity, finding that it was unnecessary for plaintiffs to prove that defendants' conduct was intentional.[86]

> "Equal protection of the laws" means more than merely the absence of governmental action designed to discriminate, as Judge J. Skelly Wright has said, "We now firmly recognize that the arbitrary quality of thoughtlessness can be as disastrous and unfair to private rights and the public interest as the perversity of a willful scheme."[87]

The court thus intimated that local officials may be held liable in damages for conduct that is unintentional but that is the product of a negligent disregard for the rights of plaintiffs.

In actual practice, the courts have found many local officials liable in damage under § 1983, including members of school boards, administrators of school districts, county health officials, and employees of building departments.[88] However, it may be necessary to sue such officials in their individual capacities as well, in order to obtain damages against them. This is due to the fiction created by the Supreme Court in *Ex Parte Young*,[89] to the effect that when a public officer acts in an unconstitutional manner, he is no longer functioning in his official capacity.[90] At least one court dismissed a § 1983 damages action due to plaintiffs' having sought money damages against defendants "solely . . . in their official capacities. . . ."[91]

The Fourteenth Amendment

The Fourteenth Amendment to the United States Constitution prohibits the state and its subdivisions from denying any person the equal protection of the laws. Recently, the United States Supreme Court held that an action for damages may be brought to vindicate the abridgment of constitutionally protected rights; such an action arises directly under the Constitution and does not require any act of Congress expressly authorizing it. *Bivens v. Six Unknown Named Agents of Federal Bureau of Narcotics.*[92]

Bivens involved an alleged violation of a citizen's Fourth Amendment rights by federal agents. There was no statute, however, which authorized an action for damages against federal officials for their infringement of an individual's constitutional rights. Title 42, U.S. Code, § 1983, the statute that creates a cause of action for violations of constitutional rights by state officials, is inapplicable to federal agents. The question presented in *Bivens* was whether, in the absence of express statutory authorization, a damages action could be maintained for such constitutional violations.

In an earlier case, the Court had suggested that where "federally protected rights have been invaded, it has been the rule from the beginning that courts will be alert to adjust their remedies so as to grant the necessary relief."[93] However, the Court there declined to decide whether a damages action was proper. In *Bivens*, the Court resolved this question, holding that "[a] violation of [the Fourth Amendment] by a federal agent acting under color of his authority gives rise to a cause of action for damages consequent upon his unconstitutional conduct."[94]

The implications of *Bivens* for municipal services litigation are far-reaching. Just as Congress had failed to provide an express damages remedy for unconstitutional conduct by federal officials, it has likewise failed to provide a remedy for similar conduct by local governmental entities; in both instances, 42 U.S.C. § 1983 precludes monetary redress against these defendants.[95] Under the rationale of *Bivens*, local governmental entities that violate the Fourteenth Amendment rights of its citizenry, may be themselves liable in damages directly under the constitutional provision.

Though *Bivens* involved only rights protected under the Fourth Amendment, the principle it enunciated has been extended to violations of rights guaranteed by other constitutional amendments; there appears no reason why the courts will refrain from similarly applying it to violations, by state and local entities, of the Fourteenth Amendment.[96] As one authority has suggested:

> *Bivens* may be read as resting upon a premise that constitutional rights have a self-executing force that not only permits but requires the courts to recognize remedies appropriate for their vindication. Under such a view, the failure of Congress to authorize suits against the Treasury may no more bar a judicially created remedy than the failure of Congress to create a cause of action against the officers barred the development of that particular remedy in *Bivens*.[97]

This view is supported by the concurring opinion of Mr. Justice Harlan in *Bivens*, in which the justice stated quite simply that "federal courts do have the power to award damages for violation of 'constitutionally protected interests'. . . ."[98] There was no suggestion that these interests were limited to those protected by any particular constitutional provision.

The federal courts are empowered by 28 U.S.C. § 1331 to take jurisdiction over any matter that "arises under the Constitution" of the United States, and that involves an amount in excess of $10,000. It was under this provision that the court took jurisdiction in *Bivens.*[99] It has long been held that equitable relief is available to protect constitutional rights in suits brought pursuant to this jurisdictional provision,[100] and in Harlan's view, a damages remedy should be equally available.

> [I]f a general grant of jurisdiction to the federal courts by Congress is thought adequate to empower a federal court to grant equitable relief for all matters of subject-matter jurisdiction enumerated therein, see 28 USC § 1331(a), then it seems to me that the same statute is sufficient to empower a federal court to grant a traditional remedy at law.[101]

Actions to protect rights under the Fourteenth Amendment's Equal Protection Clause are as much within the scope of § 1331 as are suits arising under the Fourth and Fifth Amendments. In each case, the Court, once having subject matter jurisdiction, should be able to grant whatever relief is appropriate, including damages.

The application of *Bivens* to Fourteenth Amendment rights would resolve the problem, created by *Monroe v. Pape* of obtaining damages against local governmental entities, where those bodies have violated the Constitutional rights of their citizens.

> The *Bivens* decision leads to the rather striking conclusion that Section 1983 may simply be unnecessary. Money damages, as well as equitable relief, may be obtained in suits founded directly upon the Constitution. If it is "appropriate" or "necessary" for the victim of an unconstitutional exercise of official power to have a remedy that will make good the wrong done, then it seems wholly appropriate to afford a remedy against a local treasury....[102]

The Supreme Court in *Bivens* did not reach the question of what immunities, if any, could be raised as a defense by the federal defendants. Justice Harlan, in his concurring opinion, observed that:

> ...*at the very least*, such [damages] remedy would be available for the most flagrant and patently unjustified sorts of [official] conduct. Although litigants may not often choose to seek relief, it is important, in a civilized society, that the judicial branch of the nation's government stand ready to afford a remedy in these circumstances.[103]

On remand, the Court of Appeals for the Second Circuit severely restricted the defenses available in suits arising directly under the Constitution. The Court held that the defendants "have no immunity to protect them from . . . suits charging violations of constitutional rights"[104]; according to the Court, the only defense available to defendants in such a case is to

> . . . allege and prove that the [officials] acted in the matter complained of in good faith and with a reasonable belief in the validity of the arrest and search and in the necessity for carrying out the arrest and search in the way the arrest was made and the search was conducted.[105]

It is unclear what defenses would be available to state defendants sued directly under the Fourteenth Amendment. It would seem that at most, such defendants would enjoy no better immunity than the courts have found applicable in cases arising under the Civil Rights Act. However, the fact that federal defendants have been granted absolutely no immunity in suits arising under the Constitution suggests that local governmental entities and officials may find themselves more vulnerable in actions arising under the Fourteenth Amendment than in Congressionally authorized suits under the Civil Rights Act.

State Tort Law
As we indicated earlier, in only one municipal services equalization suit did the plaintiffs seek damages in addition to declaratory and injunctive relief. *Fire v City of Winner.*[106] The claim for damages in that case was based upon a state tort law theory and was for an amount in excess of $12,000. While the District Court dismissed the damages claim as improperly pleaded, it is quite probable that future municipal services litigation will involve damages claims similar to that raised in *Fire.*

The emergence of a tort law basis for damages suits against local governmental entities parallels the gradual decline of sovereign immunity in this country over the past twenty years. The rule originally allowed an entity acting in a "governmental" capacity to claim immunity from suit in any action for damages brought by its citizenry. Certain activities of public entities, however, were classified as "proprietary," and could give rise to governmental liability in damages. The judicially created distinction between "governmental" and "proprietary" activities became hopelessly confused and illogical,[107] to the point where many courts and legislatures simply abrogated the doctrine of sovereign immunity and in its place established a legislative scheme providing for governmental liability in certain enumerated classes of cases.[108] Under these legislative tort claims systems, the usual rule was to create immunity for "discretionary" acts by governmental officials.[109]

In at least one state, the legislature has abolished sovereign immunity totally and without exception. Article II, § 2 of the Montana Constitution, as adopted in 1972, states unequivocally that: "The State, Counties, Cities, Towns, and all other local governmental entities shall have no immunity from suit for injury to a person or property."[110] The Illinois Constitution abolishes sovereign immunity "except as the General Assembly may provide by law."[111]

With the substantial inroads upon sovereign immunity, it becomes possible to frame a tort law claim against local governmental entities for the violation of federal and state constitutional rights. The success of such a claim will necessarily depend heavily upon the state of the law in the particular jurisdiction involved; obviously, Montana, which has abolished all sovereign immunity, is much more favorable than is, for example, Pennsylvania, which still maintains the "governmental-proprietary" distinction.

Under well established principles of tort law, the violation of a duty created by statute, ordinance, or appellate decision gives rise to a presumption that the party upon whom the duty rested was guilty of negligence; and unless the presumption is rebutted, that party is liable for any damages proximately caused by his act or omission.[112] This principle has been codified in some jurisdictions and is directly applicable to governmental bodies. Thus, for example, the California Tort Claims Act provides as follows:

> § 815.6 *Mandatory duty of public entity to protect against particular kinds of injuries.* Where a public entity is under a mandatory duty imposed by an *enactment* that is designed to protect against the risk of a particular kind of injury, the public entity is liable for an injury of that kind proximately caused by its failure to discharge the duty unless the public entity establishes that it exercised reasonable diligence to discharge the duty.[113]

The California Supreme Court has liberally construed this provision to hold a county liable for failing properly to supervise its employees, where the employees both violated and coerced others to violate various provisions of state and federal law.[114]

There is nothing in § 815.6 to suggest that the word "enactment" would not include the equal protection provisions of the United States and California Constitutions. There is no question that these provisions impose upon state and local governmental officials a mandatory duty not to discriminate in the provision of public services.[115] The California Law Revision Commission Comment to § 815.6 states that "enactment" includes not only statutes but also regulations. The American Law Institute's Second Restatement of Torts suggests that even ordinances and appellate court decisions might be included within the provision.[116] If this is the case, then certainly state and federal constitutional prohibitions must likewise give rise to governmental damage liability.

Even under a narrow reading of the California law[117] and of the general rule it has codified, the violation of constitutionally imposed duties will usually give rise to a negligence claim against the governmental entity. In nearly every jurisdiction, state and local governmental officials are required *by statute* to uphold the Constitution of the United States and of the particular state involved. Thus, in California, Government Code § 1360 requires public officials to bear such allegiance, and the California courts have held the requirement to be binding upon state as well as local employees.[118] Consequently, if a local official engages in conduct that violates the federal or state Constitution, he has likewise violated a duty imposed upon him by statute, and the entity may be liable under accepted principles of tort law.

It should be noted that unlike damages actions based upon 42 U.S.C. § 1983 or arising directly under the Constitution itself, claims for monetary relief under a tort theory are completely subject to state immunity rules. In some states these rules may be more liberal than the federal common law, while in others they will be more restrictive. In addition, as a general principle, punitive damages are not available in an action brought under a state tort theory.[119] Thus, depending upon the jurisdiction in question, there may be certain disadvantages to using a tort theory.

THE PLAINTIFF'S CHOICE OF FORUM: FEDERAL OR STATE COURT?

All the municipal services litigation to date has been filed in federal court. This fact reflects the generally accepted belief that for purposes of vindicating federal constitutional rights against state encroachment, the federal forum is far superior to a state court. The Supreme Court has itself recognized some of the reasons for this federal preference:

> It is abundantly clear that one reason the legislation [Section 1983] was passed was to afford a federal right in federal courts because, by reason of prejudice, passion, neglect, intolerance, or otherwise, state laws might not be enforced and the claims of citizens to the enjoyment of rights, privileges, and immunities guaranteed by the Fourteenth Amendment might be denied by the state agencies.... It is no answer that the state has a law which if enforced would give relief.[120]

Federal judges are not only more experienced at dealing with constitutional claims, but they are also less vulnerable to political pressure; federal judges effectively enjoy life tenure, whereas many of their state counterparts may be removed at the polls if their decisions meet with disfavor in the community.[121]

Municipal services litigation, if it is successful, may result in a drastic reordering of local governmental priorities, and require the expenditure of considerable sums to redress the effects of prior inequalities.[122] For these reasons it is probably no exception to the general rule that federal constitutional claims against state and local authorities are best brought in a federal district court.

Unfortunately, the federal courts are courts of limited jurisdiction. They may only hear cases expressly authorized by Act of Congress. In contrast, the state trial courts are courts of general jurisdiction; they not only may, but must, entertain all legitimate claims, whether they arise under state or federal law. And there is a presumption that a state court has the power to hear any particular claim.[123] Even in those instances where Congress has given federal courts jurisdiction to hear certain types of cases, the state courts have concurrent jurisdiction to hear the same claims if suit is filed there, unless Congress has expressly provided to the contrary.[124] Thus, all the municipal services equalization suits which were filed in federal court could have instead been filed in the appropriate state court, including those arising under the Civil Rights Act, 42 U.S.C. § 1983. The Supreme Court has held that a state court may not refuse to take jurisdiction over such claims except in very unusual circumstances,[125] and also that the state court must, in taking jurisdiction, grant all the relief to which plaintiffs are entitled, including, if necessary, money damages.[126]

State Courts for State Constitutional Decisions

Before we consider the extent to which federal courts have jurisdiction over municipal services suits, one caveat is in order. The Equal Protection Clause of the Fourteenth Amendment, which has been the basis for all the equalization litigation to date, has been subject to some narrowing by the U.S. Supreme Court.[127] Consequently, plaintiffs seeking declaratory and injunctive relief against inequities in the distribution of services may find it to their advantage to base their cause of action on the equal protection provisions of federal and state constitutions.

The constitutions of virtually every state contain the equivalent of the federal Due Process and Equal Protection Clauses.[128] If plaintiffs challenging the allocation of municipal services allege that the manner of distribution violates both the federal and the state constitutions, a favorable ruling by the state court[129] based in whole or in part on the state constitutional ground is nonreviewable by the U.S. Supreme Court, except where the state constitution is found to have denied rights protected by the federal Constitution.[130] Thus, if the state constitution grants plaintiffs greater rights than they might enjoy under the federal Equal Protection Clause, a favorable decision based upon the state provision cannot be reversed by the Supreme Court.

The California Supreme Court has used this device on several occasions to protect rulings that might otherwise have been jeopardized by the U.S. Supreme Court. In *Department of Mental Hygiene v. Kirchner*,[131] the state Supreme Court held that California's relative responsibility statute, which required the parents of an institutionalized mental patient to pay for the patient's care and maintenance, violated the Equal Protection Clause. The state appealed to the U.S. Supreme Court, which vacated the decision and remanded the matter to the state tribunal for clarification as to whether the decision was based upon state or federal constitutional grounds; in its remand order, the U.S. Supreme Court stated that "we would have jurisdiction to review only if the federal ground had been the *sole* basis for the decision or the State Constitution was interpreted under what the state court deemed the compulsion of the Federal Constitution. . . ."[132] In its decision on remand, the California Supreme Court certified that its decision has been founded on the independent equal protection provisions of both the federal and state constitutions.[133] Accordingly, the decision was not subject to review by the U.S. high court.

Similarly, in *Rios v. Cozens*,[134] the California Supreme Court declared unconstitutional the state's procedures for revoking the driver's license of uninsured motorists who were involved in an accident. A federal court in California had previously declared the same procedures to be in conformity with the U.S. Constitution; however, when the state decision was appealed to the U.S. Supreme Court, it vacated and remanded the matter for clarification as to the basis for decision.[135] In its decision on remand, the state Supreme Court certified that its decision had been independently based upon both the federal and state constitutions, and review by the U.S. Supreme Court was again precluded.[136]

These examples, while not exhaustive, suggest that poverty plaintiffs seeking to vindicate their rights vis-à-vis state and local governments should make careful use of the choice given them to select the forum in which they wish to litigate. As the climate in the Supreme Court becomes less temperate, and as more and more obstacles are erected along the path to the federal courthouse steps,[137] the state courts present an alternative arena that may be relatively more hospitable to their interests than it has been in the past.

Bases for Federal Court Jurisdiction

In some instances a plaintiff may have no choice but to bring the action in state court. There are rights guaranteed by federal law, including rights under the federal Constitution, that may be enforceable only in state courts. In order for federal court jurisdiction to exist, and for a plaintiff to thus have a choice of forums, the action must fall within one of the limited bases of federal jurisdiction. We shall consider the possible federal jurisdictional bases for causes of action that arise under 42 U.S.C. § 1983, under the Fourteenth Amendment, and under state tort law.

Claims Arising Under 42 U.S.C. § 1983

Federal courts have jurisdiction over all constitutional claims arising under the Civil Rights Act by virtue of 28 U.S.C. § 1343(3) and (4),[138] without regard to the amount in controversy. While it is uncertain whether there is federal jurisdiction under these provisions for § 1983 claims involving only federal statutory as opposed to constitutional claims,[139] all the municipal equalization suits that have been or are likely to be brought include, inter alia, claims based upon violations of federal constitutional rights. Accordingly, plaintiffs in such cases will always have the right, if they so choose, to file in federal court.

Claims Arising Under the Fourteenth Amendment

As we discussed above, actions may not be brought against a local governmental body—as distinct from its officers and employees—under the terms of 42 U.S.C. § 1983. Accordingly, to state a claim against the entity itself, it may be necessary to assert a cause of action directly under the Fourteenth Amendment. It is conceivable, but unlikely, that federal courts would have jurisdiction over all such actions. Title 28, U.S. Code, Section 1343(3) does provide on its face for federal jurisdiction over all claims alleging deprivation "of any right, privilege, or immunity secured by the Constitution of the United States. . . ."[140] This language would appear to give the courts jurisdiction over claims arising under the Fourteenth Amendment. However, the history of 28 U.S.C. § 1343(3) reveals that it was originally part of Section 1 of the Civil Rights Act of 1871,[141] which specifically limited its applicability to cases authorized by 42 U.S.C. § 1983. In other words, 28 U.S.C. § 1343(3) was the jurisdictional counterpart to § 1983; the two sections were split up in 1875 solely for purposes of codification.[142]

This history strongly suggests that a federal court might not have jurisdiction under 28 U.S.C. § 1343(3) over cases not within the scope of 42 U.S.C. § 1983. In the context of municipal services equalization units, this would mean that § 1343(3) gives federal courts jurisdiction only over Fourteenth Amendment claims against the officers and employees of local governmental entities, and not over claims against the entity itself. As we discussed earlier, such suits against local governmental entities are not authorized by 42 U.S.C. § 1983.[143]

Accordingly, Fourteenth Amendment claims against public entities would have to be brought in state court, unless another independent basis of federal jurisdiction exists. For claims exceeding $10,000, exclusive of interest and costs,[144] jurisdiction would exist under 28 U.S.C. § 1331(a), which provides for federal jurisdiction in any case satisfying that amount in controversy and which "arises under the constitution, laws, or treaties of the United States."

Satisfying the $10,000 requirement may be more difficult than would first appear. The Supreme Court has held that it is not sufficient merely to allege that amount in controversy; rather, plaintiff may have to prove this amount before the court may proceed to hear the case.[145] In addition, if the suit is to proceed as a class action, the named plaintiffs must each individually satisfy the $10,000 requirement,[146] and the unnamed members of the class must each do likewise.[147] Neither the individual nor the class plaintiffs may aggregate their claims in order to satisfy the jurisdictional requirement, except in special cases where the plaintiffs have a common interest in the funds not dependent upon their individual claims. For this reason it may be very difficult to bring a federal class action to litigate Fourteenth Amendment damages claims against public entities.

In measuring the amount in controversy, the usual method is to look to the amount of damages that plaintiffs claim to have sustained. However, in a suit against a governmental entity for declaratory and injunctive relief, the amount of plaintiffs' actual damages may be negligible; even in a suit for damages, it might be difficult to prove individual harm exceeding $10,000.

However, a number of courts have recognized that "The amount in controversy is determined not merely by the pecuniary damage to the plaintiff, but also the value of the rights they seek to protect."[148] In the case of most municipal services, the rights in question are intimately tied to the health and safety of the public. Measuring the amount in controversy in terms of the potential harm to these interests should easily satisfy the jurisdictional requirement. As one court has stated, "Certainly the right to exist in society as relatively healthy people is worth more than $10,000."[149]

Another possible approach is to measure the amount in controversy from the defendant's rather than plaintiff's point of view. In other words, rather than looking to the harm the plaintiff has or will suffer, the amount in controversy is measured by the cost to the defendant of equalizing the distribution of municipal services. Quite obviously, the difference in approach could make a drastic difference. A single individual plaintiff may be able to show only $10 damages from discrimination in the provision of public recreational facilities, say, but the cost to the city of equalizing those facilities could very easily exceed $10,000. A number of federal courts have recognized the propriety of measuring the amount in controversy from the defendant's viewpoint:

> [I]n determining the matter in controversy, we may look to the object sought to be accomplished by the plaintiff's complaint; the test for determining the amount in controversy is the pecuniary result to either party which the judgment would directly produce.[150]

If this view were more widely accepted, it would provide a ready basis for federal jurisdiction in municipal services equalization cases.

If it is not possible to allege or to prove an amount in controversy exceeding $10,000, a federal court might still take jurisdiction over a Fourteenth Amendment claim against a governmental entity under the doctrine of pendent jurisdiction. Under this doctrine, whenever there is a claim "arising under the Constitution [or] the laws of the United States" over which the federal court may take jurisdiction, it may take jurisdiction over accompanying state and federal claims as to which it would not have independent jurisdiction, if the jurisdiction conferring claim and the pendent claim derive from "a common nucleus of operative fact."[151] This test would be satisfied in any municipal services case where a claim against the municipality under the Fourteenth Amendment was pendent to a claim under 42 U.S.C. § 1983 against the city's officials or employees. The court would have jurisdiction over the latter claim under 28 U.S.C. § 1343(3) regardless of the amount in controversy, and the claim against the entity would arise from the identical facts as the jurisdiction conferring claim.

Pendent jurisdiction is not mandatory, but rather lies within the sound discretion of the court.[152] Where the pendent claim brings in a new party not involved in the jurisdiction conferring claim, some courts have declined to exercise pendent jurisdiction.[153] The Supreme Court has quite strongly suggested, however, that at least insofar as pendent federal claims are concerned, the exercise of federal jurisdiction over pendent parties is entirely proper.[154]

Claims Arising Under State Tort Law

The sole basis for federal jurisdiction over state tort law claims brought by a citizen against the local governmental entity in which he resides is under the doctrine of pendent jurisdiction. If such a state law claim stands alone, a federal court is precluded from taking jurisdiction over it. If, on the other hand, it is accompanied by a jurisdiction conferring claim, such as a § 1983 cause of action against individual government officers, a federal court, in its discretion, could take jurisdiction over both claims.

Such a use of pendent jurisdiction was attempted in *Moor v. County of Alameda*,[155] in which plaintiffs coupled a § 1983 cause of action with a state tort law claim for damages. The trial court refused to exercise pendent jurisdiction over the state law claim, and the U.S. Supreme Court affirmed. The pendent tort claim in that case was against the county, which was not (and could not be) a party to the § 1983 claim over which the court did have independent jurisdiction. Because the state law claim against a "pendent party" involved solely questions of state law, the court held that it was proper for the district court to have declined jurisdiction. The pendent claim against the county would have involved "difficult questions of California law upon which state court decisions are not legion"; with the special defenses that would be available to the county in defending against that claim, the Court ruled that by exercising pendent jurisdiction, the case "could become unduly complicated."[156]

A similar fate befell the pendent state law claim in the only municipal equalization suit in which such a claim has been made. In *Fire v. City of Winner*,[157] plaintiffs coupled a § 1983 claim against the city's officers with a tort law claim against the city itself. The district court found the latter claim to have been defectively pleaded, but went on to hold that even had the claim been properly alleged, the court would have declined to exercise pendent jurisdiction over it.[158]

This refusal to exercise pendent jurisdiction over state law claims, particularly where they are asserted against pendent parties and involve complex or relatively new questions of state law, is consistent with federal abstention practices. Ordinarily, a federal court will abstain from deciding a controversy over which it may take jurisdiction if the case presents novel or difficult questions of state law that a state court has not had an opportunity to resolve.[159] For these reasons, it would appear unlikely that federal courts will readily exercise jurisdiction over damages claims against local governmental entities that arise under state tort law. Even where these claims are pendent to jurisdiction conferring claims against individual defendants, the federal forum is likely to remain unavailable, at least until such time as the state courts have more thoroughly explored the limits of municipal liability under developing tort law doctrines.

Class Actions in Federal Court

The published reports reveal that all the municipal services equalization suits that have thus far been filed[160] were brought as class actions. The class aspect is important in that it enables a group of disadvantaged citizens to pool their resources, including available legal assistance, in a single lawsuit that will redound to the benefit of all members of the class. Were the class action device unavailable, an individual lawsuit might result in no more than improved services for one family without affecting the quality of its neighbors' environment to any appreciable extent. If others wished to benefit, they would either have to intervene in the first lawsuit, or file a subsequent action of their own. The class action device provides a means of litigating common questions of law or fact in a single proceeding, avoiding the time and expense of a multiplicity of lawsuits all of which seek the same end. Moreover, without a class action, the prospects for recovering attorneys' fees are severely diminished, due to the fact that the number of persons benefited may be too insignificant to warrant the recovery of such fees under the private attorney general theory.

The United States Supreme Court, in a very recent decision, has seriously curtailed the use of class actions where the action seeks to recover money damages on behalf of the class. In *Eisen v. Carlisle & Jacquelin*,[161] the court upheld the dismissal of a class action due to the named plaintiff's unwillingness and inability to notify each of the ascertainable members of the class individually concerning the pendency of the lawsuit. It was estimated that the class consisted of some six million persons, the names and addresses of more than two million of whom were ascertainable. The cost of providing individual notice by mail to each of these persons would have exceeded $315,000, while the named plaintiff stood to gain no more than $70 from the lawsuit;[162] moreover, the average benefit to each member of the class amounted to no more than $3.90.[163]

The size of the class in *Eisen* was much larger than that involved in most municipal services cases. Nonetheless, the size of the class in relation to the benefits to be obtained by the named plaintiffs is probably large enough to make such a notice requirement prohibitive. Thus, for example, the class in *Hawkins v. Town of Shaw*[164] consisted of 1,500 persons; in *Coleman v. Aycock*,[165] plaintiffs represented more than 2,500 people; in *Hadnot v. City of Prattville*,[166] the class comprised 2,200 persons. While the exact size of the class in *Beal v. Lindsay*[167] is not indicated, it was certainly large, consisting of all "indigent black and Puerto Rican residents of the Bronx." Were the named plaintiffs in each of these cases required to identify, locate, and then notify on an individual basis every member of the class, the suits probably could not have proceeded as class actions. The aggrieved plaintiffs in municipal services equalization suits are usually quite poor,[168] and are unable to afford costly notice requirements as a condition precedent to a class action lawsuit.[169]

GOVERNMENTAL ATTEMPTS TO AVOID LIABILITY

With the very strong likelihood that in future services equalization suits, local governmental entities will be sued for damages and attorneys' fees in addition to declaratory and injunctive relief, efforts may be made by these entities to avoid liability by attempting to shift the locus of responsibility for service provision.

For example, a municipality that currently provides certain services out of its general funds might begin to provide those services only on a user or assessment basis. The courts have held that where services are provided on a special assessment basis, and where any inequality is "due to the difference in the respective landowners' ability and willingness to pay for the property improvements," there is no equal protection violation.[170] However, in each of these cases the courts emphasized that the services in question "historically" had been provided on a special assessment basis,[171] and that the alleged inequality did not result from discriminatory conduct on the part of the city, but rather "stems primarily from the difference in the respective landowners' willingness to pay for the property improvements."[172] Thus it is unlikely the municipality could escape the legal consequences of prior discriminatory conduct simply by shifting to a special assessment system.

Another device that a municipality might employ in an effort to avoid liability for unconstitutional conduct would be to transfer those service functions it had previously performed to a private corporation or to a privately owned public utility.

The Fourteenth Amendment applies only to persons acting "under color of state law," and it is ordinarily inapplicable to the conduct of private parties. However, there are exceptions. The Supreme Court has held that where a private entity performs a "public function," the entity is subject to the same constitutional constraints as the public body itself. For example, a company town was held to be subject to the free speech requirements of the First and Fourteenth Amendments;[173] a private shopping center was held to have the same "public function" as a city business district and was therefore subject to the constraints of the Fourteenth Amendment;[174] a private "Jaybird Primary" was held to duplicate a traditional state function and was accordingly barred under the Fourteenth Amendment from excluding blacks.[175]

The "public function" doctrine, under which private conduct is brought within the scope of the Fourteenth Amendment, would apply to any attempt by local government to shift traditional public services functions to private entities and providers. Indeed, in ascertaining whether the private party is performing a "public function," the courts have often looked to whether there had been a recent transfer of control from the public to the private sector. In *Evans v. Newton*,[176] the Court held that a private park that was open to the public was subject to the Fourteenth Amendment, and in reaching its decisions, the Court emphasized that not only was the "predominant character and purpose of this park . . . municipal," but that until recently the park had been under the control and management of the city. According to the Court, the "tradition of municipal control had become firmly established"; and by merely relinquishing control and turning the park over to private parties, constitutional restrictions could not be circumvented.

These principles were applied in the context of a municipal services equalization in *Hadnot v. City of Prattville*,[177] where the district court held that the Equal Protection Clause was applicable to private parks due to their "municipal character," and due to the fact that the city was partially involved in their maintenance and upkeep. Accordingly, the court enjoined the city to equalize the "equipment, facilities, and services" provided in a private park located in a black neighborhood with those available in private parks of the city's white neighborhoods. Thus efforts to avoid constitutional proscriptions by transferring traditional governmental functions to the private sector are unlikely to succeed.

There is one device that may prove useful to municipalities, not so much for the purpose of avoiding constitutional liability but for spreading it. Municipalities that currently provide their own services might combine to establish special districts that furnish specific services to a much larger geographic area. Similarly, a municipality may contract with a county or state level public entity to supply services to its inhabitants. In these instances any discrimination in the provision of such services would in all likelihood not affect the municipality[178] but would give rise to liability on the part of the special district or other providing entity.[179] The larger entity would be better able to spread the cost of liability insurance and of any judgments recovered against it, and the burden on any particular municipality would be reduced.

Were the service district to expand to the point where it became a statewide or state level entity, plaintiffs claiming discrimination in the provision of services might be precluded from recovering monetary damages against such an entity in federal court. The Eleventh Amendment to the federal Constitution, as construed by the Supreme Court, bars a federal court from awarding damages against a state in a suit brought against it by a private citizen.[180] The Court recently held that this prohibition is applicable to retroactive compensation for benefits wrongfully withheld from a citizen by the state.[181] The Eleventh Amendment would similarly apply to damages suits brought to compensate for past inequities in the provision of services. Such a suit, however, could presumably be brought in the state court.[182] One court has held that if a state has waived immunity from suit under its tort claims act, the state may be sued for damages in the federal court, unless its tort claims act specifically excludes federal actions.[183] It should also be emphasized that the Eleventh Amendment restriction upon federal jurisdiction applies only to suits against the state and does not apply to actions brought against political subdivisions of the state, such as counties and municipalities.[184]

There is little that a municipality may do to avoid its constitutional obligation to provide services on an equal basis to its inhabitants. The devices of special assessment and transfer to private control have already been condemned by the courts in the municipal services and closely related contexts. The trend toward regionalism and the cooperative provision of traditional services by district, county, or even statewide entities will not preclude liability for unconstitutional conduct, but will simply require the naming of a different defendant, and one which may be better able to respond in damages than could a tiny municipality. Even where the discriminatory entity is a state level agency, and federal court jurisdiction is precluded by the Eleventh Amendment, a damages action on any of the bases discussed above may be litigated in state court.

CONCLUSION

The law of municipal services equalization was virtually unknown five years ago. In a relatively brief span of time, judicial challenges have been made to unequal patterns of distribution in the southern states and, more recently, in other parts of the country. With these challenges the law has developed to the point where cities and towns are now on notice that the Fourteenth Amendment will not countenance discrimination and inequality in the provision of basic public services.

The early efforts were conservative ones. Plaintiffs did not seek to be compensated for the physical deprivations and moral indignities inflicted by inadequate and unevenly distributed public services. Nor did their attorneys seek to be compensated for the hundreds of hours expended in litigating and ultimately vindicating the constitutional rights of their disadvantaged clients. The times have changed, however, and the stakes of the municipal services equalization game have been drastically increased. In future litigation, plaintiffs will not be content with merely declaratory and injunctive relief; they will seek and are likely to receive sizeable monetary judgments against public entities that have discriminated in the provision of essential services.

While the scope of the Equal Protection Clause may have been somewhat curtailed by the present Supreme Court, the risk of loss in an equal protection challenge has tremendously increased for defendant municipalities. For this reason we are optimistic as to the beneficial effects of municipal services equalization suits today and in the years just ahead. The dismissal of *Fire v. City of Winner* on the ground of mootness is a good omen.

Notes

Notes

Chapter One
Public Needs, Private Behavior, and
Metropolitan Governance:
A Summary Essay

1. Wallace Oates (Ed.), *Financing the New Federalism: Revenue Sharing, Conditional Grants and Taxation*, Washington, D.C.: Resources for the Future, 1975.

Chapter Two
Local Public Goods and
Residential Location: An
Empirical Test of the
Tiebout Hypothesis

1. Britton Harris, "Quantitative Models in Urban Development: Their Role in Metropolitan Policy-Making," in Harvey S. Perloff and Lowdon Wingo Jr. (Eds.), *Issues in Urban Economics*, Baltimore: Johns Hopkins Press, 1968, p. 393.
2. Charles M. Tiebout, "A Pure Theory of Local Expenditures," *Journal of Political Economy* (October 1956): 416-424.
3. Michael J. Ball, "Recent Empirical Work on the Determinants of Relative House Prices," *Urban Studies* (June 1973): 213-233.
4. See, for example, Wallace F. Oates, "The Effects of Property Taxes and Local Public Spending on Property Values: An Empirical Test of Tax Capitalization and the Tiebout Hypothesis," *Journal of Political Economy* (November/December 1969): 957-969.
5. See, for example, William Alonso, *Location and Land Use*, Cambridge, Mass.: Harvard University Press, 1965.
6. For a more rigorous formulation of the model described in this section, see

Stephen K. Mayo, "An Econometric Model of Residential Location," unpublished Ph.D. dissertation, Harvard University, 1972.

7. It should be noted that the form of equation (1) was suggested in John F. Kain and John R. Meyer, *A First Approximation to a Rand Model for Study of Urban Transportation*, RM-2878-FF, Santa Monica: The Rand Corporation, 1961.

8. Actually, for completeness, spatial variations in the prices of housing characteristics attributable to quasi-rents should be included as well. Because quasi-rents are not directly observable, however, they must be omitted from empirical estimates of equation (1).

9. See Mayo, *op. cit.* for further discussion.

10. John R. Meyer, "An Experiment in the Measurement of Business Motivation," *Review of Economics and Statistics* (August 1969): 304-318.

11. Note that education is included as both an expenditure category in which the relative budgetary allocation may be taken as a measure of a municipality's commitment to public education relative to other goals, and as an output measure representing the outcome of the educational process that is purchased.

12. Because school districts comprising 72 Census tracts out of the 293 in the Milwaukee SMSA failed to report achievement scores, a crude educational production function was estimated for reporting Census tracts and used to forecast scores for the nonreporting tracts the best fitting equation expressed the logarithm of the achievement score as a function of median income of families and unrelated individuals, median school years completed by the adult population, and percent of employment in three occupational categories—professional and managerial, clerical and sales, and operative and craftsman—all of which were statistically significant. Percent nonwhite occupancy in the tract was also included but was insignificant. The corrected R^2 was 0.671. Since some of the same explanatory variables are included among the principal components described above, results for the "education" variable must be interpreted cautiously.

13. See Larry L. Orr, "The Incidence of Differential Property Taxes on Urban Housing," *National Tax Journal* (September 1968): 253-262, for a more extended discussion.

14. For an example of an empirical study the conclusions of which are undoubtedly affected by this consideration, see J. P. Crecine, Otto Davis, and John Jackson, "Urban Property Markets: Some Empirical Results and Their Implications for Municipal Zoning," *Journal of Law and Economics* (October 1967).

15. It should be noted as well that the proportion of explained variance is significantly lower in equations with multiple income earners than in those with only a single income earner: about 0.14 on average for the former and about 0.32 for the latter. The discrepancy is of the same order of magnitude as the squared partial correlation coefficient between the dependent variable and T_{ij}. Were the secondary income earner's "distance from workplace" equally as important as

the primary income earner's, and if it were included as an independent variable, one would expect the discrepancy in explained variance for the two groups to almost exactly disappear.

16. One significant exception is the unpublished study by Larry Orr, "Municipal Governmental Policy and the Location of Population and Industry in a Metropolitan Area: An Econometric Study" (unpublished Ph. D. dissertation, Department of Economics, M.I.T.,1967). In that study he formulates a probabilistic model of location similar to that presented here and regresses gross density of various population subgroups, stratified by income, on the characteristics of subareas in the Boston SMSA. Considering the difference in data sources there is a remarkable similarity in his results and mine. He finds, for example, that only the two highest income groups ($10,000-24,999, and over $25,000 per year) are affected by educational expenditures, that property taxes appear to matter only for upper income groups, and that accessibility and housing variables are important in determining location.

17. See, for example, Larry L. Orr, *op. cit.*, Note 13.

18. For example Orr, *op. cit.*, concludes that little, if any shifting occurs. In a later article, however, he concludes that some (but less than half) of property tax differentials are shifted to tenants: "The Incidence of Property Taxes: A Response," *National Tax Journal* (March 1970): 99-101. A more recent study indicated that roughly 60 percent of property tax differentials were shifted, but that measured service variables were not: D. N. Hyman and E. C. Pasour, Jr., "Property Tax Differentials and Residential Rents in North Carolina," *National Tax Journal* (June 1973): 303-307.

19. See J. D. Heinberg and W. E. Oates, "The Incidence of Differential Property Taxes on Urban Housing: A Comment and Some Further Evidence," *National Tax Journal* (March 1970): 92-98; and W. E. Oates, "The Effects of Property Taxes and Local Public Spending on Property Values: An Empirical Study of Tax Capitalization and the Tiebout Hypothesis," *Journal of Political Economy* (November/ December 1969): 957-971. For a careful study of capitalization that finds "no evidence of full capitalization" of tax differentials for owned housing, however, see A. Thomas King, *Property Taxes, Amenities, and Residential Land Values*, Cambridge, Mass.: Ballinger, 1973.

20. Geoffrey Carliner, "Income Elasticity of Housing Demand," *Review of Economics and Statistics* (November 1973): 528-531.

21. Edgar W. Butler *et al.*, *Moving Behavior and Residential Choice: A National Survey*, Washington, D.C.: Highway Research Board, 1969.

22. One recent study, however, suggests that one should not be overly optimistic of discovering "Tiebout effects" even when using geographically disaggregated public service data. Thomas King (*op. cit., Property Taxes, Amenities, and Residential Land Values*)

found only limited support for tax and service capitalization in a study of property values of recent movers in New Haven.

Chapter Three
Residential Location and Local
Public Services

1. William C. Apgar and John F. Kain, "Neighborhood Attributes and the Residential Price Geography of Urban Areas," paper presented at Econometric Society, Toronto, Canada (Winter 1972); John F. Kain and John M. Quigley, "Discrimination and a Heterogeneous Housing Stock: An Economic Analysis," New York: National Bureau of Economic Research, 1973 (processed); and Mahlon R. Straszheim, "Estimation of the Demand for Urban Housing Services from Household Interview Data," *Review of Economics and Statistics* LV (1): 1-8; See Chapter Two.

2. John P. Crecine, *Governmental Problem Solving: A Computer Simulation of Municipal Budgeting*, Chicago: Rand McNally, 1970; W. E. Whitelaw, "An Econometric Analysis of a Municipal Budgetary Process Based on Time Series Data," Program on Regional and Urban Economics, Harvard University, 1968; John E. Jackson, "Politics and the Budgetary Process," *Social Science Research* 1 (1): 35-60.

3. Charles M. Tiebout, "A Pure Theory of Local Expenditures," *Journal of Political Economy* (October 1956): 416-424; also see, Albert Hirschman *Exit, Voice and Loyalty: Responses to Decline in Firms*, Cambridge, Mass.: Harvard University Press, 1971.

4. Tiebout's original article dealt with the problem of how to ration a public good that was not reproducible. His example was a public beach. The extension of the Tiebout argument to other kinds of public services occurred subsequently; see Robert Warren, "A Municipal Services Market Model of Metropolitan Organization," *Journal of the American Institute of Planners* (September 1964): 193-204.

5. Wallace E. Oates, "The Effects of Property Taxes and Local Public Spending on Property Values: An Empirical Study of Tax Capitalization and the Tiebout Hypothesis," *Journal of Political Economy* (January/February-November/December 1969): 957-971; and Brian Ellickson, "Jurisdiction Fragmentation and Residential Choice," *American Economic Review* (May 1971): 334-339.

6. Tax price is analogous to private market price and represents the price to an individual household of an additional dollar of public services.

7. Michael J. Ball, "Recent Empirical Work in the Determinants of Relative Housing Prices," *Urban Studies* (June 1973); Straszheim, *op. cit.*, Note 1; John F. Kain and John M. Quigley, "Measuring the Value of Housing Quality," *Journal of the American Statistical Association* (June 1970); and Richard Muth, *Cities and Housing*, Chicago: University of Chicago Press, 1969.

8. Oates, *op. cit.*, Note 5.
9. See Chapter Two.
10. Straszheim, *op. cit.*, Note 1, and Kain and Quigley, *op. cit.*
11. The housing stock in the sample towns is primarily single family owner occupied. The median percent renter is 22 percent. Consequently, the characteristic of owner occupied units should adequately measure each town's housing stock.
12. The 1960 U.S. Census did not publish figures for average rooms per unit separately for owner and renter occupied housing in all 65 municipalities used for the present analysis. Thus it was necessary in 24 of those municipalities to estimate these figures from data that were available. These estimates were based on the average rooms per unit for all housing in each municipality and the proportion of these units that were newly occupied. The appropriate equations are listed below. They were obtained from regressions pooling 1960 and 1970 data which were available from a large sample of 109 municipalities in the study area. Relevant *t*-statistics are listed below each coefficient. It should be noted that towns for which rooms per unit had to be calculated were the very smallest in the sample and thus according to our weighted regression procedure were much less important in the determination of our results than the municipalities for which all that data was available.

1) Rooms/Unit Owner = 0.605 + 0.897 (Rooms/Unit All) + 1.64 (Proportion

R^2 = 0.681   (1.9)   (18.2)   (9.8) Renter

N = 168   Occ.)

2) Rooms/Unit Renter = 1.24 + 0.525 (Rooms/Unit All) + 0.818 (Proportion

R^2 = 0.273   (2.7)   (7.4)   (3.4) Renter

N = 168   Occ.)

13. Vogt-Ivers and Associates, *Comprehensive Land Use Inventory Report* (for the Eastern Massachusetts Regional Planning Project), March 1967.
14. The accessibility formulation was developed and calibrated by the EMRPP for use in the EMPIRIC land use forecasting model.

Gravity Model Formulation of Accessibility to Employment

$$A_i = E_j (e^{-0.1\, T_{ij}})$$
$$\text{all}_j$$

where: A_i = Level or change in accessibility to employment of town i

E_j = Level or change in employment of town j

T_{ij} = Peak hour travel time from i to town j

15. See discussions and analysis in Frederick Mosteller and Daniel P. Moynihan, *On Equality of Educational Opportunity*, New York: Random House, 1972.

Chapter Four
Voter Demand for Public
School Expenditures

1. A sense of the variety of referendum voting can be gathered from Harlan Hahn, "Northern Referenda on Fair Housing: The Response of White Voters," *Western Political Quarterly* XXI (September 1968): 483-495; M. Kent Jennings and Harmon Ziegler, "Class, Party, and Race in Four Types of Elections: The Case of Atlanta," *The Journal of Politics* XXVIII (September 1966): 391-407; James A. Norton, "Referenda Voting in a Metropolitan Area," *Western Political Quarterly* XVI (March 1963): 195-212; and Brian Stipak, "An Analysis of the 1968 Rapid Transit Vote in Los Angeles," *Transportation* 11 (1973): 71-85.
2. A useful central reference source is Philip K. Piele and John Stuart Hall, *Budgets, Bonds, and Ballots: Voting Behavior in School Financial Elections*, Lexington, Mass.: Lexington Books, 1973.
3. Irene A. King, *Bond Sales for Public School Purposes, 1971-72*, Washington, D.C.: U.S. Department of Health, Education, and Welfare, 1973.
4. Arthur J. Alexander and Gail V. Bass, *Schools, Taxes and Voter Behavior: An Analysis of School District Property Tax Elections*, Santa Monica, Ca.: Rand Corp. R-1465-FF, 1974.
5. For discussions of some of the problems associated with the distribution of voter characteristics, see T. C. Bergstrom and R. P. Goodman, "Private Demands for Public Goods," *American Economic Review* 63 (3): 280-296; Noel M. Edelson, "Budgetary Outcomes in a Referendum Setting," Discussion Paper No. 344, University of Pennsylvania (October 1972).
6. For example, R. Barlow, "Efficiency Aspects of Local School Finance," *Journal of Political Economy* 78 (September/October 1970): 1028-1040; Thomas E. Borcherding and Robert T. Deacon, "The Demand for the Services of Nonfederal Governments," *American Economic Review* 62 (5): 891-901.
7. G. E. Peterson, "The Demand for Public Schooling: A Study in Voting and Expenditure Theory," Washington, D.C.: Urban Institute Working Paper (1973).
8. The omission of n_i probably leads to a downward bias in estimates of the price elasticity. I am presently engaged in reestimation of (2) for subsamples for which information on n_i is available. My preliminary findings confirm the predicted bias.
9. California: 138 unified school districts; Michigan: 187 school districts; New Jersey: 270 school districts; New York: 196 school districts; Kansas City, Mo.-Kansas City, Kan.: 38 school districts.

10. I am indebted to Ms. Bonnie McKellar for her assistance in analyzing the Ann Arbor data.
11. When the voting records of owners and renters were combined at the present level, the results were rendered virtually unintelligible.

Equation	R^2	$\alpha ln Y$	$\beta ln\left(\dfrac{H}{V}\right)$	α per rent	δln SCH CHILD
Combined precinct Voting, Ann Arbor	.47	−0.45 (0.9)	+0.14 (0.77)	+0.59 (1.5)	+0.19 (0.3)

12. This work has been undertaken in conjunction with Professor Daniel Rubinfeld of the University of Michigan. More complete analysis will be forthcoming in joint publications.
13. The cross-sectional estimates may also be biased because of the clustering of families with high and low demands for school spending in different communities. This stratification by taste-for-public-sector-spending will produce more variation in demand across communities (and less variation in demand within communities) than is true for the population at large. Exactly how such stratification will bias individual coefficients depends upon the relationship of the variables included in the demand function to the stratifying variables that are excluded. However, I am convinced that the principal stratification across school districts occurs according to number of school children in the family (i.e., families with school age children seek out high spending school districts to reside in). For this reason, inclusion of the school children variable would remove most of the bias.
14. G. E. Peterson, "The Public Service Demands of Owner-Occupants and Renters," Urban Institute Working Paper # 762-11 (1973).
15. Jeffrey W. Smith, "A Clear Test of Rational Voting in Intermediate Education District Budget Elections," University of Oregon, mimeo, 1973.
16. James Q. Wilson and Edward C. Banfield, "Public-Regardingness as a Value Premise in Voting Behavior," *American Political Science Review* 58 (4): 876-887; and James Q. Wilson and Edward C. Banfield, "Political Ethics Revisited," *American Political Science Review* 65 (December 1973): 1048-1062.
17. Recent shifts in actual state aid formulas for school support are summarized in National Legislative Conference, *New Programs of State School Aid* (1974).
18. For a summary of state circuit-breaker laws see John Shannon, "The Property Tax: Reform or Relief," in G. E. Peterson, *Property Tax Reform*, Washington, D.C.: Urban Institute, 1973.

Chapter Five
The Demand for Local Public
Services: An Exploratory Analysis

1. The study by Peterson in Chapter Four is very complementary to the analysis here. Another notable analysis of referenda voting (which looks at some of the same referenda as here) is James Q. Wilson and Edward C. Banfield, "Public-Regardingness as a Value Premise in Voting Behavior," *American Political Science Review* 58 (4): 876-887.

2. The estimated models are calculated using weighted regression analysis. If the underlying voter turnout model applies to individuals and the errors in the individual model are homoscedastic (i.e., have the same variance), the errors for the aggregate model which relies upon tract averages for turnout will be heteroscedastic (i.e., have different variances across observations). If the individual error variance is σ, the tract error variance will be σ/n_i where n_i is the number of potential voters in each tract i. Thus, all observations are weighted by the population over 21 years old (n_i). This also implies that the model predicts better where there are more people involved; that is, it predicts better in larger tracts.

3. The nonwhite population in this sample is overwhelmingly black.

4. The F-statistic in the welfare model is 2.4 and in the zoo model is 1.1. The critical value of F for 6 and 126 degrees of freedom is 2.17 at the 5 percent level and 2.95 at the 1 percent level.

5. The elasticity estimate indicates the percentage change in the voter turnout variable that would result from a 1 percent change in the given variable away from its mean. Note this is the percentage change in the percent voter turnout, so that an elasticity of .5 implies that a 10 percent increase in the independent variable (above its mean) would increase voter turnout 5 percent above its mean, or to 24 percent from 22.9 percent on the welfare vote.

6. Ohio has a nonpartisan registration requirement for individuals living in large cities. The tract by tract registration data are available, so it would be possible to analyze registration behavior, but that is beyond this chapter.

7. As in the "standard" case of economic theory, the individual maximizes utility by spending all of his income on the two goods and by buying quantities such that the marginal utility-price ratios on the two goods are equal.

8. Harold M. Hochman and James D. Rogers, "Pareto Optimal Redistribution," *American Economic Review* 59 (4): 542-557.

9. Wilson and Banfield, *op. cit.*, Note 1.

10. This is different than the case considered by Peterson in Chapter Four. Since the sample falls within a single jurisdiction, the effect of nonresidential property is constant for all residents, and, therefore, does not have to be considered.

11. All estimates are made using weighted regressions where the weights are the number of total votes cast in each tract. This follows the same logic as in the voter turnout models: first, we want to predict better in observations that involve more people; second, weighted regression corrects for heteroscedasticity in the aggregate models (see the voter turnout discussion).

12. These models contain separate estimates of the effects of increased rental payments and increased housing value. An alternative approach would be to combine housing value and rent. This is commonly done by capitalizing the rents to estimate the value of a rental unit. The most frequent rule is value equals 100 times the monthly rent. In the preceding estimates, since value is in hundreds of dollars, the rent and value coefficients should be equal if this aggregation is appropriate. On this score there are mixed results: the coefficients are virtually identical in three of the columns (Cols. (3) and (4) of Table 5-5, and Col. (3) of Table 5-4); in the other cases they are very different. Particularly with the large number of observations here, it does not seem wise to constrain the coefficients to equality.

13. See J. Johnston, *Econometric Methods*, New York: McGraw-Hill, 1963, pp. 168-175. The individual parameter estimates from ordinary least squares are not only biased but also inconsistent. This is the case even when the measurement errors are random.

14. The standard corrective procedures are discussed in Johnston, *op. cit.*, and in A. Madansky, "The Fitting of Straight Lines When Both Variables are Subject to Errors," *Journal of the American Statistical Association* 54: 173-203. For the specific case of systematic errors in variables of the type seen here, it seems possible to use the information gained on voter turnout to adjust the independent variables in the preference models. (Note that the errors in variables problem is not present in the voter turnout models because the relevant population is the entire population of the tract.) One possible approach is to use the parameters of the voter turnout model to adjust the variance-covariance matrix of independent variables for individuals within each tract. While the preference model is estimated on the basis of aggregate characteristics for the tracts such as tract averages, the appropriate correction must consider the distribution of individuals within each tract. This approach appears to provide consistent parameter estimates. Also, this approach seems feasible, at least in the specific problem considered here, because of the availability of Census information about the distribution of individuals within tracts. Work on the theoretical aspects of this approach is in progress, but the application of the technique is beyond the scope of this chapter.

Chapter Six
Elections and Local Fiscal Policy

1. John E. Jackson, "Politics and the Budgetary Process," *Social Science Research* 1 (1): 35-60.

2. A simple analysis of the changes in property tax revenues derived from changes in the tax rate was done. The analysis tried to relate these discretionary revenue changes to changes in the tax base, intergovernmental transfers, population, family income, the electoral cycle, and the administration in office for the period 1949-1972. The important determinants were whether it was an election year or the year following an election and the incumbent mayor. Collins had substantially smaller increases than either of the other mayors.

3. For a more complete discussion of the survey and its sample, see James Q. Wilson and Edward C. Banfield, "Political Ethos Revisited," *American Political Science Review* 65 (4): 1048-1062.

4. The unrepresentativeness of this sample should be evident from the facts that in 1970 only 27 percent of Boston households were in owner occupied dwellings and less than half of these were single family units, from which the sample was drawn.

5. See Chapter Four.

6. For an extended description of this campaign, see Murray Levin, *The Alienated Voter: Politics in Boston*, New York: Holt, Rinehart and Winston, 1960.

7. The proportion of voters in each tract supporting Collins is estimated by geographically aggregating voting precincts into Census tracts. This aggregation is done simply from visual mapping of tracts overlaid onto a map of precincts. This undoubtedly introduces some error into our dependent variable since tract and precinct boundaries overlap in most cases. The votes cast in such precincts are split between the appropriate tracts in approximate proportion to the amount of the precinct located in each tract. This process will introduce errors into our measures of Collins's support, but these errors should be random across tracts, with some tracts being overestimated and some being underestimated. By using Census tracts as the unit of analysis, however, we have relatively homogeneous areas and our measures of the characteristics of these areas are much more reliable. In the succeeding statistical analysis it is much more important to have reliable measures of the explanatory variables.

Chapter Seven
The Municipal Service Equalization Suit:
A Cause of Action in Quest of a Forum

1. Law schools situated in urban centers took an early interest in the legal services movement with these resultant developments: the modification of the formal curriculum to include course offerings dealing with the problems of the disadvantaged; the redefinition of traditional subjects such as contracts, landlord-tenant, administrative and constitutional law to incorporate an emphasis upon the position of the poor; and, the release of large numbers of law students in "clinical programs" whereby students devote time in lieu of formal

study to working within the neighborhood legal centers. In the chain of development this emphasis within the law schools has greatly heightened the interest among recent graduates in the field of poverty law with a discernible impact upon at least the initial career choice. Further evidence of this cumulative impact may be found in the formation of "public interest law firms" and the "pro bono publico" satellites inaugurated by traditional law firms which aim to attract high quality law school graduates into the private practice while incorporating an "in-house" means of participation in law reform.

2. This discussion will *not* include the discrete topic of how one might compel a municipal corporation to undertake the provision of a service which, though generally conceived as "public," it currently renders to no one within the municipal entity.

3. Section 1983 of Title 42 of the United States Code confers original jurisdiction upon the federal judiciary. The legislation provides:

> Every person who, under the color of any statute, ordinance, regulation, custom or usage, of any State or Territory, subjects, or causes to be subjected, any citizen of the United States or other person within the jurisdiction thereof to the deprivation of any rights, privileges, or immunities secured by the Constitution and laws, shall be liable to the party injured in an action at law, suit in equity, or other proper proceeding for redress.

For some time there was substantial doubt whether a municipal government could be a proper defendant under this statute. The question was whether such a governmental entity was a "person" falling under the statutory prohibition. The necessity of resolving this doubt was obviated when plaintiffs began adopting the tactic of bringing suit against the mayor and other local officials in both their personal and official capacities. Today, this practice is widespread and is sufficient to bring the activities of local government within the scrutiny of a federal court in a civil rights suit. See, *Beal et al. v. John V. Lindsay, individually and as Mayor of the City of New York, et al.*, 468 F.2d 287 (2d Cir. 1972).

4. It is now firmly settled that a United States District Court cannot deny relief in a Civil Rights Act case because the plaintiffs have failed to exhaust available state remedies. *Damico v. California*, 389 U.S. 416 (1967); and, *King v. Smith*, 392 U.S. 309 (1968).

5. A municipal services suit can be premised upon an alleged denial of Equal Protection notwithstanding the fact that neither the state nor its legislative enactments are objects of complaint. This is a nonobvious conclusion, for the Fourteenth Amendment commands that "no *state*" shall deny the equal protection of its laws to any citizen of the United States. For a time municipal governments resisted Equal Protection suits on the theory that their activities were not that of a "state." Today, such a position is untenable. In *Avery v. Midland*

County, 390 U.S. 474, 480 (1968), the Court declared: "A city, town, or county may no more deny the equal protection of the laws than it may abridge freedom of speech, establish an official religion, arrest without probable cause, or deny due process of law."

6. See generally, *Developments in the Law—Equal Protection*, 82 Harv. L. Rev. 1065 (1969). "Legislatures are presumed to have acted constitutionally even if source materials normally resorted to for ascertaining their grounds for action are otherwise silent, and their statutory classifications will be set aside only if no grounds can be conceived to justify them." *McDonald v. Board of Election Comm'rs of Chicago*, 394 U.S. 802, 809 (1969); and, *Lindsley v. National Carbonic Gas Co.*, 220 U.S. 61, 78 (1911).

By contrast, when the "strict standard" is invoked, the court tests for the indispensable presence of a "compelling governmental interest" by asking if the classification scheme is *necessary* to achieve the chief and overwhelmingly legitimate governmental goal which it is designed to effect—e.g., *Rinaldi v. Yeager*, 384 U.S. 305 (1966).

7. 394 U.S. at 633. Recognition of the legitimate status of budgetary considerations was involved in two recent decisions of the Court. *Palmer v. Thompson*, 403 U.S. 217 (1971); and, *Jefferson v. Hackney*, 406 U.S. 535 (1972). In both cases petitioners, as representatives of a class of economically disadvantaged citizens, failed in their attempts to qualify for the strict review standard.

8. Consider the observation of Mr. Chief Justice Burger concurring in *Palmer v.* (etc.) *Thompson*:

> The elimination of any needed or useful public accommodations or service is surely undesirable and this is particularly so of public recreational facilities. Unfortunately the growing burdens and shrinking revenues of municipal and state governments may lead to more and more curtailment of desirable services. . . . 403 U.S. at 227.

9. *Shapiro v. Thompson, supra* at 627. Fundamental personal interests have been identified by the Court to include the following: the right to procreate, *Skinner v. Oklahoma*, 316 U.S. 535, 541 (1942); the right to vote, *Reynolds v. Sims*, 377 U.S. 533, 561-62 (1964), *Carrington v. Rash*, 380 U.S. 89, 96 (1965), *Harper v. Virginia Bd. of Elections*, 383 U.S. 663, 670 (1966); the right to political association, *Williams v. Rhodes*, 393 U.S. 23 (1968); and the right of interstate travel, *Shapiro v. Thompson*, 394 U.S. 618 (1969).

In *Serrano v. Priest*, 487 P.2d 1241, 1258-59 (S.Ct. Calif. 1971), the court expressly added public primary and secondary education to the list of fundamental personal interests evoking the " 'strict scrutiny' equal protection standard. . . ." Accord, *Hobson v. Hansen*, 269 F.Supp. 401 (D. D.C. 1967), *aff'd sub nom. Smuck v. Hansen*, 408 F.2d 175 (D.C. Cir. 1969); *Van Dusartz v. Hatfield*, 334 F.Supp. 870, 875 (D. Minn. 1971); and, *Rodriguez v. San Antonio*

Independent School District, 337 F.Supp. 280, 282-83 (W.D. Tex. 1972).

Less than two years after the decision in *Serrano* began the trend to recognize public education as a "fundamental personal interest," the United States Supreme Court held that it was not. *San Antonio Independent School District v. Rodriguez*, 93 S.Ct. 1278, 1297-98 (1973). This express refusal to hold the provision of public education which the Court had nineteen years earlier described as ". . . perhaps the most important function of state and local government" entitled to the protection of the "New Equal Protection" bodes ill for the fate of municipal services. See *Brown v. Board of Education*, 347 U.S. 483, 493 (1954). Because it posited its holding upon both the federal and state constitutional guarantees of equal protection, *Serrano* survives in California on the non-federal ground. For further thoughts on this result see the discussion of state constitutional theories, *infra*.

Another shadow casting doubt upon an ability to convince the current majority of the Court that municipal services can qualify as "fundamental personal interests" is the opinion announced last Term in *Lindsey v. Normet*, 405 U.S. 56, 73-74 (1972). The Court, speaking through Mr. Justice White, rejected a low income tenant's bid to have Oregon's Forcible Entry and Wrongful Detainer Law examined for a denial of Equal Protection under the stringent standard. Their bid for the "New Equal Protection" was predicated upon a contention that the summary process set forth in the Oregon statute infringed upon their "fundamental personal interests" which were identified as a "need for decent shelter" and the "right to retain peaceful possession of one's home." 405 U.S. at 73. The majority expressed itself as unable to offer anything beyond sympathy. "We do not denigrate the importance of decent, safe, and sanitary housing. But the Constitution does not provide judical remedies for every social and economic ill. . . . Absent constitutional mandate, the assurance of adequate housing and the definition of landlord-tenant relationships are legislative, not judicial, functions." *Id.*, at 74.

10. Having so qualified education because of the ". . . unmatched . . . extent to which it molds the youth of society. . . ." (at 1259), the Supreme Court of California expressly declined to intimate its views on other governmental services. *Serrano v. Priest, supra*, 471 P.2d at 1262. However, it is interesting to note the court's observation that: "While police and fire protection, garbage collection and street lights are essentially neutral in their effect on the individual psyche, public education actively attempts to shape a child's personal development in a manner chosen not by the child or his parents but by the state." *Id.*, at 1259. Accord, *Van Dusartz v. Hatfield*, 334 F.Supp. 870, 875 (D. Minn. 1971). Not all would agree. The total impact of the realization that he is, for unexplained reasons, condemned to grow

up in a slum neighborhood may well work great harm to a child's "psyche."

Following reasoning not unlike that of the California Court a distinction between public education and what had been municipally operated swimming pools was articulated by Mr. Justice Black speaking for the majority in *Palmer v. Thompson, supra*, 403 U.S. at 221 n. 6. The minimum import of *Palmer* would seem to be the conclusion that recreational facilities do not constitute fundamental personal interests. This distinction was also sounded in the concurring opinion of Mr. Justice Blackman: "The pools . . . are a general municipal service of the nice-to-have but not essential variety, and they are a service, perhaps a luxury, not enjoyed by many communities." 403 U.S. at 229.

11. Citation to *McGowan v. Maryland*, 366 U.S. 420, 426 (1961). In classifying welfare benefits for purposes of a standard of equal protection review, the Court, speaking through Mr. Justice Stewart, was most explicit:

> To be sure, the cases cited, and many others enunciating this [rational relationship to any conceivable legitimate state interest] fundamental standard under the Equal Protection Clause, have in the main involved state regulation of business or industry. *The administration of public welfare assistance, by contrast, involves the most basic needs of impoverished human beings. We recognize the dramatically real factual difference between the cited cases and this one, but we can find no basis for applying a different constitutional standard.* . . . And it is a standard that is true to the principle that the Fourteenth Amendment gives the federal courts no power to impose upon the States their views of wise economic or social policy. *Id.* (Footnotes omitted; emphasis supplied.)

This noninterventionist standard of Equal Protection analysis was again applied to the claims of AFDC welfare recipients in *Jefferson v. Hackney*, 406 U.S. 535, 547 (1972). Speaking for the majority, Mr. Justice Rehnquist turned aside a bid for the strict review standard predicated on the interest of petitioners in the public assistance benefits which had been subjected to a non-evenhanded percentage reduction when compared to the other categories of assistance.

12. *Metropolis Theatre Co. v. City of Chicago*, 228 U.S. 61, 69-70 (1913).

13. In *McLaughlin v. Florida*, 379 U.S. 184 (1964), the Court spoke directly of the effect which the presence of racial classifications has upon the issue of standard selection. In the presence of a racial classification scheme, all presumptions of regularity and constitutionality of governmental actions and all indulgent speculations are to cease. "[R]acial classifications [are] 'constitutionally suspect' . . . and subject to the 'most rigid scrutiny' . . . and 'in most circumstances irrelevant' to any constitutionally acceptable legislative purpose." *Id.* at 191-92.

Generally proof of racial classifications is made out by statistical evidence of the disparity in the treatment of the races by the defendant organ of government. Such statistical evidence was adduced in *Hawkins v. Town of Shaw*, 303 F.Supp. 1162 (N.D. Miss. 1969); the failure of the District Court to accord such an evidentiary showing proper weight led to a reversal. *Hawkins v. Town of Shaw*, 437 F.2d 1286 (5th Cir.1972), reversal upheld *en banc* 461 F.2d 1171 (1972). The general impact of such statistics is to shift to the defendant the burden of meeting the *prima facie* inference of invidious discrimination by direct evidence which either disputes the statistics or, admitting their accuracy, supplies an alternative explanation of the pattern they depict which, if accepted by the trier of fact, would negate plaintiff's effort to show that the Constitution has been infringed. The continued utility of *Hawkins* to poverty law forces able to demonstrate a racial classification may be seen in *United Farmworkers of Florida Housing Project, Inc. v. City of Delray Beach*, 493 F.2d 799, 803 (5th Cir. 1974); and *Skillken v. City of Toledo*, 380 F.Supp. 228, 234 (N.D. Ohio, 1974). Additional cases are reviewed in Fessler and Haar, *Beyond the Wrong Side of the Tracks: Municipal Services in the Intersticies of Procedure*, 6 Harv. Civ. Rights-Civ. Liberties L. Rev. 441 (1971).

14. *Palmer v. Thompson*, 403 U.S. 217 (1971), *Jefferson v. Hackney*, 406 U.S. 535 (1972), and *San Antonio Independent School District v. Rodriguez*, 93 S.Ct. 1278 (1973). As previously indicated, these cases involved explicit rejection of the premise that either public assistance benefits, or publicly provided recreational facilities or education constitute "fundamental personal interests."

15. *See* note, *Discrimination Against the Poor and the Fourteenth Amendment*, 81 Harv. L. Rev. 435 (1967); *Developments in the Law—Equal Protection*, 82 Harv. L. Rev. 1065, 1087-1104 (1968); and, Michelman, *Foreward: On Protecting the Poor Through the Fourteenth Amendment, The Supreme Court, 1968 Term*, 83 Harv. L. Rev. 7, 19-33 (1969).

16. *McDonald v. Board of Election Comm'rs of Chicago*, 394 U.S. 802, 807 (1969) (emphasis added).

17. *E.g., Norris v. Alabama*, 294 U.S. 587 (1935); *McLaughlin v. Florida*, 379 U.S. 184 (1964); and, *Loving v. Virginia*, 388 U.S. 1, 10 (1967). While racial classifications have triggered the most stringent scrutiny, ancestry (*Korematsu v. United States*, 323 U.S. 214, 216 (1944)), and alienage (*Takahashi v. Fish & Game Comm'n*, 334 U.S. 410 (1948)), have also been held "suspect." Recently, legitimacy has been added to the list. *Levy v. Louisiana*, 391 U.S. 68 (1968).

18. A recent writer for the *Harvard Civil Rights-Civil Liberties Law Review* has undertaken an impressive analysis of this topic. While concluding that "public education and police and fire protection" involve interests fundamental enough to merit close scrutiny under the strict review standard, his analysis of the other services suggests some nonobvious considerations.

Inferior educational opportunities can be identified as a deprivation of the "liberty" accorded the advantaged child in his quest for employment which is, in turn, the avenue to the acquisition of "property." Adequate garbage collection and sanitary sewers are indisputably necessary to minimize health hazards to "life." Street lights contribute to a reduction in crime which is, in turn, a threat to both "life" and "property." In combination with traffic control apparatus, they minimize the accidental loss of these same interests. Similar, though less convincing, cases can be made for street paving as a means to the preservation of property, and physical and esthetic recreational facilities and opportunities as promoting both "life" and "liberty." Ratner, *Inter-Neighborhood Denials of Equal Protection in the Provision of Municipal Services*, 4 Harv. Civ. Rights-Civ. Liberties L. Rev. 1 (1968).

19. *Dandridge v. Williams, supra*, 397 U.S. at 484-85; *Jefferson v. Hackney, supra*, 406 U.S. at 547, *San Antonio Independent School Dist. v. Rodriguez, supra*, 93 S.Ct. at 1300.

20. *Reed v. Reed*, 465 P.2d 635 (S.Ct. Idaho, 1970).

21. *Reed v. Reed*, 404 U.S. 71 (1971).

22. *Korematsu v. United States*, 323 U.S. 214, 216 (1944) (racial classification "suspect," but the discrimination is not invidious given the government's "compelling interest" in an effective war effort).

Pressure upon the Court to develop an alternative can be detected in the disquiet of federal trial judges who have rightly perceived the selection of a review standard to be dispositive of the outcome of a trial thereafter reduced to the level of a near formality. An example may be found in the recorded lament of a distinguished District Judge faced with a standard selection dispute in an equal protection challenge to a municipal zoning ordinance. Under existing precedent, the trial court was confronted with a ". . . dichotomy between those classifications which enjoy every presumption of validity and those which may be said to be unlawful *per se*, unless the State carries an almost insupportable burden of proof." *Palo Alto Tenants Union v. Morgan*, 321 F.Supp. 908, 911 (N.D. Calif. 1970) (per Wollenberg, J.), *aff'd* 487 F.2d 883 (9th Cir. 1973).

23. 404 U.S. at 75-76.

24. Evidence that *Reed* has been understood to stand for a third standard may be found in several cases. In reliance upon *Reed*, the Court struck down a Massachusetts law which forbade the distribution of contraceptive materials to the unmarried. *Eisenstadt v. Baird*, 405 U.S. 438 (1972). In *Skinner v. Oklahoma*, 316 U.S. 535, 541 (1942), the Court had determined that the right to procreate constituted a fundamental personal interest. Use of the *Reed* precedent enabled the Court to avoid the further examination of *Skinner* to determine if the right to procreate a bastard achieved the same lofty plateau of constitutional dignity.

In *Police Department of Chicago v. Mosley*, 408 U.S. 94 (1972), the Court again relied upon *Reed* to strike down a Chicago city ordinance which prohibited all picketing within 150 feet of a school except peaceful picketing of any school involved in a labor dispute. In *Stanley v. Illinois*, 405 U.S. 645 (1972), the Court invoked *Reed* to hold unconstitutional an Illinois statute which provided that the children of unmarried fathers upon the death of the mother are declared dependents of the state without any hearing as to parental fitness and without proof of neglect although such a process is required before the state assumes custody of children of married or divorced parents or unwed mothers.

In all of these cases the test formulated in *Reed* proved free from the analytical strictures of either labeling criteria or placing transcending reliance upon an evaluation of the plaintiff's adversely affected personal interest. Rather, the focus of the litigation is upon the more satisfying issue of the relationship between the object sought by the government and the means selected to that end. The *Reed* test, if it achieves popularity with the bar and inferior courts will permit the litigation to demand more than a leap of judicial imagination in passing upon the ability of a classification scheme to survive an Equal Protection assault without demanding the identification of either a suspect criteria or fundamental personal interest.

25. Whether viewed as political expediency or healthy deference to the coordinate branches of government, the doctrine of "standing to sue" has been used in the United States to generally deny the judicial forum to a citizen who would contest expenditure programs or "pie dividing" functions of the state and national legislature. Both the scope of the doctrine and the dynamics of its application lie beyond the focus of this discussion. See generally, *Flast v. Cohen*, 392 U.S. 83, 92 (1968) (collecting authorities). Jaffe, "Standing to Secure Judicial Review: Private Actions," 75 Harv. L. Rev. 255 (1961).

26. But *cf.* Ratner, *supra* Note 18. There are some services so closely related to the support of constitutionally protected rights of life, liberty or property as to simply form the essence of "government." For these, no "market economy" rationale ought to be accepted by the court. The difficulty is to draw the line. In this context, a due process rationale is no more effective a divining rod than an equal protection, "fundamental personal interest" analysis.

27. *Hawkins v. Town of Shaw*, 303 F.Supp. 1162 (N.D. Miss. 1969); *rev'd.* 437 F.2d 1286 (5th Cir. 1971), reversal upheld *en banc* 461 F.2d 1171 (5th Cir. 1972); *Harris v. Town of Itta Bena*, Civ. No. GC 6756 (N.D. Miss. filed Nov. 21, 1967); *Coleman v. Aycock*, 304 F.Supp. 132 (N.D. Miss. 1969); *Hadnott v. City of Prattville*, 309 F.Supp. 967 (M.D. Ala. 1970); *Selmont Improvement Ass'n. v. Dallas County Com'n.*, 339 F.Supp. 477 (S.D. Ala. 1972); *Dupree v. City of Chattanooga*, 362 F.Supp. 1136 (E.D. Tenn. 1973); *Beal v. Lindsay*, 468 F.2d 287 (2d Cir. 1972); *Maye v. Lindsay*, 352

F.Supp. 1120 (S.D. N.Y. 1972); and, *Fire v. City of Winner*, 352 F.Supp. 925 (D. S.D. 1972).

28. The original complaint in *Hawkins v. Town of Shaw, supra*, posited discrimination upon race and "wealth." The issue of wealth discrimination was specifically abandoned on appeal. 431 F.2d at 1287 n. 1. The original complaint in *Fire v. City of Winner* alleged race discrimination but the claim was dropped. Note 56, *infra*.

29. *Selmont Improvement Ass'n v. Dallas County Com'n.*, 339 F.Supp. 477 (S.D. Ala. 1972) (street paving); *Beal v. Lindsay*, 468 F.2d 287 (2d Cir. 1972) (park facilities); and, *Maye v. Lindsay*, 352 F.Supp. 1120 (S.D. N.Y. 1972) (fire protection). *Dupree v. City of Chattanooga*, 362 F.Supp. 1136 (E.D. Tenn. 1973) assailed a variety of alleged service inequalities, but bore principally upon an attempt to check the defendant city's plan to merge the local Model Cities Program with other federally funded urban programs to the claimed prejudice of black residents.

30. Notwithstanding the presence of plaintiffs' undisputed statistics, coupled with their allegation that the documented pattern was typical of a history of unequal provision, the trial court felt itself free to adopt "all legitimate deductions to be made from the evidence running counter to statistical racial disparity." *Hawkins v. Town of Shaw*, 303 F.Supp. at 1168. The court did not find fault with plaintiffs' statistics, and apparently the defendants did not dispute most of them. Rather, the defendants offered evidence of the city's static population which historically had shown little popular interest in modern improvements; limited finances; cautious fiscal policy; and the lack of modern zoning codes which would have required individual property owners to prepare their premises for the reception of municipal services. Without attempting to explain or citing any efforts on the part of the defendants to explain how all of these impediments had been substantially overcome in white neighborhoods, the court was able to discern "rational considerations, irrespective of race or poverty . . . [which] are not within the condemnation of the Fourteenth Amendment, and may not be properly condemned upon judicial review." *Id.*, at 1168.

31. 437 F.2d 1286 (1971), *en banc* 461 F.2d 1171 (1972).

32. *Id.*, at 1239. Specifically, the panel decision ruled that the District Court had fallen into reversible error in failing to recognize the presence of a "prima facie case of racial discrimination." *Id.*, at 1288.

33. 461 F.2d 1171 (1972).

34. *Coleman v. Aycock*, 304 F.Supp. 132 (N.D. Miss. 1969).

35. *Hadnott v. City of Prattville*, 309 F.Supp. 967 (M.D. Ala. 1970).

36. *Coleman v. Aycock, supra*, Note 34; *Hawkins v. Town of Shaw*, 303 F.Supp. 1162 (N.D. Miss. 1969).

37. *Hadnott v. City of Prattville, supra* 309 F.Supp. at 971. Regarding street lights, the defendants admitted that until recently they had pursued policies which had resulted in discrimination against black neighbor-

hoods in the provision of this service which was undertaken out of general funds. However, the city contended that these policies had been voluntarily abandoned so that present policy and usage admitted an obligation to provide street lighting on a nondiscriminatory basis. What is particularly interesting is that the court accepted the defendants' assertion. While it found that black neighborhoods still did not enjoy parity with white areas, it declined to enter any decree because "no pattern of discrimination [exists] at this time. . . ." *Id.*

38. *Id.* Plaintiffs complained that 35 percent of the dwelling units fronting on unpaved streets were black occupied while only 3 percent of Prattville's white residents existed under similar conditions. The District Court concluded that it was the ability and willingness of local property owners to pay for improvements, and not any form of racial discrimination, which accounted for these statistics. This same rationale was applied to sanitary sewers also covered by plaintiffs' complaint. The absence of water lines provided through special assessments was accepted by the court as a sufficient explanation for the lower incidence of fire hydrants in the black neighborhoods of Prattville.

39. *Hawkins v. Town of Shaw, supra,* 461 F.2d at 1172. On the basis of precedent, the total elimination of "motive" as an element in plaintiffs' case is unassailable. The immateriality of this factor stems from the "positive, affirmative" (*United States ex rel. Seals v. Wiman,* 304 F.2d 53, 66 (5th Cir. 1962)) "constitutional duty" (*Avery v. Georgia,* 345 U.S. 559, 561 (1953)) of the defendant municipal officials to pursue a "course of conduct" (*Hill v. Texas,* 316 U.S. 400, 404 (1942)) in the provision of municipal services which would not "result . . . [in] racial discrimination." (*Cassell v. Texas,* 339 U.S. 282, 289 (1950) (plurality opinion). Their failure to do so, however motivated, is actionable.

40. *Selmont Improvement Association et al. v. Dallas County Commission et al.,* 339 F.Supp. 477 (S.D. Ala. 1972). "The court finds that since the adoption of the foregoing resolutions by the Dallas County Commission in 1955 and 1966, no discrimination had been shown in the application of these resolutions with reference to subdivisions. However, to hold that these resolutions are a defense to the present suit would permit the resolutions to freeze in past discriminatory actions against these plaintiffs in violation of their rights under the Fourteenth Amendment. This the court refuses to do." *Id.,* at 481.

41. *Fire v. City of Winner,* 352 F.Supp. 925 (D. S.D. 1972).

42. *Id.,* at 927. "The remaining areas to which Plaintiff attributes discrimination—street paving, sidewalks and sewerage facilities—although somewhat inferior to other areas of Winner, are improvements associated with property ownership. Any difference, therefore, in the quality of such improvements stems primarily from the difference in the respective landowner's willingness to pay for the property improvements."

43. *Beal v. Lindsay*, 468 F.2d 287 (2d Cir. 1972).
44. *Id.*, at 291.
45. "[F]igures speak and when they do, Courts listen. . . ." *Brooks v. Beto*, 366 F.2d 1, 9 (5th Cir. 1966). For an excellent example of the impact of statistics on the relative levels in per unit allocation of physical services see: *Selmont Improvement Association v. Dallas County Com'n.*, 339 F.Supp. 477 (S.D. Ala. 1972). The certitude imparted by such figures not only enabled the court to determine the presence of constitutionally forbidden racial discrimination, but provided the highly specific details of the injunction entered against the city whereby defendant was ordered to plan, appropriate funds, and pave enumerated lengths of designated streets in West Selmont.
46. *Maye v. Lindsay*, 352 F.Supp. 1120 (S.D. N.Y. 1972).
47. *Brown v. Board of Education of Topeka*, 347 U.S. 483 (1954), and 349 U.S. 294 (1955).
48. *Bell v. Rippy*, 133 F.Supp. 811 (N.D. Tex. 1955), *rev'd sub nom. Brown v. Rippy*, 233 F.2d 796 (5th Cir. 1956); *Bell v. Rippy*, 146 F.Supp. 485 (N.D. Tex. 1956), *rev'd sub nom, Borders v. Rippy*, 247 F.2d 268 (5th Cir. 1967); *Rippy v. Borders*, 250 F.2d 690 (5th Cir. 1957); and, *Boson v. Rippy*, 275 F.2d 850 (5th Cir. 1960).
49. *See, e.g., Hecht Co. v. Bowles*, 321 U.S. 321 (1944); and, *United States v. Morgan*, 307 U.S. 183 (1939).
50. Deserving of final emphasis is one further point. Though relatively few in number, each of the service equalization suits bottomed on the Equal Protection Clause reveals a similar propensity to distort all of the governance issues into the standard selection process. As indicated earlier, a conclusion that the strict review standard is the appropriate vehicle for analysis is tantamount to a verdict for plaintiff. Relegation of the complaint to review under the noninterventionist standard renders further consideration an exercise in formality prior to entry of a judgment of dismissal. Such a procedure may be tolerable as a price to pay for the annihilation of racial discrimination, but the Venus fly trap exercise of standard selection is a weighty reason to look with suspicion upon any further advance of the "suspect criteria" route to the strict review standard.
51. See Note 27, *supra*.
52. 352 F.Supp. 925 (D. S.D. 1972).
53. The court found that plaintiffs had not properly pleaded their cause of action for damages and stated that, even had the cause been correctly pleaded, the matter was one for litigation in the state court rather than for exercise of the federal court's pendent jurisdiction. See part VI(B)(3) *infra*.
54. 352 F.Supp. at 928.
55. Plaintiffs' amended complaint was filed on September 13, 1971; defendants made all of the improvements specified prior to the trial of the action held 11 months later on August 9, 1972. 352 F.Supp. at 926.
56. The action was originally filed on a class basis, alleging invidious discrimina-

tion against the Indian residents of Winner; however, the class action was dropped and the race discrimination claim withdrawn in the amended complaint. *Ibid.*

57. 303 F.Supp. 1162 (N.D. Miss. 1969), rev'd, 437 F.2d 1286 (5th Cir. 1971). reversal aff'd *en banc*, 461 F.2d 1171 (5th Cir. 1972).

58. Of the eight reported equalization suits (see Note 27, *supra*), at least five involved plaintiffs who were represented by either OEO funded legal services attorneys or by the NAACP Legal Defense and Educational Fund, Inc. ("Inc. Fund"): *Hawkins v. Town of Shaw, supra* (Inc. Fund); *Hadnot v. City of Prattville, supra* (Inc. Fund and O.E.O.-funded Columbia Center on Social Welfare Policy and Law); *Beal v. Lindsay, supra* (OEO funded Morrisania Legal Services); *Fire v. City of Winner, supra* (OEO funded Rosebud Legal Services); *Coleman v. Aycock, supra* (Inc. Fund).

59. See generally, Nussbaum, *Attorney's Fees in Public Interest Litigation*, 48 N.Y.U. L. Rev. 301 (1973).

60. See, for example, *Taylor v. City of Millington,* F.Supp. Civ. No. 71-249 (W.D. Tenn. April 25, 1972) [O.E.O.-funded legal services program awarded $400.00 attorney's fee in suit challenging segregationist policies in a city housing program]; *Trout v. Carleson*, 37 C.A.3d 337, 112 Cal. Rptr. 282 (Ct. App. 1974) [O.E.O.-funded attorney awarded $600.000 in suit against state welfare department to compel payment of statutory benefits to indigent]; *DeLeon v. Operating Engineers Local No. 3,* F.Supp. , No. C-71-974 RFP (N.D. Calif. June 27, 1973) [O.E.O. legal services attorneys awarded fee of $65,000.00 in suit to enjoin employment discrimination by labor union]. In each of these cases, the order that defendants pay plaintiff's attorney's fees was based upon a statute which authorized such an award to a successful litigant. See generally, Note, *Awards of Attorneys Fees to Legal Aid Offices*, 87 Harv. L. Rev. 411 (1973).

61. See, for example, *Gates v. Collier*, 349 F.Supp. 881 (N.D. Miss. 1972), aff'd 489 F.2d 298 (5th Cir. 1973) [Lawyer's Committee on Civil Rights awarded $52,736 attorney's fee in § 1983 civil rights action against state officials to vindicate constitutional rights of state prisoners]; *Brandenburger v. Thompson*, 494 F.2d 885 (9th Cir. 1974) [ACLU awarded attorneys fees in § 1983 action against state officials to vindicate constitutional rights of welfare recipients]; *La Raza Unida v. Volpe*, 57 F.R.D. 94 (N.D. Calif. 1972) [public interest law firm funded by Ford Foundation awarded attorney's fees in environmental suit to enjoin state officials from displacing persons in order to build a highway].

62. *Gates v. Collier, supra* Note 61; *Sims v. Amos*, 336 F.Supp. 924, 340 F.Supp. 691 (M.D. Ala. 1972) (three-judge ct.), aff'd 409 U.S. 942 (1972) [attorney's fees awarded against Alabama governor, attorney general and state legislators]; *Ojeda v. Hackney*, 452 F.2d 947 (5th Cir. 1972) [attorney's fees awarded against state welfare department]; *Bassett v. Atlanta Ind. School Dist.*, 347 F.Supp. 1191 (E.D.

Tex. 1972) [teacher dismissal case awarding plaintiff $16,000 attorney's fee]; *Sterzing v. Fort Bend Ind. School Dist.*,   F.Supp.
(S.D. Tex. 1972) [teacher dismissal case in which plaintiff awarded $5000 in attorney's fees]; *Newman v. Alabama*, 349 F.Supp. 278 (M.D. Ala. 1972) [$12,000 attorney's fee awarded against state prison officials in suit challenging adequacy of medical facilities]; *Roberts v. Brian*, 30 C.A.3d 427, 106 Cal. Rptr. 360 (Ct. App. 1973) [$9,000 attorney's fee awarded against state welfare department in action on behalf of single welfare claimant]; and, see generally, Lawyers' Committee for Civil Rights, *Attorney's Fees in Pro Bono Publico Cases* (1972).

63. See, McLaughlin, *The Recovery of Attorney's Fees: A New Method of Financing Legal Services*, 40 Ford. L. Rev. 761 (1972).

64. *Bell v. School Bd.*, 321 F.2d 494 (4th Cir. 1963); *Bell v. Alamatt Motel*, 243 F.Supp. 472, 474 (N.D. Miss. 1965).

65. 352 F.Supp. 925 (D. S.D. 1972).

66. 489 F.2d 298 (5th Cir. 1973).

67. *Id.*, at 301; accord, *Brandenburger v. Thompson*, 494 F.2d 885, 890 (9th Cir. 1974) (Koelsch, J., concurring).

68. The federal courts have split on the question of whether an award of attorneys fees against the state is barred by the Eleventh Amendment. See Note 184, *infra*.

69. This provision is set forth in full at Note 3 , *supra*.

70. *Sullivan v. Little Hunting Park*, 396 U.S. 229, 238-40 (1969); *Meyers v. Anderson*, 238 U.S. 368 (1915); *Kerr v. City of Chicago*, 424 F.2d 1134 (7th Cir. 1970), cert. den. 400 U.S. 833 (1970); *Rolfe v. County Bd. of Educ.*, 391 F.2d 77 (6th Cir. 1968); *Basista v. Weir*, 340 F.2d 74 (3d Cir. 1965); *Marshall v. Sawyer*, 301 F.2d 639 (9th Cir. 1962); *Jackson v. Duke*, 259 F.2d 3 (5th Cir. 1958).

71. In one case, plaintiffs sought monetary damages under a state tort law theory. *Fire v. City of Winner*, Note 27, *supra*.

72. 365 U.S. 167 (1961).

73. *City of Kenosha v. Bruno*, 412 U.S. 507 (1973).

74. *Scher v. Board of Educ. of Town of West Orange*, 424 F.2d 741 (3d Cir. 1970) [§ 1983 damage claim allowed against school board].

75. 411 U.S. 693 (1973).

76. See, for example, *Hawkins v. Town of Shaw, supra* Note 27; *Hadnot v. City of Prattville, supra* Note 27; *Fire v. City of Winner, supra* Note 27; *Dupree v. City of Chattanooga, supra* Note 27; *Selmont Improvement Ass'n v. Dallas County Comm'n, supra* Note 27.

77. See, for example, *Coleman v. Aycock, Maye v. Lindsay*, and *Beal v. Lindsay, supra* Note 27. In *Hawkins v. Town of Shaw*, Note 27 *supra*, 303 F.Supp. at 1163 n. 1, the court dismissed the action against the city on the ground that "injunctive relief was not obtainable against a municipal corporation under § 1983." A similar ruling was made in *Dupree v. City of Chattanooga, supra* Note 27, 362 F.Supp. at 1138-39; however, jurisdiction over the city was

found to exist under 28 U.S.C. § 1331, providing for federal jurisdiction of suits to redress violations of constitutional rights where the amount in controversy exceeds $10,000. See text *infra.*

78. *Dupree v. City of Chattanooga, supra* Note 27, 362 F.Supp. at 1140.

79. Comment, *Toward State and Municipal Liability in Damages for Denial of Racial Equal Protection,* 57 Calif. L. Rev. 1142, 1158 (1969); Kates and Kouba, *Liability of Public Entities Under Section 1983 of the Civil Rights Act,* 45 So. Calif. L. Rev. 131, 136-37, 157 (1972); and, see, *Moor v. County of Alameda,* 411 U.S. 693 at n. 10 (1973).

80. *McDaniel v. Carroll,* 457 F.2d 968, 969 (6th Cir. 1972); *Caperci v. Huntoon,* 397 F.2d 799, 801 (1st Cir. 1968, cert. den. 393 U.S. 940 (1968); *Basista v. Weir,* 340 F.2d 74, 87-88 (3d Cir. 1965); *Stringer v. Dilger,* 313 F.2d 536 (10th Cir. 1963); *Washington v. Official Court Stenographer,* 251 F.Supp. 945, 947 (E.D. Pa. 1966); *United States ex rel. Motley v. Rundle,* 340 F.Supp. 807, 810-11 (E.D. Pa. 1972).

81. *Ex parte Young,* 209 U.S. 123, 159-60 (1907); *Pierson v. Ray,* 386 U.S. 547 (1967); *Kletschka v. Driver,* 411 F.2d 436, 448 (2d Cir. 1969); *Jobson v. Henne,* 355 F.2d 129, 133-34 (2d Cir. 1966); *Anderson v. Nosser,* 438 F.2d 183, 201, mod. on other grnds. 456 F.2d 835 (5th Cir. 1972). This contrasts with actions founded in tort, where immunity from suit is governed exclusively by state law (part V(B)(3), *infra.*). However, a federal court may apply state rules on official immunity if they are more restrictive than the applicable federal standards. *McCray v. State of Maryland,* 456 F.2d 1 (4th Cir. 1972). *McCray* is consistent with the Supreme Court's decision in *Sullivan v. Little Hunting Park,* 396 U.S. 229, 240 (1969), holding that in actions brought under the Civil Rights Acts, 42 U.S.C. § 1988 authorizes use of "both federal and state rules on damages . . . whichever better serves the policies expressed in the federal statutes." See generally, Comment, *The Doctrine of Offical Immunity and Section 1983: A New Look at an Old Problem,* 30 Wash. & Lee L. Rev. 344 (1973).

82. *Scheuer v. Rhodes,* 416 U.S. 232 (1974); *Franklin v. Meredith,* 386 F.2d 958, 960 (10th Cir. 1967); *Hoffman v. Halden,* 268 F.2d 280, 300 (9th Cir. 1959).

83. *Littleton v. Berbling,* 468 F.2d 389, 412 (7th Cir. 1972), cert. den. 94 S.Ct. 894 (1974); *Wolfe v. O'Neill,* 336 F.Supp. 1255 (D. Alaska 1972).

84. *Jobson v. Henne,* Note 81 *supra,* 355 F.2d at 133-34; *McCray v. State of Maryland,* Note 81 *supra.*

85. *Scheuer v. Rhodes, supra* Note 82, 416 U.S. at 247.

86. *Dupre v. City of Chattanooga,* Note 27 *supra,* 362 F.Supp. at 1140.

87. *Ibid.,* quoting from *Norwalk Core v. Norwalk Redevelopment Agency,* 395 F.2d 920 (2d Cir. 1968).

88. See, C.J. Antieau, *Federal Civil Rights Acts: Civil Practice,* § 42 (San Francisco, 1971) (collecting authorities).

89. 209 U.S. 123 (1908).

90. The fiction was created to avoid the Eleventh Amendment prohibition against federal damages suits by a citizen against a state (see *infra*). See also, *Scheuer v. Rhodes, supra* Note 82, 416 U.S. at 237-38.
91. *Williams v. Eaton*, 443 F.2d 422, 429 (10th Cir. 1971); and, see Schwartz, *Municipal Services Litigation After Rodriguez*, 40 Brooklyn L. Rev. 93, 109-10 (1973).
92. 403 U.S. 388 (1971).
93. *Bell v. Hood*, 327 U.S. 678, 684 (1946).
94. 403 U.S. at 389. Since *Bivens* was decided, numerous courts have held that a damages action was proper against federal officials who violated the Fourth Amendment. See, e.g., *Bethea v. Reid*, 445 F.2d 1163, 1164 (3d Cir. 1971), cert. den. 404 U.S. 1061 (1971); *Williams v. Rogers*, 449 F.2d 513 (8th Cir. 1971), cert. den. 405 (U.S. 926 (1972).
95. *Monroe v. Pape*, 365 U.S. 167 (1961); *Moor v. County of Alameda*, 411 U.S. 693 (1973) (see part V(B)(1) *supra*).
96. *Moore v. Koelzer*, 457 F.2d 892 (3d Cir. 1972) (Fifth Amendment); *States Marine Lines v. Shultz*, 498 F.2d 1146 (4th Cir. 1974) (Fifth Amendment); *Butler v. United States* 365 F.Supp. 1035 (D. Haw. 1973) (First and Fifth Amendments); *Gardels v. Murphy*, 377 F.Supp. 1389 (N.D. Ill. 1974) (First and Fifth Amendments); and see, *Singleton v. Vance County Board of Education*, 501 F.2d 429, 432-33 (4th Cir. 1974) (Winter, J., concurring and dissenting), in which it was suggested that the rationale of *Bivens* applied to violations of the Fourteenth Amendment Equal Protection Clause by a county entity.
97. Dellinger, *Of Rights and Remedies: The Constitution as a Sword*, 85 Harv. L. Rev. 1532, 1557 (1972).
98. 403 U.S. at 399.
99. Bivens sought damages of $15,000 from each of the federal agents. 403 U.S. at 390, 398.
100. See, for example, *City of Kenosha v. Bruno, supra* Note 73.
101. 403 U.S. at 405.
102. Dellinger, Note 97 *supra*, at 1559. Not all such actions authorized by *Bivens* could be brought in federal courts; in some instances, plaintiffs might have to resort to a state forum. See *infra*.
103. 403 U.S. at 411 (emphasis added).
104. *Bivens v. Six Unknown Named Agents*, 456 F.2d 1339, 1341 (2d Cir. 1972).
105. *Ibid.* And see, text accompanying Notes 81-87, *supra*.
106. 352 F.Supp. 925 (D. S.D. 1972).
107. For an interesting discussion as to the absurdity of the governmental proprietary distinction, see, Comment, *Governmental Tort Immunity in Pennsylvania*, 46 Temple L. Q. 345 (1973).
108. See, for example, Note, *The New Jersey Tort Claims Act*, 26 Rut. L. Rev. 838 (1973).
109. See generally, Van Alstyne, *Governmental Tort Liability: A Decade of*

Change, 1966 U. Ill. L. F. 919 (1966) [state by state analysis of developments to 1965]; Comment, *Toward State and Municipal Liability in Damages for Denial of Racial Equal Protection,* 57 Calif. L. Rev. 1142, 1145-53 (1969).

110. For a discussion of the adoption and possible effects of the provision, see, Comment, *The Passing of Sovereign Immunity in Montana: The King is Dead!,* 34 Mont. L. Rev. 283 (1973).

111. Ill. Const., art. 13, § 4.

112. W. Prosser, *Law of Torts,* § 36 (4th ed. 1971); *Restatement (Second) of Torts,* § § 285, 286 (1965).

113. Calif. Gov't Code, § 815.6 (West 1966) (emphasis added); see, A. Van Alstyne, *California Government Tort Liability,* § 815.6 (Cont. Educ. of the Bar, 1964).

114. *Ramos v. County of Madera,* 4 Cal.3d 685, 695-96, 94 Cal. Rptr. 421, 484 P.2d 93 (1971).

115. *Avery v. Midland County,* 390 U.S. 474, 480 (1968).

116. *Restatement (Second) of Torts,* § 285 (1965).

117. The California Supreme Court has indicated that the state tort claims act is to be liberally construed against the public entity. "[I]n governmental tort cases, 'the rule is liability, immunity is the exception.' . . . 'Accordingly, courts should not casually decree governmental immunity; * * *' Unless the Legislature has clearly provided for immunity, the important societal goal of compensating injured parties for damages caused by willful or negligent acts must prevail." *Ramos v. County of Madera,* Note 114 *supra,* 4 Cal.3d at 692.

118. *Pockman v. Leonard,* 39 Cal.2d 676, 249 P.2d 267 (1952).

119. See, Van Alstyne, *Government Tort Liability: A Decade of Change,* Note 109 *supra,* at 976; Calif. Gov't Code, § 818 (West 1966) [exemplary and punitive damages not available against public entity].

120. *Monroe v. Pape,* 365 U.S. 167, 180, 183 (1961).

121. Kates and Kouba, Note 79 *supra,* at 145-46.

122. See, for example, the extensive injunctive relief granted in two municipal services cases: *Hawkins v. Town of Shaw,* Note 27 *supra*; *Hadnot v. City of Prattville,* Note 27, *supra.*

123. *Dred Scott v. Sanford,* 19 How. 393, 401 (1856).

124. *Claflin v. Houseman,* 93 U.S. 130 (1876).

125. *Testa v. Katt,* 330 U.S. 386 (1947).

126. *Sullivan v. Little Hunting Park,* Note 81 *supra* [state court must take jurisdiction over civil rights case and grant monetary damages where appropriate]; but see Notes 182 and 184 *infra.* The California Supreme Court, in an action brought in state court under 42 U.S.C. § 1983 by inmates of a county jail against their keepers, has held that federal and state courts have "concurrent" jurisdiction of suits brought under § 1983, and that if plaintiffs choose to file such a suit in the state forum, the state court has a duty to take jurisdiction. *Brown v. Pitchess,* 112 Cal. Rptr. 350, 37 Cal. App. 3d 461 (Ct. App. 1974), *affirmed,* Cal.3d (2/19/75).

127. See part IV(A)(1)(b), *supra.*
128. See, for example, Calif. Const., art I, § § 11 and 21, which have been held to be "substantially the equivalent of the equal protection clause of the Fourteenth Amendment to the United States Constitution." *Dep't of Mental Hygiene v. Kirchner*, 62 Cal.2d 586, 588, 43 Cal. Rptr. 329, 400 P.2d 321 (1965); N.Y. Const., art. 1, § § 6, 11; see, generally, Legis. Drafting Research Fund, *Constitutions of the United States* (2d ed. 1974).
129. Such an action alleging violation of federal and state constitutional provisions could be brought in federal court, but that court would not be required to exercise its pendent jurisdiction over the state law claim; in the alternative, the federal court might abstain until a state court had been given a chance to rule on the matter. See, for example, *Reetz v. Bozanich*, 397 U.S. 82 (1970).
130. *Reitman v. Mulkey*, 387 U.S. 369 (1967).
131. 60 Cal.2d 716, 36 Cal. Rptr. 488, 388 P.2d 720 (1964).
132. *Dep't of Mental Hygiene v. Kirchner*, 380 U.S. 194, 198 (1965).
133. *Dep't of Mental Hygiene v. Kirchner*, 62 Cal.2d 586, 588, 43 Cal. Rptr. 329, 400 P.2d 321 (1965).
134. 7 Cal.3d 792, 103 Cal. Rptr. 299, 499 P.2d 979 (1972).
135. *Dep't of Motor Vehicles v. Rios*, 410 U.S. 425 (1973).
136. *Rios v. Cozens*, 9 Cal.3d 454, 455, 107 Cal. Rptr. 784, 500 P.2d 696 (1973). Another vivid example of a state constitution providing greater protection than the U.S. Constitution is presented by *Sail'er Inn, Inc. v. Kirby*, 5 Cal.3d 1, 96 Cal. Rptr. 329, 485 P.2d 529 (1971), in which the California Supreme Court held that under the state constitution, classifications based upon sex are inherently suspect and thus subject to strict scrutiny. 5 Cal.3d at 15-20. The United States Supreme Court has declined to hold that such classification require strict scrutiny under the Fourteenth Amendment Equal Protection Clause. In *Frontiero v. Richardson*, 411 U.S. 677 (1974), only four justices agreed that sex was a suspect classification; the majority rejected such a holding. See also, *Reed v. Reed*, Note 21 *supra*, and *Kahn v. Shevin*, 416 U.S. 351 (1974). Another example of a state constitution providing greater protection than is provided by the Fourteenth Amendment Equal Protection Clause is *Serrano v. Priest*, 5 Cal.3d 584, 487 P.2d 1241 (1971), in which the California Supreme Court declared wealth to be a suspect classification, and education to be a fundamental interest under the state equal protection provisions; the U.S. Supreme Court has not gone this far. See, *San Antonio Independent School District v. Rodriguez*, 411 U.S. 1 (1973), and see, part IV(A)(1)(b) *supra*. In a recent decision, however, the California Supreme Court has intimated that in the future it may interpret the state equal protection provision in conformity with U.S. Supreme Court decisions construing the federal constitution. *D'Amico v. Board of Medical Examiners*, 11 Cal.3d 1, 18, 112 Cal. Rptr. 786 (1974).

137. See *infra.*
138. Title 28, United States Code, Section 1343, provides in pertinent part as follows:

> "The district courts shall have original jurisdiction of any civil action authorized by law to be commenced by any person: * * *
> (3) To redress the deprivation, under color of any State law, statute, ordinance, regulation, custom or usage, of any right, privilege or immunity secured by the Constitution of the United States or by any Act of Congress providing for equal rights of citizens or of all persons within the jurisdiction of the United States;
> (4) To recover damages or to secure equitable or other relief under any Act of Congress providing for the protection of civil rights, including the right to vote."

139. See, for example, *King v. Smith*, 392 U.S. 309, 312 n. 3 (1968); *Hagans v. Lavine*, 415 U.S. 528 (1974), and *Edelman v. Jordan*, 415 U.S. 651, 653 n. 1 (1974) [both suggesting that a federal court has jurisdiction over federal statutory claims only under exercise of pendent jurisdiction, and that there would be no federal jurisdiction over the statutory claim were it presented alone]; Note, *Federal Judicial Review of State Welfare Practices*, 67 Colum. L. Rev. 84 (1967).
140. See Note 138 *supra.*
141. Ch. 22, § 1, 17 Stat. 13 (1871).
142. See, Comment, *Federal Jurisdiction over Challenges to State Welfare Programs*, 72 Colum. L. Rev. 1404, 1406 et seq. (1972); *Lynch v. Household Finance Corp.*, 405 U.S. 538, 540, 543-44 n. 7 (1972) [indicating that 28 U.S.C. § 1343(3) is the jurisdictional counterpart to 42 U.S.C. § 1983].
143. *Monroe v. Pape*, 365 U.S. 167 (1961); *City of Kenosha v. Bruno*, 412 U.S. 507 (1973); see *supra.*
144. This would include both claims for declaratory and injunctive relief, and claims for damages.
145. *City of Kenosha v. Bruno*, Note 143 *supra.*
146. *Snyder v. Harris*, 394 U.S. 332 (1969).
147. *Zahn v. International Paper Co.*, 414 U.S. 291 (1973).
148. *Bass v. Rockefeller*, 331 F.Supp. 945, 952-53 n. 6 (S.D.N.Y. 1971), remanded for dismissal as moot, 1 CCH Pov. L. Rep., para. 1505.61 (2d Cir. 1971).
149. *Ibid.*
150. *Ronzio v. Denver & R.G.W. R.R. Co.*, 116 F.2d 604, 606 (10th Cir. 1940); see also, *Tatum v. Laird*, 444 F.2d 947, 951 n. 6 (D.C. Cir. 1971), rev'd on other grounds, 408 U.S. 1 (1972); and see, Comment, *Federal Jurisdiction over Challenges to State Welfare Programs*, Note 142 *supra*, at 1432-34.
151. *United Mine Workers v. Gibbs*, 383 U.S. 715, 725 (1966).
152. *Id.*, at 726.
153. See, for example, *Hymer v. Chai*, 407 F.2d 136 (9th Cir. 1969).

154. *Moor v. County of Alameda*, 411 U.S. 693, 710-17 (1973).
155. *Ibid.*
156. *Id.*, at 716.
157. 352 F.Supp. 925 (D S.D. 1972).
158. *Id.*, at 928.
159. See, for example, *Reetz v. Bozanich*, Note 129 *supra*; *Dep't of Social Services v. Dimery*, 398 U.S. 322 (1970); *Wisconsin v. Constantineau*, 400 U.S. 433 (1971) (Burger, C.J., dissenting); but see, *Hagans v. Lavine*, Note 139 *supra*, 415 U.S. at 545-48.
160. See Note 27 *supra.*
161. 417 U.S. 156 (1974). The *Eisen* ruling is limited to class actions brought pursuant to Rule 23(b)(3) of the Federal Rules of Civil Procedure. To the extent that plaintiffs in municipal services equalization suits seek only declaratory and injunctive relief, a class action is probably maintainable under Rule 23(b)(2) which is not subject to the notice requirements dealt with in *Eisen.* However, where damages are also sought, the action must in all likelihood proceed under Rule 23(b)(3); the court has indicated that a (b)(2) class action is ordinarily limited "to actions exclusively or predominantly for injunctive or declaratory relief." *Eisen, supra*, 417 U.S. at 163-64 n. 4.
162. 417 U.S. at 167-68.
163. *Eisen v. Carlisle & Jacquelin*, 479 F.2d 1005, 1010 (2d Cir. 1973).
164. 303 F.Supp. 1162 (N.D. Miss. 1969).
165. 304 F.Supp. 132 (N.D. Miss. 1969).
166. 309 F.Supp. 967 (M.D. Ala. 1970).
167. 468 F.2d 287 (2d Cir. 1972).
168. As mentioned earlier, Note 60 *supra*, plaintiffs in *Hawkins, Hadnot* and *Beal* could not even afford to pay private counsel.
169. In *Fire v. City of Winner*, Note 27 *supra*, the class consisted of only 138 persons. In situations where the class is this small, either due to the size of the city or the size of the neighborhood involved, notice requirements of the type at issue in *Eisen* would probably have no real effect on the litigation.
170. *Hadnot v. City of Prattville*, Note 27 *supra*, at 970 [street paving]; *Fire v. City of Winner*, Note 27 *supra*, at 927 [street paving, sidewalks, and sewerage facilities].
171. 309 F.Supp. at 970.
172. 352 F.Supp. at 927.
173. *March v. Alabama*, 326 U.S. 501, 505-06 (1946).
174. *Food Employees Local 590 v. Logan Valley Plaza*, 391 U.S. 308 (1968).
175. *Terry v. Adams*, 345 U.S. 461 (1953).
176. 382 U.S. 296 (1966). It should be noted that in a recent decision, the U.S. Supreme Court held that a privately owned and operated public utility does not act "under color of state law," and is thus not subject to the restraints of the Fourteenth Amendment. *Jackson v. Metropolitan Edison Company,*   U.S.   , 95 S.Ct. 449 (1974).

The Court found that the utility was not performing a "public function," in that it did not exercise "power delegated to it by the State which is traditionally associated with sovereignty. . . ." 95 S.Ct. at 454. This language seems to suggest that perhaps there are functions, performed by a state or one of its political subdivisions, which could be transferred to a private entity and thereby lose their public character, to the extent that a court might find those functions not to be "traditionally associated with sovereignty." In the *Jackson* case, the utility provided electrical services. Thus, if a municipality currently providing residents with electrical services opted to transfer this function to a private utility, the latter might not be subject to the Fourteenth Amendment.

177. 309 F.Supp. 967, 973 (M.D. Ala. 1970).

178. The municipality would of course be liable as well if it was in any way responsible for the challenged inequities. As a related point, it should be noted that the courts have held a deprivation of services which resulted from a municipality's refusal to annex an adjoining area does not violate the Equal Protection Clause. *Wilkerson v. City of Coralville*, 478 F.2d 709 (8th Cir. 1973); thus, the larger service entity cannot be held liable on the basis of inequalities in services which it is not obligated to provide and does not in fact provide to plaintiffs.

179. See, for example, *Selmont Improvement Ass'n v. Dallas County Comm'n*, Note 27 *supra*, in which residents of an unincorporated area sued the governing board of the county with respect to services the county was obligated to provide.

180. *Hans v. Louisiana*, 134 U.S. 1 (1890) [holding that Eleventh Amendment's prohibition of federal jurisdiction over suits against a state brought by citizens of another state applied as well to suits brought against a state by one of its own citizens]. The Eleventh Amendment has been held not to bar suits by a citizen against his state seeking only prospective injunctive relief. *Ex parte Young*, 209 U.S. 123 (1908).

181. *Edelman v. Jordan*, Note 139 *supra*.

182. The majority opinion in *Edelman v. Jordan, supra*, appears to suggest that a § 1983 damages action against a state may be improper even if filed in state court, perhaps on the theory that Congress could not, simply by enacting the Civil Rights Act from which § 1983 derives, cause a state to waive its sovereign immunity. The court did not reach the question of whether a violation of the Fourteenth Amendment would give rise to a damages action notwithstanding the Eleventh Amendment on the theory that the subsequent amendment limited the state's Eleventh Amendment sovereign immunity. See, 415 U.S. at 694 n. 2 (Marshall, J., dissenting).

183. *Flores v. Norton & Ramsey Lines, Inc.*, 352 F.Supp. 150, 153-54 (W.D. Tex. 1972). However, the Supreme Court's decision in *Edelman v. Jordan*, Note 139 *supra*, casts considerable doubt on the validity of

this holding, for the high court held that a waiver of Eleventh
Amendment rights by a state must be so clear as to "leave no room
for any other reasonable construction."

184. *Lincoln County v. Luning*, 133 U.S. 529 (1890); *Hopkins v. Clemson
College*, 221 U.S. 636, 645-46 (1911); *Edelman v. Jordan, supra*
Note 139, 415 U.S. at 667 n. 12. However, it should be noted with
caution that the precedents which exempt local governmental
entities from the protection of the Eleventh Amendment are ancient
indeed. The Supreme Court has quite candidly admitted, in the
context of prior Eleventh Amendment decisions, that when "we deal
with a constitutional question, we are less constrained by the
principle of *stare decisis* than we are in other areas of the law."
Edelman v. Jordan, supra, 415 U.S. at 671. It is very possible that
the Court could extend the protections of the Eleventh Amendment
to the political subdivisions of the state. In this event, damages
actions in the federal courts would be precluded, in the absence of
consent by the governmental entity. In addition, the federal courts
might be barred from awarding attorneys fees against such entities;
since the Supreme Court's decision in *Edelman*, a number of lower
federal courts have held that the Eleventh Amendment bars any
monetary award against a state in federal court, whether couched in
terms of damages or attorneys fees. *Jordan v. Gilligan*, 500 F.2d 701
(6th Cir. 1974), cert. filed 10/9/74 (Dkt. #74-403); *Skehan v.
Board of Trustees of Bloomsburg State College*, 501 F.2d 31 (3d Cir.
1974), cert. filed 11/8/74 (Dkt. #74-558). *Contra: Gates v. Collier*,
489 F.2d 298 (5th Cir. 1973) and *Brandenburger v. Thompson* 494
F.2d 885 (9th Cir. 1974), both decided before *Edelman*. And see,
Downs v. Department of Public Welfare,   F. Supp.   (E.D. Pa.
1974), 43 U.S.L.W. 2270 (1/7/75).

About the Authors

Howard S. Bloom, Ph.D. candidate in Political Economy and Government, John F. Kennedy School of Government, Harvard University. Mr. Bloom has worked as a consultant to the Framingham (Mass.) School Committee.

H. James Brown, Associate Professor of City Planning, Graduate School of Design, Harvard University. Mr. Brown has contributed to the development of the Urban Simulation Model of the National Bureau of Economic Research.

Daniel Wm. Fessler, Professor of Law, Law School of the University of California at Davis. Mr. Fessler, with Professor Charles M. Haar, acted as council *amicus curiae* in *Hawkins v. Town of Shaw.*

Eric A. Hanushek, Associate Professor of Economics, Yale University. Mr. Hanushek is the author of *Education and Race*, and formerly Senior Staff Economist, Council of Economic Advisors.

John E. Jackson, Associate Professor of Government, Harvard University.

Christopher N. May, Professor of Law and Associate Dean, Loyola University School of Law, Los Angeles, Mr. May is the former Director of the San Francisco Neighborhood Legal Assistance Foundation.

Stephen K. Mayo, Senior Economist, Abt Associates. Mr. Mayo is currently working on the Housing Allowance Demand Experiment.

George E. Peterson, Director of Economic Research, the Land Use Center of the Urban Institute. Mr. Peterson is currently working on a study of federal tax influence on metropolitan development for the Council on Environmental Quality.

DA